Routledge Revivals

I0121530

From Military to Civilian Rule

Military disengagement from power in favour of a civilian government is not an uncommon phenomenon, especially in the developing world. First published in 1992, *From Military to Civilian Rule* is the first comparative study of the motives behind military withdrawal and the establishment of sustainable civilian rule.

Using case studies from Africa, Central and South America, the Caribbean and Europe written by regional specialists, the book looks at the future of civil–military relations in the post-disengagement state. It reviews the factors—organizational, societal, and international—necessary for maintaining civilian rule, and it establishes conceptual themes common to the countries discussed.

This volume will appeal to academics and advanced students with interests in Third World Politics, Latin American Politics, and the role of the military in the State.

From Military to Civilian Rule

Edited by Constantine P. Danopoulos

Routledge
Taylor & Francis Group
REVIVALS

First published in 1992
by Routledge

This edition first published in 2024 by Routledge
4 Park Square, Milton Park, Abingdon, Oxon, OX14 4RN

and by Routledge
605 Third Avenue, New York, NY 10017

Routledge is an imprint of the Taylor & Francis Group, an informa business

© 1992 Constantine P. Danopoulos

All rights reserved. No part of this book may be reprinted or reproduced or utilised in any form or by any electronic, mechanical, or other means, now known or hereafter invented, including photocopying and recording, or in any information storage or retrieval system, without permission in writing from the publishers.

Publisher's Note
The publisher has gone to great lengths to ensure the quality of this reprint but points out that some imperfections in the original copies may be apparent.

Disclaimer
The publisher has made every effort to trace copyright holders and welcomes correspondence from those they have been unable to contact.

A Library of Congress record exists under LCCN: 91011160

ISBN: 978-1-032-84246-2 (hbk)
ISBN: 978-1-003-51209-7 (ebk)
ISBN: 978-1-032-84291-2 (pbk)

Book DOI 10.4324/9781003512097

From military to civilian rule

Edited by
Constantine P. Danopoulos

ROUTLEDGE

London and New York

First published 1992
by Routledge
11 New Fetter Lane, London EC4P 4EE

Simultaneously published in the USA and Canada
by Routledge
a division of Routledge, Chapman and Hall, Inc.
29 West 35th Street, New York, NY 10001

© 1992 Constantine P. Danopoulos

Typeset by
Michael Mepham, Frome, Somerset
Printed and bound in Great Britain by
Biddles Ltd, Guildford and King's Lynn

All rights reserved. No part of this book may be reprinted or reproduced
or utilized in any form or by any electronic, mechanical, or other means,
now known or hereafter invented including photocopying and recording,
or in any information storage or retrieval system, without permission in
writing from the publishers.

British Library Cataloguing in Publication Data
From military to civilian rule.
   1. Government. Role of military forces
   I. Danopoulos, Constantine P.
   322.5
   ISBN 0–415–04333–6

Library of Congress Cataloging in Publication Data
From military to civilian rule / edited by
Constantine P. Danopoulos.
      p.   cm.
   Includes bibliographical references and index.
   ISBN 0–415–04333–6
   1. Civil–military relations—Case studies. 2. Civil–military
   relations—Developing countries—Case studies.
   I. Danopoulos, Constantine P. (Constantine Panos)
   JF195.C5F6   1991
   322'.5'0722—dc20   91–11160
                                                                  CIP

Στή μνήμη
τοῦ Νίκου Τζιρίτη
καί
τῆς Σούλας Ντανοπούλου-Παρασκευοπούλου

Contents

Contributors

CONSTANTINE P. DANOPOULOS teaches Political Science at San Jose State University. He received his Ph.D. in Political Science from the University of Missouri, Columbia and has written extensively on international security and civil–military relations. He is the author of *Warriors and Politicians in Modern Greece* (1984), and editor of *The Decline of Military Regimes – The Civilian Influence,* and *Military Withdrawal from Politics.* Dr Danopoulos' numerous articles have appeared in journals such as *Armed Forces and Society, Political Science Quarterly, West European Politics,* the *Journal of Political and Military Sociology, The Journal of Security Studies* and *Public Administration and Development.* He is Associate Editor of the *Journal of Political and Military Sociology* and is presently writing on international relations a textbook preliminarily entitled *International Relations in a Technological Age.*

JAN KNIPPERS BLACK, formerly at the University of New Mexico is now Professor of International Policy at the Monterey Institute of International Studies. Previously, she was Senior Research Scientist and Chairperson of the Latin American Research Team in the Foreign Area Studies Division of American University. A former Peace Corps Volunteer in Chile, she holds a Ph.D. in international studies from American University in Washington, DC. Her publications include: *United States Penetration of Brazil* (1977); *Sentinels of Empire; the United States and Latin American Militarism* (1986); *The Dominican Republic; Politics and Development in an Unsovereign State* (1986); and a two-volume work entitled *Development in Theory and Practice.* She has also published several dozen chapters and articles in reference books and anthologies, journals, magazines, and newspapers.

RODERIC AI CAMP, Director of Latin American Studies at Central University of Iowa, Pella, has engaged in field research on Mexico since

1966. A former Fulbright Fellow to Mexico, Dr Camp has been a visiting researcher at the Colegio de Mexico and a fellow at the Woodrow Wilson Center for International Scholars, Smithsonian Institution. He is the author of numerous articles and books on Mexico. His most recent works included *Memoirs of the Mexican Politician*, (1988), *Who's Who in Mexico Today*, (1988), and *Entrepreneurs and Politics in Twentieth Century Mexico* (1989). His current research interests on Mexico include the Catholic Church, the military and political generations.

ELENA V. DORABJI received her Ph.D. in Comparative Politics from the University of California at Berkeley. Her areas of interest include African politics and the impact of Western imperialism on former colonies. Dr Dorabji has taught at Santa Clara University and San Jose State University and is at present pursuing the publication of her book on the African National Congress's (ANC) change from nonviolence to sabotage in the 1950s.

JOHN FELLS took his BA in Philosophy and Politics from the University of Durham (UK) and his MA from the London School of Economics and Political Science. He then returned to the University of Durham where he obtained his Ph.D. in 1984. Dr Fells has taught Political Science at the Polytechnic of North London and Santa Clara University (US). His current academic interests include the study of European political parties and movements, and of political ideas which inform them.

RITA GIACALONE holds a Ph.D. in History from Indiana University. Presently, she is Associate Professor at the Center for Social and Political Studies of Latin America (CEPSAL) and Graduate School of Political Science, University of the Andes, Merida, Venezuela. Her most recent publications include: *Estudios del Caribe en Venezuela* (1988); 'La politica centroamericana de Venezuela, 1979–87', in C. Eguizábal, ed., *América Latina y la crisis centroamericana: En busca de una solución regional* (1988); 'El Caribe oriental de habla inglesa en la politica exterior de Venezuela y Cuba', *El Caribe Contemporáneo* (México), no. 16 (enero-junio 1988); 'Venezuela's Relations with Curacao and Aruba: Historical Linkages and Geopolitical Interests', in B. Sedoc- Dahlberg, ed., *The Dutch in the Caribbean: Old and New Connections*, forthcoming.

REXENE HANES DE ACEVEDO holds a Ph.D. in Political Science (Latin American Politics), from the University of Texas at Austin. Fornerly Associate Professor, Center for Social and Political Studies of Latin America (CEPSAL), and Graduate Program in Political Science, University of the Andes, Merida, Venezuela. Dr Hanes is now with IESA in Caracas. Among her publications in these areas can be found: *El Clientelismo Politico En America Latina: Una Critica a La Teoria De La Dependencia* (1984); 'El clientelismo politico en el modelo venezolano: un análisis preliminar', in *Secuencia, Revista Americans De Ciencias Sociales* (México, no. 10, January–April, 1988); 'La evasión del conflicto en la universidad venezolana' in Julián Aguirre Pe. ed., *Hacer y Rehacer La Universidad*, forthcoming.

BENJAMIN KLINE is a graduate of San Jose State University and received his Ph.D. in History from the University College Cork in Ireland in 1980. He has taught as an Assistant Professor of History at San Jose State University and at California State University at Chico. In 1988–9 he taught at Fourah Bay College, the University of Sierra Leone, as a Fulbright Scholar. His present appointment is as an Assistant Professor in the History Department at the University of Alaska. Dr Kline is the author of *Genesis of Apartheid: British African Policy in the Colony of Natal, 1845–93*, and *Imperialism and its Legacy: Aspects and Perspectives*, as well as numerous articles on imperial subjects. Presently he is completing a work on United States–South African relations since 1948.

KARL P. MAGYAR is currently Associate Professor and Research Associate at Air University Maxwell Air Force Base in Alabama. He holds a Ph.D. in Political Science from Johns Hopkins University. He also completed additional training at the university of Munich and Mexico City College. He lived in Africa for many years and taught at the Universities of Durban–Westville and Witwatersrand in South Africa. Dr Magyar served as economic advisor to the President of Bophuthatswana (1982) and lecturer at the US State Department and the US Information Agency. He has written numerous publications on the politics and society of a variety of African countries.

N. PATRICK PERITORE is Associate Professor of Political Science at the University of Missouri–Columbia, where he teaches political theory, methodology, and Latin American Studies. He has done fieldwork in Brazil, Mexico, Nicaragua, and Cuba on political parties and the Catholic Church, utilizing interviews and Q-Methodology opinion modelling protocols. He is the author of *Socialism, Communism, and Liberation Theology in Brazil* (1989). Dr Peritore is currently researching the political ecology of Amazon deforestation and Latin American ocean management.

DANIEL L. PREMO is Professor of Political Science and Department Chair at Washington College, Maryland. He earned his Ph.D. in Latin

American studies at the University of Texas at Austin. Before joining academia, he served with the US Information Agency in Guatemala and Colombia. He has contributed to scholarly journals and has written chapters on Colombia, military and insurgency movements in Latin America, and political assassination and violence in Guatemala. He is a regular contributor to the Hoover Institution's *Yearbook on International Communist Affairs.*

FERNANDO RODRIGO teaches Sociology at the Universidad Complutense in Madrid where he also received his Ph.D. in Political Science. He is also associate researcher at the Instituto Universitario Ortega y Gasset in Madrid and former Senior Associate Member of St. Anthony's College at Oxford University. Dr Rodrigo is a member of the Inter-University Seminar on Armed Forces and Society and the International Institute for Strategic Studies. He has published several articles dealing with the role armed forces have played during the Spanish political transition, and currently is finishing a book titled *El camino hacia la democracia. Militares y política en la transición española.*

Acknowledgements

Many generous people deserve special thanks for their assistance in the preparation and completion of this project. I wish to express my gratitude to each of the contributors who, often at very short notice, agreed to tackle a difficult and inherently controversial subject. The Third World and the military of all nations – developed, developing, authoritarian, or democratic – remain difficult grape vines that do not lend themselves to an easy harvest. Many colleagues and friends read all or part of the manuscript; I am grateful to Professors Roy Christman of San Jose State University who offered numerous helpful comments. My parents, Panos and Athanasia Danopoulos; my brother George, his wife Niki and their children, Panos and Soula, my aunt Areti Panaskeropoulou; and my *koumbaro* George Nikoletopoulos have provided boundless moral support and love. Special thanks are also in order for Naomi Ruffin, Tim and Corine Zaracotas, Fotis and Sophia Salamanis, George and Debbie Reid, Father John Asimacopoulos, my in-laws Francis and Gladys Reid, and Frank Agnost with whom I have had numerous enlightening conversations over the years. Emi Nobuhiro, Stella Melgoza and Linda Chromik's expert typing added significantly to the aesthetic value of the book. Last but certainly not least, my wife Vickie and our two sons Panos and Andreas, deserve special praise for their willingness to endure the long hours that writing and manuscript preparation entail. Though helpful, none of these people bear any responsibility for any deficiencies associated with this volume. Responsibility for the accuracy and scholastic quality of what follows belongs to the contributors and myself.

Constantine P. Danopoulos
Fremont, California

1 Intervention and withdrawal: notes and perspectives

Constantine P. Danopoulos

Military intervention or praetorianism, i.e., 'a situation in which military officers are major or predominant actors by virtue of their actual or threatened use of force',[1] has preoccupied the attention of those interested in the politics of changing or developing societies of the Third World. A host of theoretical explanations have been advanced including loss of legitimacy on the part of the supplanted civilian regime, lack of institutionalization, political decay, low levels of political culture, ethnic and factional rivalries and professional military concerns to explain the causes which prompt the armed forces to leave the barracks and to assume the levers of political authority. The literature is also replete with studies evaluating the performance of the military as political governors in such critical areas as regime legitimacy, social change, national integration, and modernization. More recently, responding to the tendency of the armed forces of many Latin American, Asian, and even African countries to return to the barracks and to make room for some kind of civilian rule, civil–military relations specialists produced an ever-increasing body of literature seeking to understand and analyse the causes and processes of military withdrawal or disengagement, defined as 'the substitution of praetorian policies and personnel with these advocated by the recognized civilian authorities'.[2]

However, recent experiments with military disengagement, although proliferating in numbers, are still too fresh to allow for any definitive conclusions to be drawn regarding the long-term survival and supremacy of the newly installed civilian authorities. Long-term military disengagement or withdrawal from politics is characterized by 'a minimum period of ten years during which at least one successful "regular" executive transition has occurred'.[3] Moreover, scholars of civil–military relations are almost unanimous in their assessment that when the armed forces intervene the moral barrier against praetorianism has been broken, and 'the most frequent sequel of military coups and governments is more of the same'.[4]

This rather pervasive view belittles the fact that long-term withdrawal has taken place in a variety of countries who experienced military intervention at some point in their history. The list includes a number of typical Third World countries in Central and Latin America, the Caribbean and Africa, as well as more 'Western' nations such as France, Spain and Greece. Though relatively few in number and with varying degrees of military withdrawal and civilian supremacy, these experiments can teach us a great deal regarding the processes and the travails of re-establishing and maintaining civilian rule that may be applicable to nations that recently followed their example as well as those still ruled by the military. Finally, understanding how long-term military disengagement is accomplished can help us get a better comprehension of why military coups occur in the first place.

THE CASE STUDIES

The countries chosen for this volume include: 3 European (France, Greece, and Spain); 2 South American (Columbia and Venezuela); 2 Central American (Mexico and Costa Rica); 1 Caribbean (Dominican Republic); and 2 African (Sierra Leone and Gabon). Although restricted by the relatively short list of countries with successful long-term disengagement experiences, the single most important criterion in the selection of countries for inclusion was balance, both geographic as well as proportional.

An effort was made to include as many of the world's major geographic regions. Thus, in addition to a number of 'typical' Third World nations, 3 European countries with praetorian experiences are also included. Of these, Greece and Spain, although displaying some characteristics associated with the developing world, such as weak political institutions, fragmented social organizations and unevenly developed economies, have none the less made giant strides towards development. A 'developed' country 'is one that can provide its citizens with goods and services roughly equivalent to the highest level of goods and services available at that time'.[5] The third European country, France, is considered a leading example in the 'developed' category. Notably absent from the list are the Middle East and Asia, for none of the nations in these two regions (with the possible exception of Japan) appear to meet the criteria of long-term disengagement outlined at the beginning of this chapter.

In addition, a conscious attempt was made to give a proportional balance by giving more emphasis to geographic regions with the greatest number of long-term military disengagement from the levers of political authority. As a result, Latin America and Africa are more heavily represented. With regard to Africa, in addition to chapters on Gabon and Sierra Leone, given the distinct and on-going involvement of the armed forces in politics, the editor decided to include a more comprehensive piece on the problems and perspectives of African experiences with praetorianism and long-term disengagement, as well as the applicability of civil–military relations concepts in the African setting. Lastly, care was taken to offer examples of varying degrees of disengagement in order to highlight the different degrees of civilian supremacy, the factors that promoted and are responsible for maintaining long-term disengagement, and the nature of the successor set up and the role of the armed forces in it.

IN THE BARRACKS TO STAY

Long-term military disengagement or withdrawal from politics cannot be seen as an isolated phenomenon. Instead, it can properly be understood and analysed in the context of military intervention, praetorian rule, and disengagement. Broadly speaking, students of civil–military relations have advanced two general explanations regarding the causes of praetorianism: one external or societal, and the other internal or organizational. The first seeks to explain military involvement in politics by looking at such societal considerations as political decay, economic backwardness, corruption, factionalism, and loss of legitimacy. The internalists on the other hand, regard organizational imperatives such as the level of military professionalism or perceived threats to the military's corporate interests as the real culprits of intervention.

In recent years, however, the externalist/internalist dichotomy has been criticized as more apparent than real. Prefacing the second edition of his much acclaimed essay on *The Military in the Political Development of New Nations*, the late Morris Janowitz, regarded as the leading internalist, emphatically dissociated himself from the externalist/internalist debate:

> I do not know of any empirically oriented study of civil–military relations that would accept or limit itself to one of these approaches. Certainly, that was not the strategy of my original essay, which focused on the interplay between military institutions and societal political processes.[6]

Agreeing with Janowitz's basic argument, Nordlinger,[7] and Welch and Smith[8] have concluded that military coups take place in societies where economic difficulties, social fragmentation and political instability lead to legitimacy loss, and occur when the professional or corporate interests of the military are threatened. Corporate interests include adequate budgetary support, institutional autonomy and exclusiveness, protection against encroachments from rival institutions and the survival and viability of the military as social institutions.[9]

The experiences of the case studies included in this volume make it abundantly clear that societal as well as professional (military) concerns were responsible for instigating military interventions in these countries. Long-term disengagement is tied to the very nature of intervention and, as Talukder Maniruzzaman emphatically states, '[t]he factors and trends in any particular society that lead to military intervention have to be eliminated and reversed if that society ever hopes to achieve military withdrawal from politics'[10] – an argument echoed by S. E. Finer in the second edition of his classic work on *The Man on Horseback.*[11]

The experience of the military as political governors, especially in situations where praetorian rule was of considerable duration, cannot help but impact on the attitudes, perceptions and the corporate interests of the armed forces as well as on societal, political, economic and psychological conditions of the countries concerned. The role of the military in the post-disengagement era is inseparably linked to the lessons and experiences drawn by the officer corps, their civilian successors, as well as society at large.

Last but not least, in an era of ever increasing technological and economic dependence and expanding communications capabilities, domestic, political, social, economic and psychological developments can no longer be divorced from the international environment.[12] Indeed never before have international developments influenced domestic developments, and vice-versa, as they do today. Civil–military relations and the role of the military are not immune from what is fast becoming a symbiotic and synergic relationship. In this changing environment adaptations, experiences, attitudes and problems involving leading international financial institutions (such as the World Bank and the International Monetary Fund) and dominant nations have and continue to influence events and processes in the developing world; but the opposite is also increasingly true.

The contributors to this volume effectively demonstrate that societal, professional military as well as international factors are responsible for bringing about and maintaining long-term military disengagement from the politics of the countries included in this work. Let us address each factor separately and in greater detail.

Societal

The authors of the following essays make it abundantly clear that military interventions occur when the political elites and the popular forces they represent disagree as to the proper role of the state and the division of power between the different sectors, classes or ethnic groups of a given society; and when the governing forces fail to resolve national questions and/or address major policy or societal concerns. Under such circumstances civilian authorities suffer legitimacy deflation and the military either takes upon itself to become the saviour of its client, the state, and/or is formally or informally invited to step in and assume the reins of power.

Conversely, the armed forces relinquish the levers of authority when: political elites resolve their differences, reach a consensus on key policy questions, and present a viable and acceptable alternative; popular forces demand the return of civilian rule; and the military as political governors fail to meet expectations and are unable or unwilling to address major societal concerns such as improving economic conditions, checking social violence, and defending the nation against outside threats. Long-term disengagement is established and maintained when the civilian authorities build institutions capable of: gaining popular allegiance, managing social conflict, attaining the goals of the regime, and making decisions that are properly implemented and enforced.[13] The latter includes 'the extent to which authority patterns of social units [including the military] actually attain the goals they pursue'.[14] And, as Welch has correctly pointed out, the consistent but limited participation of the military in politics is an important factor that keeps the armed forces in the barracks.[15]

In Central and South America interventionism and long-term disengagement is explained in the context of conflict and cooperation depicting the conservative forces backed by the Catholic Church and the landlords on one side and popular strata on the other. Analysing the interventionist role of the Mexican military, Professor Roderic Camp attributes General Porfirio Diaz's 1877 coup to concerns that the newly achieved electoral victory by the reformist liberal forces would not suffice to contain the threat emanating from the reactionary conservatives and their allies. But in spite of Diaz's military background, his presidency (1877–1911) was marked by 'a gradual but persistent decline in career military backgrounds among his most influential collaborators'.

The 1910 Revolution resulted in the eventual dominance of the political forces and 'destroyed the influence and legitimacy' of the military. In the eyes of the public, says Camp, the armed forces became 'a paper force ... feared but not respected' – nothing more than 'one of several quasi-state institutions with its [own] political interests' which was defeated by a civilian competitor. The new authorities eventually 'opened up their leadership ranks to dissident groups willing to join the system'; established a strong, civilian-dominated presidency and a broad-based political party (Institutional Revolutionary Party–PRI); restricted the role of the Catholic Church; and instituted land and social reform advocated by the popular forces. At the same time, the civilian authorities gave the armed forces autonomy in 'internal matters' and transformed 'military participation in politics ... into military influence in politics, based on the increasing legitimacy of civilian and governmental institutions'. The Mexican armed forces, argues Professor Camp, have become 'one of several state-co-opted interest groups, sharing some similarities with labour, peasants, intellectuals and business people'. Camp concludes that Mexican political leaders are 'both singularly united in the military and successful in gaining military acquiescence to this role definition' – positions that the Mexican public supports overwhelmingly.

Venezuela and Colombia displayed societal conflicts similar to those that dominated the Mexican landscape, although the reasons for military intervention in these two South American countries as well as the process of withdrawal displayed striking differences from those of their Central American neighbour. Professors Giacalone and Hanes argue that political fractionalization and social divisions in Venezuela provided the background to a series of military coups. Mobilization and incorporation of labour and peasants into the political system propelled Romulo Gallegos, candidate of the Accion Democratica (AD) party, to the presidency of Venezuela in 1948 by an overwhelming 74.4 per cent of the vote. The sheer size of his victory led Gallegos to introduce social and economic reforms, and made him feel 'no great commitment to maintain the privileged role of the military'. Under the circumstances the declining political parties, the church, and the privileged mobilized the army against the popularly elected president.

Eventually the army-backed regime turned into a personalistic dictatorship under General Marcos Perez Jiménez. Jiménez sought to legitimize his rule through a plebiscite. Held in 1957, the plebiscite angered many officers who were 'asked ... to participate actively in electoral fraud', and became 'the catalyst which mobilized both civilian and military opposition to the Jiménez dictatorship'. The armed forces joined the Junta Patriotica, a coalition of the four principal political parties (AD, COPEI, URD, and PCV), to overthrow Jiménez. In turn, Venezuela's major political parties, minus the Communists (PDV), worked out a minimum programme, known as Pact Punto Fijo, aimed at consolidating the newly re-established democratic regime. The pact included 'social and economic reforms and an ambitious industrialization programme, which together would assure political stability and economic development'. Huge oil revenues made possible the implementation of many of the provisions included in the agreement.

Dubbed by Giacolone and Hanes as 'subsidized democracy', Venezuela's civilian-dominated regime made possible the integration of different sectors in the new political system after 1958, 'obtaining their support by means of the resources available to the state'. Venezuelan politics, in the words of Giacalone and Hanes are 'characterized, at the top, by compromise, conciliation and bargaining among elites ... including the armed forces'. Political leaders have and continue the pattern of noninterference in internal military matters established under the leadership of President Rómulho Betancourt.

In neighbouring Colombia the military traditionally has been kept under civilian control and its 'political significance ... has been considerably less than any other Latin American country except Costa Rica'. Yet Colombia experienced military rule in the 1950s (1953–8), when the armed forces reluctantly assumed the task of governing the country at the behest of the divided political elites, in the face of what Professor Premo describes as 'unprecedented levels of partisan rural violence', political intrigue by President Laureano Gómez, and 'the breakdown in Colombia's social and political order' – all of which caused legitimacy deflation and 'threatened the institutional autonomy of the military'.

The armed forces with the help of the civilians removed Gómez and established a quasi-military government, which General Gustavo Rojas Panilla sought to turn into a personalistic dictatorship. However, Rojas's efforts to create an organized base 'to confront the Liberal–Conservative coalition forming against him' failed. Much like neighbouring Venezuela, Colombia's military removed Rojas and the nation's main political parties (Liberals and Conservatives) 'agreed to share power in a unique experiment in "controlled democracy" known as the National Front'.

In spite of recent drug-related violence, Colombia's post 1958 civilian-dominated political system is characterized by a broad consensus among the nation's political forces to maintain the present political system, but also to recognize the military as 'a major pressure group in Colombian politics'. And Colombian presidents, in Professor Premo's terms, 'have not been insensitive to the institutional concerns of the military'.

Finally, tiny Costa Rica shares with the rest of her Latin sisters many of the factors that led to military intervention and subsequent withdrawal, but parts company with regard to the role of the armed forces in post-disengagement politics. The takeover and the establishment of the Ticono dictatorship in 1917 was the result of rivalries between political elites and declining coffee prices which led the landed oligarchy to employ violence in order to suppress popular discontent. The reaction was similar in the mid-1930s when a similar economic crisis generated social strife and radicalization of the masses forced the oligarchy 'to take refuge in an authoritarian government'.

After considerable machination and coalition politics, often involving strange bedfellows, Costa Rica's political elites, like those of Mexico, Colombia and Venezuela, patched up their differences and reached a consensus which resulted in the growth and expansion of the role of the state, and, as Professor Peritore points out, to the establishment of a 'sophisticated welfare state'. Unlike their other Latin neighbours, Costa Rican leaders, led by the charismatic and dominant personality of the late José Figueres, declared in 1948 their nation 'formally neutral in foreign relations' and, in an unprecedented step for Latin American politics, 'abolished the army'. Today Costa Rica has a police force for internal security functions but no organized military institution.

Half-way around the world economic difficulties, political divisions, regionalism and class struggle between the landed aristocracy and the landless peasantry propelled the Spanish army into a privileged position and initiated an era of *pronunciamentos* that continued well into the twentieth century. The same factors accounted for the Spanish civil war (1936–9) which culminated in the defeat of the republican forces and the inauguration of the Francoist dictatorship. The latter was supported by the nation's conservative sectors including the Catholic Church, the financial and industrial elites, and the armed forces. The Francoist regime lasted until General Franco's death in 1975.

The post-dictatorship period saw a gradual effort by Prime Minister Adolfo Suárez's government to institute a democratic political system in which Spain's nervous military would accept the supremacy of the constitutional authorities. As in Latin America, Spain's political forces displayed a remarkably 'positive attitude towards the military ... facilitating by every means available the integration of the armed forces in the new political system'. Professor Fernando Rodrigo refers to this as 'a democratic strategy towards the military' and considers it 'essential to the noninterventionist behavior of the military' in Spain's transition to and consolidation of democracy. The major elements of this strategy, in Rodrigo's mind, included: remilitarizing the military, creating a defence ministry, demilitarizing law enforcement, giving the armed forces substantial pay increases and autonomy to manage their own affairs, and opportunities to influence the making of the nation's defence policy through normative, group, or institutional processes.

Intervention in the Dominican Republic and Greece occurred because the politicized military sought to prevent the rise to power of political forces who they considered potentially damaging to the armed forces' prerogatives and corporate interests. In the Dominican setting the American trained, corrupt, and factionalized officers corps stepped in to prevent the election of Antonio Guzmán (1978), candidate of the centre-left Dominican Revolutionary Party (PRD) to the presidency. The military considered the PRD a 'socially disruptive, if not communistic element', and moved to interrupt the ballot count 'with the apparent intent of nullifying the election'. In a similar vein the thoroughly sanitized, right-wing but politically powerful Greek military staged a coup in 1967 to prevent the rise to power of that nation's centrist political forces whom they regarded as threatening the professional interests and the privileged position the armed forces held in Greece's post-war political equation.

The two nations, however, parted company with regard to the nature of civilian supremacy and the role of the military in post-disengagement politics. In the Dominican Republic, as Professor Black sees it, the armed forces continue to be factionalized and have yet to divorce themselves from the political arena. The civilian institutions manage to maintain power by manipulating, corrupting and buying off the nation's military establishment. Even the age-long duel between the country's two octogenarian politicians Juán Bosch and Joaquin Balanguer continues unabated, as evidenced by the recent electoral contest between them.

Post-junta Greece on the other hand represents a different picture. In the wake of seven years of corrupt dictatorial rule and the Cyprus debacle, the nation's political elites formed a consensus and managed to put many of the divisive issues of previous decades to rest. The issue of the monarchy was decisively resolved in late 1974 (with the Greeks opting for a presidential republic), steps were taken to heal the wounds of the Civil War (1946–9), and the country has gone through a number of electoral contests in which power shifted away from the conservatives to the socialists, and back to the conservatives.

In spite of present economic difficulties, the Greek public is supportive of the nation's democratic political institutions and the officer corps, though exercising considerable influence in defence-related matters, accepts civilian supremacy and appears devoted to its professional mission. Greek political leaders have shown sensitivity to military concerns and, partly due to continuing difficulties with neighbouring Turkey, budgetary appropriations for defence consume almost a quarter of total government spending.

Indecision and inability to resolve the Algerian issue caused the French military stationed in that colony to make 'a series of forays into the political arena' in the 1950s. Though the French military did not establish a military government, it nevertheless forced the political forces to line up behind General de Gaulle who, in turn, proceeded to replace the Fourth Republic's stalemated and weak political system with a strong presidential government (Fifth Republic). The general also acted boldly to sever France's presence in Algeria and, as Professor John Fells sees it, strengthened the military's professional mission, giving it 'a new role under a popular regime'. Civilian supremacy in France is beyond question and 'officers pushed beyond the limits of their endurance find relief for their exasperation by writing letters of resignation'.

The African landscape of civil–military relations represents a different dimension. Tribalism, underdevelopment, client–patron relationships, social fragmentation, corruption, absence of democratic ethos, and often a lack of national consciousness characterize the politics of African countries most of which attained their independence in the 1950s. Thus, as Professor Magyar correctly observes, 'coups are merely the most frequent expression of the utter frustrations encountered in nation-building in Africa, attempted under the most severe socio-political conditions'. Whenever long-term military withdrawal has occurred it has been accomplished not because African governments have been able to reverse the social economic, and historic conditions that prompted praetorianism, but by establishing and maintaining a close relationship between the ruling elites and the military, based on tribal or personal connections, and by purging the officer corps or drastically reducing its size.

Social divisions based on tribal or ethnic considerations and economic underdevelopment dominated Sierra Leone's political landscape and have made nation-building and the functioning of democratic processes very problematic. When Sierra Leone gained its independence in 1960 these social divisions manifested themselves in the formation of political parties. The Sierra Leone People's Party (SLPP) represented the Merle hinderlanders, and the Creoles formed the backbone of the All People's Party (APP). The new country's armed forces were not immune to these divisions and, as Professor Kline states, rendered Sierra Leone's 'officer corps in disarray'. When the opposition APC, under the leadership of Siaka Stevens won the 1967 elections, military officers sympathetic to the ruling SLPP staged a coup to prevent Stevens's appointment to the premiership of Sierra Leone. The intervention was instigated out of fear that Stevens would purge pro-SLPP elements in the military, but was supported by many civilian politicians who joined hands to 'impede the transfer of power to the victorious APC'.

However, Brigadier David Lansana who led the coup, was perceived ready 'to defend the ruling circle at any cost', and was removed by fellow officers. A National Reformation Council (NRC) was formed under Lt Col. Andrew Juxon-Smith to lead the country back to normalcy. But the NRC's authoritarian tendencies and corruption, in Kline's terms, generated 'a great deal of opposition to its continuation in office'. Moreover, the Sierra Leone public, as Professor Magyar contends, 'saw the military as obstructionists' and feared that the 'economy would not be developed under military rule'. Under the circumstances, lower-echelon officers conspired with Stevens, who also managed to obtain military assistance from neighbouring Guinea in the form of a force, prevailed on the NSC to relinquish power and to accept Stevens's accession to the premiership of Sierra Leone in April 1968.

To consolidate his position Stevens purged his political opponents, declared Sierra Leone a one-party state (APP), eliminated officers suspected of insubordination and, in Professor Kline's words, nurtured 'pro-government cliques in the army and tribal loyalties'. Moreover, as Magyar discovered, Stevens rewarded loyalty by extending 'generous benefits ... to the armed forces'. Finally, the APP formed a de facto coalition with the military – referred to by Kline as a civilian-military republic – which Stevens augmented in 1985 by personally selecting the head of the armed forces, Brigadier General Joseph Momoh, as his successor as leader of the party and President of Sierra Leone. Momoh and the APP, concludes Kline, 'have filled the ranks of the military with those tribes and supporters who will continue their support as long as the special privileges they enjoy continue'.

With an average per capita income of $5500 (1987), little-known Gabon contrasts sharply with Sierra Leone and most of its destitute neighbours. Yet, as Professor Dorabji points out, colonial legacies, dependency, and 'neocolonialism' prevented the emergence of a Gabonese 'national vision' and 'made divisive sectional politics a problem from the very start'. Faced with those difficulties and unable to resist the temptation of governing with anything 'less than total loyalty and obedience', President Mba moved in 1964 to 'close down loyal opposition' and, copying many of his African counterparts, resorted to a one-party state. However, under French 'protection' Mba concentrated his efforts on economic matters and in the process neglected the needs of Gabon's small army. 'Outraged at being excluded from the bounty harvested' military officers 'stormed the presidential palace' in February 1964, seized President Mba and governed the country for a brief 48-hour period. France's immediate intervention forced the disgruntled officers to return to the barracks and Mba was reinstated as the country's chief executive.

Mba acted forcefully to consolidate his position and to prevent another coup. He 'dismantled the entire army and dismissed every soldier'. Then, he turned around and created a new military force 'containing only tribal groupings loyal to him'. But unlike Siaka Stevens, Mba and his successor, El Hadj Bongo, have carefully refrained from using 'the army to strengthen their power base'. Given the fact that Gabon is becoming 'steadily wealthier – an anomaly for Africa', coupled with foreign (mainly French) influence, and the small size (1900 men) of the country's army, Professor Dorabji feels that civilian rule is likely to stay in place.

In a pioneering piece of scholarship Samuel P. Huntington suggested two methods of civilian control over the military: subjective and objective. Subjective implies 'maximizing the power of the ruling group in relation to the military', which is accomplished through 'instrumental slogans' exalting the supremacy of 'particular governmental institutions particular social classes, and particular constitutional forms'. Subjective control then is based on the 'identity of thought and outlook between the civilian and military groups'. Objective control, on the other hand, denotes depoliticizing or 'militarizing' the military. This can be accomplished by a clear delineation between political and military roles, creating for the military a climate 'most conducive' for the development of *esprit de corps* and devotion to strictly military-related matters and preparedness, thus 'making them the tool of the state'. Objective control, Huntington concludes, depends on the 'compatibility of the professional military ethic with the political ideologies prevailing in society'.[16]

Building on Huntington's scheme, Claude E. Welch identifies 'five means of civilian control [that] have been devised and utilized by governments': (1) constitutional constraints on the role of the armed forces; (2) ascriptive factors, implying either integration or separation of the military from society depending on the idiosyncrasies of each individual case; (3) penetration of the military by the ruling party (usually communist or single party systems); (4) maintaining a small military establishment, whenever geographic and historical factors permit; and (5) delineation of clear spheres of responsibility, similar to Huntington's objective type.[17]

As the contributions to this volume make clear, civilian regimes use one or a combination of the means mentioned by Huntington and Welch. European nations (France, Spain and Greece) as well as Central and Latin American countries, whose societies are divided along class but not tribal lines, tend to utilize methods that come closer to Huntington's objective type, without altogether staying away from such subjective factors as constitutionalism. African countries, and to a lesser extent the Dominican Republic, seem to be more subjective types of controls. Given the fact that African societies are deeply divided along tribal lines and national consciousness is often lacking, delineation between military and political roles, so crucial to objective means of civilian control, is almost impossible at this stage of their development.

The role of the military

Establishing and sustaining long-term military disengagement from politics is not the exclusive domain of the civilian elites, but the military as well. After all, the armed forces may have relinquished the levers of authority, but by virtue of their unchallenged force, still maintain the ability to reoccupy the offices of government almost at will. Societal considerations, as outlined above, go a long way towards keeping the army in the barracks, so do lessons drawn by civilian elites who have come to accept the military as an important element in a nation's polity. But the attitudes and behaviour of the armed forces should not and cannot be neglected.

Scholars of civil–military relations agree that professionalism – defined in terms of role specialization, responsibility and corporateness – is a salient characteristic of modern soldiery and plays a pivotal role in determining the political posture of the armed forces.[18] However, scholars disagree as to the nature of professionalism's impact regarding intervention as well as during post disengagement. Two distinct but opposing views have emerged: one sees professionalism as a factor inhibiting intervention; the other, as a stimulant to praetorianism. The first thesis, advanced by Samuel Huntington, stipulates that a professionalized army concentrates all its efforts to perfect its fighting ability and 'stands ready to carry out the wishes of any civilian government'. Professionalism, therefore, renders the military into 'politically sterile and neutral' servants of the state.[19]

The other view advances the theory that professionalism makes the military group-conscious, instilling the ability and the will to intervene, in order to protect its corporate interests which, as stated earlier, include: adequate budgetary support, institutional autonomy, protection against outside encroachments, and survival and viability of the armed forces as an institution. Interference with corporate interests constitute 'the most important interventicnist motive'.[20]

The experiences of the case studies that follow and Professor Magyar's more comprehensive chapter on Africa bear out the second position. In almost every example the record shows that interventions occurred when the officer corps felt that less of legitimacy on the part of the ruling civilian governments, were unable to forge a consensus, tackle major national questions, or undesirable opposition groups rose to power. Under such conditions the armed forces seize power in order to protect their corporate interests. By the same token, in order to forestall recurring interventionist motives, successor civilian regimes have shown considerable sensitivity to the corporate interests of the officer corps which includes influencing the making and implementation of the country's security policy.

The non-interventionist posture and the sustenance of long-term disengagement also seems to be connected to two related professional concerns: praetorian rule can damage the military's prestige, social standing and internal cohesion; and the armed forces can best protect their corporate interests from the barracks acting as a respected social group rather than political governors. Central to the latter factor is the well-founded conclusion that the rough and tumble of politics and choice-making that governing entails divide the officer corps, warps the military's professionalism and alienates the armed forces from important sectors of the society. Thus, one can agree that the armed forces of nations who have experienced long-term military disengagement have chosen to stay in the barracks because they perceive the civilian alternative acceptable and non-threatening to their corporate interests; and when civilian authorities allow the military influence in matters relating to national defence and other related concerns. It takes two to tango and the following chapters substantiate it rather persuasively.

The international factor

The role of forces lying outside national boundaries on military intervention, subsequent withdrawal and long-term disengagement is certainly not new, but remains a controversial subject. National sovereignty, territorial integrity, political independence and other well-known components of modern international law and international relations discourage nations with geographic strategic, historical, economic or political ties from interfering in the internal affairs of other (usually weaker) states.

Yet there is ample evidence suggesting that such intrusions (direct, indirect or by proxy) have and continue to occur when strategic, economic, or geopolitical factors are at stake. Guatemala, the Dominican Republic, Nicaragua and Greece are but a few examples where the USA used its power or influence to help overthrow reform-oriented governments, considered dangerous or unacceptable to American interests. The Kremlin was even harsher and moved ferociously against liberalization attempts within its bloc in the 1950s, 1960s and 1970s.

On the more positive side, Professor Kline credits the 'Guinean factor' as having played a key role enabling Siaka Stevens to bring about the fall of the NCR regime, and to forestall the recurrence of military intervention in Sierra Leone. The 'timely intercession of United States diplomats and military officers' is cited by Professor Black as having been instrumental in forcing the Dominican armed forces not to proceed with their intention to nullify the election of Antonio Guzmán. In 1974 Washington acted in a similar vein and 'openly encouraged' the Greek junta to withdraw and allow the return of civilian rule. France moved expeditiously in 1964 forcing the coup makers in Gabon to return power to the overthrown civilian authorities; and 'through an unpleasant affirmation of Gabonese sovereignty, permitted the growth of a politically stable government'. Finally, the recent and on-going historic changes in Eastern Europe could not have taken place without Moscow's acquiescence, and, to some extent, encouragement.

Moreover, in an era of increasing technological and economic interdependence the role of international factors on domestic developments has never been greater, although the opposite is also true. In this environment developing nations – beset by a myriad of economic social, and political problems – are now more vulnerable to outside pressures than ever before. Under such circumstances the ability of developed countries and leading international financial institutions, such as the IMF and the World Bank, to influence processes in changing societies has never been greater. In the Dominican Republic, for example, by ensuring that the nation's debt is serviced, the IMF protects the interests of the economic elites and the military. At the same time when foreign creditors demand sacrifices these sacrifices fall on the poor and the political elites absolve themselves by 'passing the buck to the mysterious and seemingly omnipotent IMF'.

What we are witnessing is a shift in the nature of influence peddling on the part of developed nations. Gunboat diplomacy and 'fraternal assistance' is giving way to economic and diplomatic intercession threatening to cut off the flow of aid, take other punitive measures such as freezing assets, imposing trade or tourist embargoes, or refusing to provide badly needed loans to keep the economies of needy nations afloat.

This shift emanates from the realization that dictatorships (military or otherwise) may be strategically beneficial in the short term but run the risk of damaging the long-term interests of influential nations. Events in Portugal, Greece, Spain and Ethiopia in the mid-1970s challenged its long-held view in Washington that a right-wing anti-Communist dictatorship of the Salazar, Franco, Haile Selassie, or Papadopoulos type would prevent 'radicalization' of these countries and keep them firmly in the Western camp. The 1974–6 Portuguese Revolution showed that a reactionary dictatorship can plant the seeds of social discontent and radicalization in the ranks of the military, and cause an upheaval which nearly delivered a NATO member into the arms of the Soviet Union. The botching of the Cyprus issue by the Greek junta created severe difficulties in the southern flank of the Atlantic Alliance, led to the rise of popular discontent and damaged Greek–American relations. An even more discouraging outcome took place in Ethiopia, where the armed forces overthrew Emperor Selassie and installed a Leninist-type regime. Conversely, the Spanish experience revealed that reform, liberalization, and democratization are not synonymous with radicalization, instability and a neutralist foreign policy. Professor Rodrigo credits NATO membership as a major factor contributing to Spain's relatively smooth democratization and civilian supremacy in the post-Franco era.

Technological advances in warfare, coupled with the Soviet Union's economic problems, recently led Moscow to realize that 'friendly' governments in Eastern Europe were no longer strategically necessary and economically advantageous. In fact Gorbachev appears to have concluded that maintaining in power the old Communist rulers in Prague, Warsaw and East Berlin might thicken the lines of those at home who oppose *perestroika* and *glasnost*. All these developments, in turn, rendered the confrontational temper of the Cold War obsolete and propelled forward a spirit of cooperation in international relations. In spite of the increasing ascendancy of hardline elements and the slowing down of the pace of reform in Moscow, the spirit of cooperation continues as exemplified by the Kremlin's support of the United Nations' resolution calling on Saddam Hussein to withdraw his troops from Kuwait.

A more amicable international environment, technological advances, economic independence, lessons learned by all involved, and growing ills led developing countries to reach out and in the process become more susceptible to outside influence. Given the West's growing preference for civilian rule and competitive politics, one can see how long-term military disengagement from politics has been sustained, in part, by factors lying beyond national boundaries.

On the flip side of the coin, international developments may also serve as a means of creating a climate conducive to military re-intervention in politics. This is likely to occur when excessive dependence on outside actors hampers the ability of that country's ruling elites to perform to expectations and thus suffer legitimacy deflation. Sharply declining revenues resulting from the dramatic fall of the price of oil in the international market in recent years is viewed by Professors Giacalone and Hanes as having eroded the ability of Venezuela's political system to 'sustain the co-optation of every major social sector.... [and] has also weakened its capacity to control or avoid conflict within the society'. Dwindling oil revenues have also been partly blamed for Mexico's recent economic ills and the corresponding losses suffered by the once unchallenged PRI, although Camp sees no erosion in the ability of the civilians to control the military.

American and international bank 'mismanagement' of the Costa Rican debt as well as 'US pressure to coordinate with the Contra programme' have led the 'Switzerland of Central America ... into a socioeconomic and political impasse which may stretch its tolerant democratic culture to a violent breaking point', and bring about 'indirect militarization of the Tico society'. Finally, international demand for drugs and the huge profits they generate have dramatically increased the level of violence and threaten the fabric of Colombian society. However, Professor Premo is optimistic arguing that, given the long-held tradition of non-involvement, that nation's military would intervene only 'if Colombia's civilian elites fail to provide the inspired moral and political leadership'.

BRINGING IT ALL TOGETHER

Establishing and maintaining civilian control of the military, especially in societies that have experienced praetorianism, is no easy matter, and the essays in this volume make that very clear. Societal, institutional as well as international factors undoubtedly play significant roles. However, it is the quality of leadership exercised by those in key positions that often determines whether these factors are recognized and properly implemented. Inspired and effective stewardship can pick the right time, make the necessary concessions, display toughness and determination, show compassion, and touch the sensitive rational and emotional chords of civilians and the military alike. Leadership, says Thomas Cronin,

> is all about making things happen that otherwise might not happen and preventing things from happening that ordinarily would happen. It is the process of getting people to work together to achieve common goals and aspirations. It involves the infusion of vision and purpose into an enterprise and entails mobilizing both people and resources to undertake and achieve desired ends.[21]

Almost all of the countries included in this book were endowed with inspired and flexible leaders at crucial points in the transition from military to civilian rule, who made the proper decisions and set the foundations which contributed to re-establishing and maintaining civilian control of the military.

Notes

1. Eric A. Nordlinger, *Soldiers in Politics: Military Coups and Governments* (Englewood Cliffs, NJ: Prentice-Hall, Inc., 1977), p. 2.
2. Constantine P. Danopoulos, 'Military Dictatorships in Retreat: Problems and Perspectives', in Constantine P. Danopoulos, ed., *The Decline of Military Regimes – The Civilian Influence* (Boulder, CO: Westview Press, 1988), p. 3.
3. Claude E. Welch, Jr, *No Farewell to Arms? Military Disengagement from Politics in Africa and Latin America* (Boulder: Westview Press, 1987), p. 20. Also see S. E. Finer, *The Man on Horseback: The Role of the Military in Politics*, 2nd enlarged edition (Boulder: Westview Press, 1988), p. 305.
4. Eric A. Nordlinger, *Soldiers in Politics: Military Coups and Governments* (Englewood Cliffs, NJ: Prentice-Hall, Inc., 1977), p. 207. Also see: Finer, *The Man on Horseback*, pp. 110–39; and Ulf Sundhaussen, 'Military Withdrawal from Government Responsibility', *Armed Forces and Society*, 10: 4 (Summer 1984), p. 559.
5. Monte Palmer, *Dilemmas of Development*, 3rd edition (Itasca, Ill. : F. E. Peacock Publishers, 1985), p. 2
6. Morris Janowitz's second edition of the book appeared under the title *Military Institution and Coercion in the Developing Nations* (Chicago: The University of Chicago Press, 1977), pp. VIII and IX.
7. Nordlinger, *Soldiers in Politics*.
8. Claude E. Welch, Jr and Arthur K. Smith, *Military Role and Rule: Perspectives on Civil–Military Relations* (North Scituate: Duxbury Press, 1974).
9. Nordlinger, *Soldiers in Politics*, pp. 65–78.
10. Talukder Maniruzzaman, *Military Withdrawal From Politics: A Comparative Study* (Cambridge: Bollinger Publishing Company, 1987), p. 29.
11. Finer, *The Man on Horseback*, pp. 305–6.
12. See: Maniruzzaman, *Military Withdrawal*, ch. 9; and Lawrence Whitehead, 'International Aspects of Democratization', in Guillermo O'Donnell, Philippe Schmitter and Lawrence Whitehead, eds, *Transitions from Authoritarian Rule: Comparative Perspectives* (Baltimore: Johns Hopkins University Press, 1986), pp. 3–46; and Constantine P. Danopoulos, 'Withdrawal and After: A One Way

Street or a Revolving Door?', in Danopoulos, ed., *The Decline of Military Regimes*, ch. 11.

13. Harry Eckstein and Ted Robert Gurr, *Patterns of Authority: A Structural Basis for Political Inquiry* (New York: John Wiley and Sons, 1975), pp. 445–74.
14. Ibid., p. 458.
15. Welch, *No Farewell to Arms?*, p. 13.
16. Samuel P. Huntington, 'Civilian Control of the Military: A Theoretical Statement', in Heinz Eulau, Samuel J. Eldersveld, and Morris Janowitz, eds, *Political Behaviour: A Reader in Theory and Research* (Glencoe, Ill. : The Free Press, 1956), pp. 380–81.
17. Claude E. Welch, Jr, 'Civilian Control of the Military: Myth and Reality', in Claude E. Welch, Jr, *Civilian Control of the Military: Theory and Cases from Developing Countries* (Albany, NY: State University of New York Press, 1976), pp. 5–34.
18. Bengt Abrahamsson, *Military Professionalization and Political Power* (Beverly Hills: Sage Publications, 1972), pp. 15–18.
19. Samuel P. Huntington, *The Soldier and the State: The Theory and Politics of Civil–Military Relations* (New York: Random House, 1957), p. 84.
20. Nordlinger, *Soldiers in Politics*, p. 65.
21. Thomas E. Cronin, 'Foreword', in William E. Rosenbach and Robert L. Taylor, eds., *Contemporary Issues in Leadership*, 2nd edition (Boulder: Westview Press, 1989), p. XIII.

2 In the wrong republic: civil–military relations in modern France

John Fells

Shortly after France's 1988 presidential election Reuters reported the Defence Minister, Jean Pierre Chevenement as issuing 'a stern warning to forty-five generals, most of them retired, who supported the conservative candidate, Jacques Chirac, in the presidential election'. According to this report, 'Military sources said he warned them that they would be stripped of military honours if they again "contravened the principle of the army's neutrality by publicly contesting the state's legitimacy"'.[1] That principle of military 'neutrality' stoutly defended by a recent minister of defence was asserted and consolidated during the Third Republic with very little serious threat from the military either in the last years of the nineteenth century, or in the present century before World War II. The same, however, is not true of the following three decades. Something had changed.

The military establishment of the reconstructed French democracy obediently played its allotted role in the Third Republic, but it did so with a strong sense of its own uniqueness within French national life. Reference to the Dreyfus Affair is all that is required to remind us that the army saw itself as concerned above all with honour, its own as well as that of France. Clearly, if the army of France was to be an obedient instrument of the will of the French nation, it could not be called upon to act in a way whereby honour might be compromised.

Widespread questioning of the compatibility of loyalty and honour could not be avoided after the capitulation of France and the establishment of the collaborationist Vichy Republic in 1940. The renegade de Gaulle's subsequent call upon French soldiery to cease to honour their oaths of loyalty to the government of France, and instead to continue to resist by joining the Free French is only the clearest of the conflicting demands made upon a traditionally obedient and traditionally nationalistic officer corps during World War II. Allied victory, moreover, provided a lesson about the consequences of such 'disloyalty' that could not easily be ignored.

The ending of World War II was not, however, the beginning of a period of world peace. French armies were called upon to continue fighting to maintain an empire (renamed the French Union) whose peoples had supplied attentive observers of the recent spectacles of French military defeat and the division of French imperial power into two opposing camps. In Indo-China the French military learned that French territory and loyal peoples could be abandoned by a France which harboured among its population and in its National Assembly supporters of the Viet Minh enemy. When the Algerian independence movement resorted to armed struggle, the army was determined to avoid any ignominious repetition of its experience in South East Asia. To that end it was ready to defend France against its external enemies and, if necessary, against the misguided amongst its politicians and citizens.

In Algeria the stage was set for military intervention in French political life. That neither the imposition of military government in France, nor the institution of a government subservient to the military establishment were the outcome of events in Algeria in the late 1950s and early 1960s can to a large extent be attributed to Gaullist policy, to which must also be given a measure of credit for the re-establishment of the tradition of obedience of the military (apart from a few vocal pensioners) to the civil power in France. However, the particular circumstances of the revolt of the military in Algeria must also figure largely in any explanation of the course of military intervention in French politics.

ALGERIA

The discontent of the armed forces in Algeria manifested itself in a series of forays into the political arena over a period of 3 years.[2] The events of the late spring and early summer of 1950 when the generals found themselves at the head of rebellious *colons* brought about the demise of the Fourth Republic and the institution of the Fifth Republic under the presidency of Charles de Gaulle. Dissatisfaction with the policies of the new regime led to a plotted coup being called off in October 1959,[3] followed by the Barricades Affair in Algiers in January of the next year when paratroops failed to act promptly and decisively against armed European settlers and territorial units occupying government buildings in an attempt to advance the cause of French Algeria. The final outbreak of military unrest was the failed putsch of April 1961, an attempt at direct action by a small part of the Algerian garrison who, in the event, were supported neither by the majority of French citizenry nor by the conscripts who formed much of the army in Algeria.

The key to this catalogue of military unrest is the Algerian struggle for independence from France. The removal of the Algerian 'problem' from French political life brought the series of interventions to an end. The

Algerian war was the last battle of the old French colonial army, and its end the beginning of a new role for the French armed forces.

When the Algerian war of independence began in 1957, the French troops who arrived to confront the insurgents were determined not to repeat the debacle of Indo-China. Algeria after all was part of France. It had been invaded by the forces of Charles X in 1830, conquered and settled by Frenchmen and other Europeans. Algeria now elected representatives to the French parliament. The enemy in Algeria, however, was soon seen to be part of the same global Communist threat. If, in the recent past Europe had been freed by troops invading from North Africa, so it could be enslaved by the same route. A Communist Algeria would threaten France and the West. Algeria, the home of the foreign legion, represented a vital bridgehead as well as a source of manpower for the French army. It could not be abandoned.

If this reasoning seems bizarre, we should remember that the cause of Arab nationalism was supported by Egypt's Colonel Nasser who, after the nationalization of the Suez Canal, was supported solely by Communist states. Arab nationalism was thus perceived to be the latest manifestation of the struggle for world Communism.[4] Military defeat of the nationalists would both thrust back Communism and restore the prestige of an army whose officers were facing a decline in both social and financial position in metropolitan France.[5] That victory could be denied them by two adversaries: the insurgents in Algeria and the politicians at home. The latter had already given Morocco independence in a sudden reversal of policy, and if the insurgents in Algeria were their opponents, so must be the Communists in the 'other part' of France. Still, the army had learned how to fight Communism during the war in Indo-China. It knew how to 'win hearts and minds' (or at least deny them to the enemy) by setting up its own social hierarchies to resist Communist organization; and it knew how to attack terrorist networks by police actions. General Massu's 'Battle of Algiers' furnishes an example of the controversial methods employed to make such actions successful. The 'Communists', it was maintained, could be beaten back if engaged by an opponent with sufficient resolve.

The policy of 'beating Communism at its own game' had a number of consequences which further committed the military to the policy of French Algeria, while increasing their involvement in the administration and day to day politics of Algeria. As the war continued, junior officers organized schools and public works in protected villages in an attempt to engage the sympathies of the Moslem population. If the involvement of such officers in day to day government was less than that of say, General Massu, they nevertheless had to offer guarantees, sometimes personal, to those who cooperated with them that they would not be abandoned to reprisals like the loyal peoples of Indo-China.[6] This is not to say that the personal honour of the officers in Algeria was not also staked on victory. The army, of course, needed to restore its prestige after recent defeats, but, during police actions by soldiers in Algiers in particular, recourse to torture had been routine and had been condoned by very senior officers. A victorious army would not be reproached for such excesses. There were protests from metropolitan France against alleged incidences of torture, but these could only confirm, in the minds of many officers, the view that the national spirit was failing under the onslaught of the left, and that the army was now its only guardian.[7]

By early 1958 France had the upper hand militarily in Algeria. The border had been sealed, and, while terrorist activity continued, it did so at a much reduced level. It still remained to be seen, however, how the politicians would use the army's achievement; it could still be wasted effort. A political solution which defended the position of the Europeans but which could also win the support of the majority Moslem population still had to be found. The Paris government had already explored the possibility of negotiations with the rebels, who were to be offered a measure of autonomy for Algeria. Enabling legislation was drafted, but the discontent of the army was beginning to show. 'The anguish which could be removed only by a government resolutely decided to maintain our flag in Algeria' was made clear to the government by leading officers in Algeria still friendly to the regime.[8] Soon after, the Fourth Republic was wound up, and the Fifth Republic inaugurated under the leadership of de Gaulle.

The collapse of the Fourth Republic stems indirectly from military action. A French bombing raid against Algerian rebels in Sakhiet in Tunisia in February 1958 killed many civilians, and became the subject of an international quarrel.[9] Negotiations over the incident between France and Tunisia were conducted with the aid of mediation by France's British and American allies in NATO. The perception that this was an 'internationalization' of the Algerian question resulted in a vote of no confidence which brought about the fall of the government. The ensuing interregnum was chosen by right-wingers as the moment to lead European settlers, already gathered for a rally in homage to soldiers killed by insurgents, in the occupation of government headquarters in Algiers. The Commander-in-Chief in Algiers (Gen. Salan) was given the powers of the Minister for Algeria by Paris, and the commander in Algiers itself (Massu), claiming that this was the only means to maintain public order, soon allowed himself to be put at the head of a committee of public safety. Salan's position was confirmed by Pierre Pflimlin after his eventual investiture as the new prime minister. Two days after the start of the insurrection, and the day after Pflimlin became premier, de Gaulle announced his own willingness to lead a government, encouraged no doubt by the same tide of Gaullist enthusiasm which led Gen. Salan to shout 'vive de Gaulle' to an Algerian crowd on the same day. The Deputy Chief of the General Staff was arrested in Paris, and troops from Algeria taking advantage of extra transport aircraft he had supplied from France, occupied Corsica. An attempt to occupy Paris seemed imminent. On 28 May, encouraged by President Coty, and despite the support of the National Assembly, Pflimlin resigned. Coty then threatened to resign too if de Gaulle were not made premier, a measure which, given the anti-Gaullist views of his constitutionally assigned successor, many feared would lead to a situation reminiscent of the outbreak of the Spanish Civil War in which the army defied a popular front government with bloody consequences. On 1 June the National Assembly invested de Gaulle as prime minister and gave him the task of furnishing a new constitution to be approved by referendum.

Clearly the military had intervened in political life, but it is difficult to assess the extent to which de Gaulle could be said to be the army's man rather than a candidate more or less acceptable to all parties. His degree of complicity in the plot is uncertain. Certainly, many of the plotters, mostly officers below the rank of general were decorated or promoted. Yet de Gaulle's subsequent policy of de-colonization could hardly be said to be that favoured by the officers of the army, a number of whom were soon to experience divided loyalties again when European settlers occupied government buildings in Algiers in what became known as the Barricades Affair.

The disaffected settlers called again for Algeria to remain French, this time to be met by a resolute government, and to succeed only in tainting the army with their own reputation for right-wing extremism. At the beginning, General de Gaulle seemed to be the leader the army needed, but the honeymoon was short.

In autumn 1958 the army, its political stance made clear, buried itself with the organization of a constitutional referendum, both officiating over the vote and organizing the campaign in support of a 'yes' vote for a new constitution establishing a new kind of president. The man destined for the part, however, was making his position with regard to French Algeria and its supporters studiedly ambiguous.

Within the year President de Gaulle had offered self-determination to Algeria. The army's immediate response was the abandoned coup plot of October 1959, a warning to those who knew of it of renewed military discontent. In June 1960, paratroops called in to restore order were reluctant to intervene in the Barricades Affair. Although the new Commander-in-Chief in Algiers, General Challe, and his staff were still clearly loyal, the political sympathies of the troops who fraternized with the right-wing European settlers were clearly suspect. Officers implicated in the affair were transferred to France.[10] De Gaulle toured Algeria some weeks later in an attempt to mollify the army, but the value of his assurances became clear when on 4 November 1960 he talked of an Algerian Republic.[11] Negotiations with the insurgents continued, and by January 1961 Algerian self-determination was the subject of a referendum on which de Gaulle staked his prestige by issuing the threat of resignation in the event of a 'no' vote. Despite Communist efforts to obtain this result, de Gaulle gained a majority in metropolitan France and within 3 months stated his preference for rapid French disengagement from Algeria. What the army had dreaded: the abandonment of loyal Moslems to inevitable reprisals, and the rejection of the possibility of military victory towards which end much sacrifice and some progress had been made; this was now openly entertained.

The final attempt by the army to force the hand of government took place in April 1961, but with little real chance of success. The *colons* had espoused right-wing extremism thereby reducing sympathy for their cause in metro-politan France. Many of the officers implicated in the Barricades Affair were transferred to posts outside Algeria, where they could be expected to be less able to be active on behalf of French Algeria. The widely respected Generals Salan and Challe and other familiar figures of May 1958 were now in retirement. Together they could perhaps gain support in French barracks and among French civilians, but what a coup could have achieved is unclear. In the event, the army in Europe remained loyal, and in Algeria where three-quarters of the troops were now conscripts[12] the occupation of Algiers by the First Paratroop Regiment of the Foreign Legion received little support. It was the paratroop regiments who had brought with them the legacy of the retreat from Indo-China, and who had borne the brunt of the fighting in Algeria. The foreign legion as a whole, moreover, stood to lose its traditional home, and together with other career soldiers would suffer the loss of adventure in exotic lands.[13] The conscripts by their inaction dissociated themselves from the allies of torturers and colon extremists. In addition, a policy of loyalty and obedience to a strong and popular government did not impair a conscript's chances of timely release from military service. For the generals, the need to preserve the unity of the armed forces dictated loyalty, just as 3 years before that some unity demanded support of the army in revolt. The coup failed. Its leaders were tried and condemned, though none were executed, and some escaped to continue the battle for French Algeria fought by the Organization Armée Secrète (OAS), which was unable to delay Algerian independence beyond September 1962.

Algeria's independence brought an end to the army's traditional imperial role, and to the circumstances which had goaded it to intervene in metropoli-tan politics. The army did not come to rule during the crises of the Algerian war, but it was instrumental in changing the nature of the regime. The new regime had new strategic priorities and a new role for the armed forces.

THE FIFTH REPUBLIC

The Fourth Republic was abandoned when its parliament in Paris was unable to choose a prime minister and while its army, growing accustomed to governing in Algeria, sought to influence the process in favour of its own policy. Clearly, to be successful the Fifth Republic required the means to ensure strong and stable government and an obedient army. Gaullism promised a means to both. What de Gaulle offered and attempted to realize was a vision of himself at the head of a powerful French nation with influence in the counsels of the world. Implicit in this vision of the nation is a diminution of the influence of political parties which were seen by de Gaulle as representatives of sectional interests often over and against those of the nation as a whole. Also implicit, and of more direct concern to the army, was the shedding of direct control over the territories which made up the French Union, the post-war successor to the French Empire. De Gaulle foresaw a technically trained force armed with nuclear weapons paid for by economic growth brought about by the policies of a resolute government. If this could be attained France's claim to recognition as a world power would be impossible to ignore. It was not enough to solve the Algerian problem; the army had to be rehabilitated and weaned from its colonial role by a strong government. De Gaulle supplied a constitution and the accompanying political practice by which this could be achieved.

In the Fourth Republic parliament had been pre-eminent, but party rivalries and divisions within parties had rendered it ineffectual. The new constitution shifted the balance of power from parliament to government. Henceforth Deputies would be less able to bring down a government or interfere with its legislative programme. The position of the president was also transformed by de Gaulle from that of a state figurehead and 'honest broker' between parties to that of national leader.

On 1 June 1958 de Gaulle became prime minister with powers to govern until the end of the year while the constitution was being prepared (by loyal Gaullist Michel Debré). Approval of the new constitution by referendum was followed by a general election in November in which the Gaullists took 206 of the 578 seats.[14] This was a striking success in view of the poor showing by the Gaullists in the previous National Assembly.[15] The result was also a clear success for the two ballot *scrutin uninominal* system which enhances polarization of the Assembly into a government and an opposition rather than a variety of disparate political groups. On 21 December de Gaulle was elected president by an electoral college, and with the powers conferred upon him by the new constitution he selected Michel Debré as his first prime minister. The difficulty which had loomed large over the Fourth Republic, that of finding a prime minister acceptable to parliament, had been removed.

The prime minister was now to be appointed by the president, and his security of tenure was improved by further provisions of the new constitution. The Gaillard government, like several governments before it, had been brought down by a vote of censure on 15 April 1958, less than four months after its formation, precipitating the crisis which brought de Gaulle to power. In the Fifth Republic, votes of censure succeed less frequently. Abstentions are counted as votes for the government thereby turning doubters into supporters and thus making votes against the government a matter of declaration of commitment. Abstentions as a speculative attempt to improve the position of a deputy or his party are no longer a threat to the government. Censure motions, moreover, must be signed by 10 per cent of deputies who then may not sign another such motion during the parliamentary session unless in opposition to a bill or a statement of policy which the government has made a matter of confidence (has pledged its responsibility, [Art. 19]).[16]

The stability of governing coalitions, which in the Fourth Republic had been hostage to the conflicting interests of rival constituent parties with the consequent subordination of policy to coalition politics, was further enhanced by the stipulation that ministers could not also be deputies. This 'separation of powers' [Art. 23] was designed to make ministers more wary of destroying coalitions in order to pursue party advantage. A minister leaving a wrecked coalition has no parliamentary seat unless another deputy is willing to resign and so create a vacancy. The same provision of the constitution also forbids ministers to represent 'interest groups' in the attempt to diminish further the influence of party in parliament.

The deliberative powers of parliament itself were also diminished by Article 34 of the constitution, which limits the range of subjects on which parliament is competent to legislate, leaving all other subjects to be dealt with by the government, with the further restriction that on many of these subjects parliament is limited to the framing only of outlines of policy, leaving the detailed regulations and provisions to be drawn up by the administration. Moreover, the government can at any time seek the consent of parliament to issue ordinances on any of the subjects listed in Article 34 'with a view to carrying out its own programme' [Art. 38].[17] Government control over debate was also increased. For example, the agenda is set by the government which can insist on a vote on its own text of a bill at any time. Debate over the budget, often the occasion for lengthy wrangling in the Fourth Republic, can now last no longer than forty days in the National Assembly, with a further two weeks allowed in the Senate. In the event of the whole procedure being incomplete after seventy days the bill may be put into force 'by ordinance' [Art. 47].

The locus of constitutionally conferred powers, then, was shifted away from the legislature into the hands of the government, but within the government itself the prime minister is not the all powerful figure to which Britons, for example, seem recently to have grown accustomed. There has been a transfer of power from the premier to the president who has been transformed thereby from a largely symbolic head of state to the incumbent of an executive presidency with a number of new responsibilities defined by the new constitution. Here, also, we meet a timely reminder that political habits can be as significant a factor in political practice as the stipulations of a written constitution.[18]

After the end of the Algerian crisis, de Gaulle established a number of practices which enhanced the power of the presidency at the expense of the prime minister. According to the constitution the president, apart from the usual ceremonial functions of a head of state, is responsible for the appointment of the prime minister and for terminating his period of office on resignation of the government. The president is to appoint and dismiss the remainder of the government on the premier's recommendation. In practice de Gaulle also dismissed his prime ministers (starting with Debré) without waiting for parliament's disapproval of them, and removed ministers without advice from the prime minister. The Council of Ministers, too, is less important than it might first appear. Real decision making more usually takes place in smaller *conseils restreints* in which the president confers solely with the ministers and advisers relevant to the issue under discussion. De Gaulle, in addition, 'reserved' for himself a number of areas of policy making including foreign affairs and defence.[19]

Areas of competence are, of course, given to the president explicitly by the constitution. Article 16 provides the president with emergency powers. This provision of the constitution, although apparently framed with June 1960 in mind, is of particular interest for its use during the Algerian crisis, which revealed a number of failures of precision in its wording.[20]

De Gaulle's invocation of Article 16 between April and September 1961 was politically astute even if it was of doubtful constitutionality.[21] Once the coup had failed, the powers were used to purge the armed and public services, and to set up special courts to try those alleged to have committed crimes during the rebellion. The use of the special powers is controversial because of their duration and because of de Gaulle's treatment of parliament towards the end of the Emergency. However, General de Gaulle found himself at the centre of more serious constitutional disputes during the following year. His role in these disputes reveals much about de Gaulle's approach to the tasks of government.

In April 1962 a referendum was held to endorse or reject the Evian agreement with the Algerian National Liberation Front, and, in the event of acceptance, to give de Gaulle special powers to implement the agreement. Special courts were set up under these powers as successors to those established under Article 16. Their purpose was to try alleged OAS terrorists, but the courts themselves were declared illegal by the Conseil d'Etat on the grounds that those convicted were given no right of appeal. Initially de Gaulle responded by simply having a new law passed by the tamed National Assembly which legalized the courts and took them out of the sphere of competence of the Conseil d'Etat which deals only with matters relating to the executive. Subsequently, however, a court was set up which would have met with the Conseil d'Etat's approval, but de Gaulle's single mindedness and his impatience with legal niceties in the face of what he saw as political necessity was clearly displayed.

The other important constitutional clash of the period also involves a referendum, but in this case de Gaulle used the plebiscite in circumstances of doubtful constitutionality to change the constitution itself, allowing the president to be elected directly in future, rather than by electoral college. (The procedure used for introducing the referendum was that laid down under Article 11 which deals with referenda, rather than under Article 89 which deals with constitutional amendment. Article 11 does not, of course, allow for changes of the constitution by referendum.) Characteristically, the General warned that his resignation would follow a 'no' vote. In the ensuing row the prime minister, Georges Pompidou, was forced to resign by a vote of censure, but was immediately reinstated by his president who won the populace's 'vote of confidence' on his 'policy'. De Gaulle was using his popularity and indispensability during the Algerian crisis, which was barely settled, to make provisions for the further terms in office which he would require in order to establish a new France according to his vision of a great nation in direct communication with its leader, unmediated by party politics. This vision, with its redefined world role for France, was the basis of plans to re-shape the armed forces and to make French Algeria truly *l'Algerie de Papa*: firmly in the past rather than remaining as a continued stimulus to military and political atavism.

THE SOLDIER AND THE VISION

De Gaulle's position could not be secure, nor could he achieve his more distant goals, until he had removed the threat of further military intervention. In Algeria, the army had claimed to be fighting the modern enemy, Communism, using the most modern methods of psychological warfare. It was also fighting to expunge past defeats and to vindicate its technique for combating threats to the French Union and to Western Civilization. The war in Algeria came to monopolize the efforts of both the army and the metropolitan government so that little could be achieved to give a new direction to France until the Algerian problem had been solved. For withdrawal from Algeria to be successful, the army would have to be offered and, if necessary, forced to accept a new role. The 1958 Constitution enabled a strengthened government to disengage from North Africa in spite of the resistance of some officers, and to contain the OAS terrorist backlash. De Gaulle's subsequent manoeuvrings to secure Gaullist rule into the second half of the decade were complementary to his attempts to ensure the cooperation of the army. The Gaullist enterprise, in which the army was expected to participate, was portrayed as a serious attempt to fulfil a new national destiny.

After World War II, the age of the great colonial empires was clearly over, and France was no longer a great power. Pre-eminence now belonged to the possessors of nuclear weapons: first the Americans, and then also the Soviet Union and the British developed nuclear technology. Possession of such weapons by Britain, itself a waning power, was clear evidence of Anglo-Saxon collusion to diminish French power. It was impossible to forget the sinking of the Vichy fleet at Mers el Kebir, and the American patronage of her Anglo-Saxon ally, which gave the bigger of the two powers influence over the smaller turning Britain into the (more) unreliable ally which had withdrawn from the Suez conflict. Nevertheless, the French and the Anglo-Saxons had, since 1949, committed themselves to the North Atlantic Treaty Organization which had rearmed (and France hoped, tamed) western Germany to counter the power of a Soviet Union armed with nuclear weapons. The old adversary, Germany, was occupied and divided. Its western zone, although rearmed, had renounced atomic, biological and chemical weapons, and control of its strategically vital coal and steel industries had been delegated to one of the three European communities which had the Fourth Republic as a founder member and supporter. The Soviet Union had appeared as the enemy in the Cold War, but its very ability to pose a nuclear threat gave rise to a stalemate making an advance by either side unlikely.

The outcomes of the crises over Soviet missiles in Cuba, and over the status of Berlin suggested a certain security for France that would allow her to pursue her own goals even if these did not accord with those of the allies that had snubbed her at Potsdam and Yalta, and had withheld access to nuclear technology. At the same time, the now familiar doubt whether the United States would risk massive destruction at home in order to defend Europe, suggested that a national deterrent was also necessary. France would have to be transformed into a modern power in Europe in order to win new global influence. After 1958 France was rapidly divested of her empire. The Community that was to be its successor, giving France a world role coordinating the defence, foreign and economic policies of its former colonies was announced in title twelve of the 1958 Constitution, but the governments of the proposed member states soon chose to exercise full sovereignty. France's destiny lay in Europe. The nuclear stalemate left France some freedom to pursue a policy independent of that of the United States to which she was allied, and which still extended the shelter of its nuclear umbrella to her. Russia, which had in the past provided a counter weight to German power, was not to be presumed to be an enemy. France, in a strategy popular with the nonaligned movement, began to speak of working to establish a future Europe comprised of independent nations between the Atlantic and the Urals.

De Gaulle put the nation first, running counter to a tide of post-war enthusiasm for international organizations. Objecting that NATO as an organization restricted its participating forces to a European role under American tutelage, he sought an equal partnership with Britain and the United States in a Western Alliance in which France could play a world role without loss of sovereignty. Similar reservations were voiced about the supranationalism of the European Communities which was perceived as a threat to the integrity of the French nation, and a similar solution was entertained; membership of a European Community of closely cooperating states could only enhance the status of France.

France's ambition to be first among the second-rank nations demanded possession of a nuclear arsenal. With such weaponry the prestige of France was assured. The armed forces, who represented the essence of nationhood, and who had rebelled rather than acquiesce in the alienation of the North African Departments, would secure France's destined status as a world power.[22] Of course the loyalty of the army was still in doubt, but it now would have a new enterprise to absorb its energies. The technically skilled officers rather than the veterans of colonial wars would become the new elite as soon as battlefield nuclear weapons could be provided. In the meantime, the navy and the air force, both of which incidentally had held themselves aloof from the 1961 plot, would have to be the custodians of the bulky equipment of France's rudimentary nuclear arms.

It was officially decided to create a French nuclear force in late 1960, after the successful test of February of that year, but the reorganization of the armed forces, which had been planned soon after de Gaulle came to power, had to be delayed because of the situation in Algeria.[23] The events of 1960 and 1961, however, made reorganization imperative. The 'problem of the army' was not confined to the troops stationed in Algeria. Veterans' organizations, meetings of reservists and even military classes in *lycées* had been used to promote the cause of French Algeria, and once the revolt of the army had been diverted into the terrorism of the OAS, it was clear that serving officers were closely linked with the campaign, even when it extended to the attempted assassination of de Gaulle.[24] No doubt the officers involved could claim in their defence that their activities under the orders of the condemned renegade General Salan had parallels to resistance action under de Gaulle, but the old rhyme that tells us why treason never prospers should have been better remembered. Admittedly, the special tribunals which were set up to try captured OAS members handed down erratic verdicts, but it should be noted that no-one convicted served more than eight years, largely as a result of a series of presidential pardons, and of thirteen sentenced to death only four were executed.[25] The penalties imposed for the more overt military interventions of the early 1960s also included changes of posting and the regrouping of units. The latter reorganization included the dissolution (after the Barricades Affair) of the Fifth Bureau which had been established in all military headquarters in Algeria and elsewhere to advise on 'psychological action'. It had sought to indoctrinate both civilians and soldiers about the need for the struggle to maintain French Algeria, and had tried to impress on each reserve officer the need for him to continue the fight even after ceasing active duty.[26] The three paratroop regiments most closely involved in the 1961 putsch were, of course, broken up and regrouped. The paratroops were also deprived of the distinctive uniforms which formed part of their mystique.

The reorganization of the armed forces, when it came, afforded an opportunity for loyalty to be rewarded. A new chief of staff was chosen from among the generals who had refused to join the revolt, and an air force general, Michel Fourquet, who loyally refused the 'Algerian' generals access to aircraft for paratroop landings in France, became head of the General Secretariat established in 1962 to offer advice and information to the Committee of Defence chaired by the president (the General Secretariat thus replaced the General Staff of National Defence established in 1958).[27]

Once the Algerian crisis and its aftermath had been cleared away, the postponed redefinition of the role of the military could begin. By early 1952 France had just under 14,000 troops left in its former possessions in Africa. The independence of the colonies reduced the overseas duties of the armed forces to little more than the tasks of training the new national forces, and of assisting in the defence of the Community. This was hardly a new world role, especially in view of the planned reduction by a further 10,000 men by the end of the decade.[28] In pursuit of a new world role for France as first among Francophone and European equals, the armed forces, including the more loyal navy and air force, had to be returned to Europe. There was to be an intervention force, capable of carrying out what remained of France's global commitments, but the primary role foreseen for the reorganized military establishment was the defence of France itself.

Defence of the 'hexagon' involved both the defence of its frontiers, a purpose for which the Fourth Republic had undertaken the NATO membership that was becoming so burdensome to de Gaulle, and the in-depth defence of the French countryside, an assignment which would prove to be a source of unexpected difficulties. Frontier defence would require a new technologically skilled force equipped with the most modern weapons. The strategy for the defence of the French interior, however, seemed more like a return to a familiar past. It called for regional garrisons, skilled in the defence of local terrain, to join forces with the gendarmerie to resist attack. The 1962 manoeuvres in which this plan of action was to be tested involved a landing by 'enemy' paratroops. This was hardly a reorientation of the army towards modern warfare. Worse still, if the exercise was designed to calm military disquiet about the politicians' ability to understand the modern army and its needs, the exercise presupposed a loyal civilian population.[29] This, the veterans of Indo-China and Algeria knew, was something rather to be actively striven for than presupposed. Even the unloved Fourth Republic had enacted legislation that allowed the army to take over regional government once a state of siege had been declared. It was recognized that preventative measures would have to be taken against subversion by the local populace. In the Fifth Republic the best solution to Juvenal's riddle of '*Quis custodiet custodes*' was to retain responsibility for internal defence in the hands of the interior ministry and its representatives in the regions, leaving local commanders to establish what those needs were.[30] Juvenal notwithstanding, the armed forces of the Fifth Republic also continued to exercise their traditional vocation as tutor of the nation's youth. The value of this training and education in civic virtue, combined with the weight of the myth of 'the nation under arms' ensured the continuance of the institution of conscription despite its cost and questionable utility to modern warfare. After all, the persistence of conscription provided job security for the junior ranks, and could again provide, as in 1961, a brake on the political ambitions of their seniors who might feel uncomfortable adjusting to the demands of European rather than colonial service.

The reorganized metropolitan force was almost exclusively dedicated to the defence of France. Two divisions were committed to NATO while a further four remained under French control although available for NATO deployment. Full participation by the Mediterranean fleet was similarly withheld. French forces were to remain as much as possible at the disposal of France rather than be obedient to the orders of foreigners. Still, even without Gaullist suspicions about Anglo-Saxon hegemonic ambitions, obligations to NATO and to the ill-starred Western European Union would have been in danger of underfulfilment as the reviving French economy strained to fund a national nuclear force. The military usefulness of such a force either to deter an attack or inflict unacceptable retaliation must always be doubtful in view of Soviet nuclear firepower, but its other advantages would have been immediately obvious. Possession of an independent nuclear force would contribute to the prestige of France. It would also serve as a channel for the energies of the newer officers who could be expected to be seduced by the technical intricacies of the new weapons, and by the more abstract delights of strategic theory. The colonial experience of older officers would be rendered clearly obsolete. Provision of the expensive new weapons could be expected to stimulate some areas of the economy such as the aircraft industry. However, abandonment of the programme once begun, apart from the obvious cost in prestige, would, of course, mean that much of what had already been spent would have to be written off as a dead loss. It would also mean that the industries stimulated by those funds would probably face decline.

These considerations shed some light on de Gaulle's response to the Nassau proposals of late 1962, and his pursuit of military autarky. Polaris was of little value without warheads or submarines. A France technically capable of producing the latter would, no doubt, easily design and manufacture missiles too. Testing of prototypes had already begun.[31] Acceptance of polaris could be seen from the French point of view as an obstacle to the development of suitable technology in France. Until French missiles were available French bombs would be delivered by Mirage IV bombers. Curiously, this option was only credible when Boeing tanker aircraft capable of refuelling the Mirages en route became available to France in the summer of 1962.[32] French troops also gained training in the use of the new weapons through NATO after 1961, but by 1963 France was clearly ready to pursue her destiny in earnest.[33] The Atlantic fleet was removed from NATO command as a prelude to the full withdrawal from the Organization (but not the alliance) which came in 1966. The Franco–German pact, also of 1963, though providing little by way of concrete results signalled a determination to play a continental role through intergovernmental rather than supranational organizations.

De Gaulle offered the army a part in his grand design. Aspects of the enterprise remained vague, but development of the required equipment had begun, although questions remained about the feasibility of the later stages of these projects. If there were no others, cost alone would be a formidable obstacle. The army had little choice but to accept. There was no longer an empire to defend. If its appointed task was to fight Communism here was another way to do it.

Resistance in the form of military intervention in the political process was no longer feasible. The Fifth Republic, although it had more in common with the Fourth than is at first apparent, had a powerful and popular leader. In the first general election of the Fifth Republic in 1958 the Gaullists gained more seats than any party had done in the Fourth.[34] In the next general election in 1962, the Gaullists were even more successful, although they were still just short of an overall majority without help from V. Giscard d'Estaing's Independent Republicans.[35]

In 1958 the army, although not providing a classic example of praetorianism, had been able to influence politicians unable to choose a prime minister to direct policy. In 1961 they had failed to influence the new power in France. Since then, de Gaulle had consolidated his position, and had redeployed the army. Serious military intervention in the political life of France was over, at least for the incumbency of de Gaulle. This much was clear to the would-be assassins of the OAS. De Gaulle survived their attacks, but a few years later his political career was brought to an end by his own miscalculation.

By the time de Gaulle left office, the army had already been given an opportunity to show that it had returned to its traditional obedience. At the end of May 1968 as social and political unrest found expression in strikes and demonstrations, de Gaulle flew to Baden to hold secret talks with the commander of the French army in West Germany, General Massu. Massu claims to have reassured the dispirited president, and to have encouraged him to continue in office rather than resign. This visit could, perhaps, have been a ploy by de Gaulle to sound Massu's true feelings.[36] Whatever the true purpose of the visit, it seems that the army was loyal to de Gaulle. Of course, in 1968 the challenges to the existing order were more easily identifiable with the left rather than the right in French politics; hence the army was unlikely to be sympathetic to them.

It soon became clear that the Fifth Republic could survive without de Gaulle. The Gaullists were highly successful in the National Assembly election of June 1968. Bastille Day that year was marked by a general amnesty for those still serving sentences connected with the unrest in Algeria that had marred the beginning of the decade. De Gaulle, nevertheless, was forced out of office by his own threat to resign in the event of a 'no' vote to his further proposed constitutional changes offered to, and rejected by, the electorate in the referendum of spring 1969. France without de Gaulle, however, would no longer be the France ripe for the military intervention for which the OAS activists strove in 1961 and 1962. The army seemed to have changed, and certainly the Gaullists were firmly in power. However, the doubt lingered whether the army could accept a change of political leadership which brought the left, particularly the Communists, to power.

The long rule of the French right finally ended in 1981. France elected first a Socialist president, and then, a month later, a new National Assembly in which the Socialists and their left Radical allies had an absolute majority. The new government included four Communists, although none were in 'sensitive' ministries. Fears about the discipline of the army proved groundless.

Clearly de Gaulle's attempts to reform the armed forces had been successful. The army had sought to justify many of its actions in Algeria by referring to the fight against Communism. The influence of the latter in Metropolitan France was taken as a clear indication of the degeneration of the French nation. The army attempted unsuccessfully to impose its will in the political process, and was withdrawn from Algeria. In the 1970s it had continued to take up the new duties assigned to it by de Gaulle. The promised nuclear arsenal became more of a reality, and overseas adventure came with French intervention in the political upheavals of Francophone Africa. By the 1980s, it seems, the armed forces of France once again merited the soubriquet of *La Grande Muette* given to it in the nineteenth century. The endorsement by some of France's retired generals of a candidate of the right against François Mitterrand, an old adversary of the 1950s and 1960s, in the 1988 presidential election hardly constitutes evidence of military recidivism. Still, as Dorothy Pickles remarks:

> The trouble about the French political past, however, is that it so often turns out to be far from dead, which makes prediction of its future a more than usually hazardous undertaking.[37]

Nevertheless, at the moment it is hard to envisage a likely set of circumstances which could plausibly be said to be a return to a past in which a French colonial army, seeking to regain its honour and put an end to a series of defeats for which it blamed inept politicians and the hostility of a section of the metropolitan population, took action against its own government. No doubt the future will vouchsafe to France other politicians whom the army will regard as inept, and a number (at the moment decreasing) of French voters will continue to give their allegiance to a Communist 'fifth column', but the military intervention of 1958 also required for its success the presence of a paralysed political system unloved by the population at large. The importance of this factor was clear from the failure of the coup staged by three rebellious regiments and four renegade generals in 1961. The main factor in the strained civil–military relations of the whole period was, of course, the Algerian problem. Now the cause of French Algeria lies in the past. Officers pushed beyond the limits of their endurance nowadays find relief for their exasperation by writing letters of resignation.[38]

The army has been given a new role under a new and popular regime. It continues to perform those new functions even when required to accept left-wing political masters. French governments rule according to a constitution that has begun to stand the test of time. Military plotters attempting to intervene under these circumstances would be embarking upon a project whose only precedents for success have been in the previous, that is, the wrong Republic.

NOTES

1. *Independent* (London) 9 July 1988.
2. It was the army which took a leading role. This puts the Vichy experience into perspective. The navy was heavily involved in Vichy France, and could therefore be expected to have most taken to heart any lesson about the advantages of disloyalty.
3. Maurice Larkin, *France Since the Popular Front*, (Oxford: Oxford University Press, 1988), pp. 274–5.
4. General Raoul Salan, a former Delegate General of the Government in Algeria, made a similar connection in 1960. *Le Monde* (Paris) 13 October, 1960 quoted in Edgar S. Furniss Jr, *De Gaulle and the French Army* (New York: The Twentieth Century Fund, 1964), p. 51.
5. John Steward Ambler, *The French Army in Politics 1945–1962* (Columbus: Ohio State University Press, 1966) ch. 4. passim.
6. Paul Marie de la Gorce, *The French Army*, trans. Kenneth Douglas (New York: George Braziller, 1963), p. 404 and p. 464.
7. While some officers espoused the cause of Catholic reaction, it should be noted that the Catholic church was vociferous in its protests against the use of torture, and that many officers despised the entrenched privileges and racism of the right-wing *colons*.
8. Telegram to General Ely quoted in de la Gorce, *The French Army*, p. 464.
9. The raid had not been cleared with the government first. Already the armed forces were acting independently of government in actions which inevitably had serious political consequences.
10. A number of colonels had sent the rebels a message of support. Challe too was transferred, presumably for lack of vigour during the Affair.
11. Quoted in de la Gorce, *The French Army*, p. 515.
12. Dorothy Maud Pickles, *Algeria and France*, (New York: F. A. Praeger, 1963; reprinted, n.p.: Greenwood Press, 1976), p. 88 n. 45.
13. Pickles, *Algeria and France*, p. 67. Twelve African colonies (including Madagascar) had become independent in the first two years of the Fifth Republic.
14. Dorothy Maud Pickles, *The Government and Politics of France*, 1 vol. (London: Methuen, University Paperback, 1973) 2: 28 n. 1.
15. Larkin, *France*, p. 270.
16. M. Pompidou lost such a vote in 1962 over the proposed changes by referendum to articles 6 and 7 of the constitution. See p. 28. The text of the constitution used in this chapter is that appearing in Pickles, *Government and Politics*, 1: 307–20.
17. Pickles, *Government and Politics*, 1: 91 notes that this article resembles a Fourth Republic law of August 1948.
18. Neighbouring Britain, of course, presents an example in which political habits are all-important, and a written constitution is thought to be of little value by most politicians.
19. See Pickles, *Government and Politics*, 1: 133. Compare, too, articles 5, 15 and 21 of the constitution. An ordinance of 7 January, 1959 shifted responsibility for defence policy to the Council of Ministers. A later ordinance (July 1962) gives overall direction of defence policy to the president. (Furniss, *De Gaulle*, p. 133.)
20. Article 17 ('The President of the Republic has the right of pardon') was used to good effect in dealing with the aftermath of the rebellion.
21. Pickles, *Government and Politics*, 1: 123.

22. Furniss, *De Gaulle*, p. 35 gives the following quotation from General Salan in August 1960: 'It is not the prerogative of any authority to decide on the abandonment of a portion of territory where France exercises sovereignty. No one has this right; no one has received such a mandate from the country'.

23. The first French atom bomb was exploded in May 1962.

24. There were at least eight other attempts. See Furniss, *De Gaulle*, pp. 60–1. This was the price de Gaulle had to pay for taking such a large part in the policy making of the Republic.

25. Pickles, *Government and Politics*, 2: 48–9. By early 1963 each tribunal included two officers, giving rise to fears that the army was insufficiently distanced from politics while officers sat in judgement on 'political crimes'. (Furniss, *De Gaulle*, p. 57.)

26. Ambler, *The French Army*, p. 220.

27. The new chief of staff was General Charles Ailleret (see Furniss, *De Gaulle*, p. 134).

28. Furniss, *De Gaulle*, p. 240.

29. Ibid. pp. 235–6.

30. Ibid. pp. 230–1.

31. Ibid. p. 191.

32. Ibid. p. 273.

33. Pickles, *Government and Politics*, 2: 280.

34. Ibid. 2: 32.

35. Ibid. 2: 67.

36. Larkin, *France*, pp. 325–6.

37. Pickles, *Government and Politics*, 2: 27.

38. Alistair Horne in *The French Army and Politics 1870–1970* (London: Macmillan, 1984), p. 91 gives the example of General Delaunay, the Chief of Staff who resigned in 1984.

3 Farewell to man on horseback: intervention and civilian supremacy in modern Greece[1]

Constantine P. Danopoulos

Long-term military disengagement or withdrawal from politics, i.e., 'a minimum period of ten years during which at least one successful "regular" executive transition has occurred',[2] cannot be seen as an isolated phenomenon. Instead, it can properly be understood and analysed in the context of military intervention, praetorian rule, and disengagement. As Maniruzzaman and Finer have each pointed out, civilian supremacy can be re-established and sustained only when the factors, trends, and conditions which prompted intervention have been reversed.[3]

Broadly speaking, students of civil–military relations have advanced two general explanations regarding the causes of praetorianism that have characterized the majority of the developing or changing societies of the Third World: one external or societal and the other internal or organizational. The first seeks to explain military involvement in politics by looking at societal considerations such as political decay, corruption, factionalism, and loss of legitimacy.[4] The internalists, on the other hand, regard organizational imperatives such as the level of military professionalism[5] or perceived threats to the military's corporate interests as the real culprits of intervention.[6]

In recent years, however, the dichotomy between internalists and externalists has been criticized as more apparent than real. Prefacing the second edition of his much acclaimed essay on *The Military in the Political Development of New Nations*, the late Morris Janowitz, a leading internalist, emphatically dissociated himself from the externalist–internalist dichotomy: 'I do not know of any empirically oriented study of civil–military relations that would accept or limit itself to one of these approaches. Certainly, that was not the strategy of my original essay, which focused on the interplay between military institutions and societal political processes'.[7] Agreeing with Janowitz's basic argument, Nordlinger,[8] Welch and Smith[9] have concluded that military coups take place in societies where economic difficulties, social fragmentation and political instability lead to legitimacy loss, and occur when the professional interests of the military are threatened. The latter includes adequate budgetary support, institutional autonomy and exclusiveness, protection against encroachments from rival institutions and the survival and viability of the military as a social institution.[10]

The experience of the military as political governors, especially in situations where praetorian rule was of considerable duration, cannot help but have an impact on the attitudes, perceptions and the corporate interests of the armed forces, as well as on the societal, political, economic and psychological conditions of the countries concerned. The role of the military in the post-disengagement era is inseparably connected to the lessons and experiences drawn by the officer corps, their civilian successors, as well as society at large.

As a consequence, to identify, analyse, and understand the reasons why a relatively small group of nations, of which Greece is a prime example, have managed to experience long-term military disengagement from politics, one would have to seek explanations at both levels: societal and organizational. This essay will aim to do exactly that. The following pages will provide a short history of the role of the armed forces in Greek politics emphasizing the causes of the 21 April 1967 coup d'état, evaluate the role of the military as political governors (1967–74), and analyse post disengagement civil-military relations in that country.

THE BACKGROUND

Since the late 1820s when Greece became a 'sovereign' nation, the country has witnessed numerous military coups, both direct and indirect. The intervention of 21 April 1967 was by far the most protracted in terms of time and the most independent in terms of initiative and goals. The 1967 coup and the ensuing 7-year rule stand out as praetorianism undertaken by the newly professionalized and highly autonomous military institution seeking to protect its corporate interests. Past military interventions, with the possible exception of the 1909 coup which resulted in a new elite coming to power, were nothing more than putsches – direct, indirect, or abortive – launched by the military acting as a surrogate for a political party and/or the monarchy.

From the late 1820s until World War II, professionalization in the Hellenic army, although improved, remained at relatively low levels. The Greek military was characterized by lack of corporate spirit, expertise, and responsibility; all reflecting the country's weak agricultural economy, parochial political culture, and unorganized institutions and social groups. One should also add the role of the great powers that managed to penetrate and even dominate Greek politics.

Although the Greek military sought and obtained professional advice, training, weapons, and supplies from French, British, and (to a lesser extent)

Italian counterparts, these inducements were neither persistent nor massive enough to professionalize and autonomize the services. Thus, while the armed forces intervened on numerous occasions, such coups do not seem to have been stimulated by professional concerns on the military's part. Instead, they reflected the cleavages and ambitions of political elites and the corresponding clientalization and weakness of the Greek military.

The advent of World War II ushered Greece into a new period. The country was occupied by the Germans; King George II, accompanied by his government and the remnants of the Greek army, fled to the Middle East. While there, the more reactionary elements formed an organization called ENA (Union of Young Officers). They labelled themselves as *ethnikó-phrones* (nationally minded) and set out to eliminate their republican counterparts from the armed forces, branding them Communists or fellow-travellers. The civil war that followed provided IDEA (formerly ENA) the opportunity to dominate the Greek services. So pervasive was this penetration that Brigadier Patakos, one of the leaders of the 1967 coup, asserted that '[IDEA] ... encompassed every officer with the exception of those burdened by incidents of improper execution of their duties'.[11] The Greek military became a homogeneous, die-hard, right-wing organization no longer 'reflecting the contradictions of the political society'.[12]

The massive and long-continuing American military and economic aid that flowed in as a result of the Truman Doctrine and the Marshall Plan had a decisive impact on the civil war and subsequent developments. Viewing Greece as 'merely one aspect of a considerably more elaborate picture involving the future of the Near and Middle East',[13] US policymakers proceeded to provide the right-wing military with sophisticated training, equipment, and support – transforming it into 'an independent political force within the country'.[14] The professionalization of the Greek military, at long last, became a reality.

Even though American aid eventually tapered off, the Greek army continued to enjoy considerable autonomy, and a hefty slice of the country's budget went on defence. This was made possible because the Greek economy was undergoing considerable (albeit dependent) development, marked by investment increases, a rise in per capita output, and significant improvements in production techniques and rates. The armed forces used this newly acquired muscle to maintain right-wing governments, from 1952 on, by engaging in electoral fraud, intimidation, and violence. Unlike previous periods, the armed forces were independent and did not hesitate to conspire even against the very government they had helped re-elect when they perceived its actions as harmful to their own interests. Civil–military relations in Greece in the post-World War II period fell in the 'praetorian guardians' category: the military intervened in order to preserve the status quo.[15]

From the early 1950s to 1963, Greece was governed by a puppet parliamentary regime. Behind the ruling political forces of the right stood the palace and particularly the military establishment. But in the early 1960s the ruling coalition came under attack from the rising middle class, those who had not benefited from the economic activity of the past decade, and workers, most of whom lived in the large metropolitan centres of Athens and Salonika who demanded greater participation in the decision-making process. The severely restricted left could only lend its support to the centrist political forces. Led by George Papandreou and his son Andreas, the latter seemed willing to challenge the repressive regime. They demanded democratization of the country's political life, participation in the decision-making process, and a more equitable distribution of wealth. Realizing that these demands would be doomed without a parallel 'democratization' in the armed forces, the Papandreous stated their intention to bring the army under the control of the elected civilian authorities. This would mean purging officers belonging to cliques such as IDEA, dismantling paramilitary clans closely aligned with the military, and breaking the armed forces' exclusiveness as a right-wing, watertight compartment beyond the bounds of legal state authority.

Naturally, the ruling establishment objected and in the ensuing political conflict the fragile political system suffered severe legitimacy deflation. The military perceived this and the strong possibility of a centrist electoral victory in the scheduled May 1967 elections as a direct threat to its supremacy and corporate interests, including diminishing appropriations for defence, and autonomy to manage its internal affairs. Army officers also saw alleged conspiracies within the military supported by forces loyal to Andreas Papandreou as threatening the institution's internal unity.[16] And as Nordlinger has correctly pointed out, interference with the military's corporate interests constitute 'the most important interventionist motive'.[17]

These developments, however, did not occur in a vacuum. Instead they were inseparably connected to the economic and corresponding social change generated in Greece in the years following the civil war. Beginning with the 1950s, if not before, successive Greek governments sought to alter the agricultural and underdeveloped state of Greece's economy by emphasizing industrial development and the service sector of the nation's economy. Lacking an adequate infrastructure, domestic capital, and an investment ethos, industrialization efforts did not manage to bring about a strong and autonomous industrial economic base. What was generated instead was a widespread and not always efficient small manufacturing sector which, along with ever increasing tourist revenues and remittances of seamen and Greeks living abroad, sufficed to bring about considerable increases in gross national product, per capita income, urbanization, consumerism, media and communications development, and diversification of the occupational structure of Greek society.

As a result of this socio-economic development and participation the educational system, however archaic and inefficient, promoted social mobility, greater awareness, and political consciousness; led to social and political diversity; increased the number of professional groups and associations; expanded the functions of the state; and brought about a closer identification and dependence between the individual and the state.[18] The more reactionary elements and the anti-Communist military perceived these changes as harmful to the moral fabric of Greek society and sought to arrest them by supporting the Colonels' repressive military dictatorship. All these plus a sluggish economy, social unrest, political instability, and concern about Greece's future role in NATO prompted a band of junior officers to stage a coup, thus sealing Greece's experiment with parliamentary democracy.

THE COLONELS ENTER AND EXIT

As is common among praetorians, the Greek coup-makers announced at first that their mission was to clean up the mess and return the country to normalcy (presumably civilian rule) at the earliest possible opportunity. But it soon became apparent that the Colonels, as the Greek military rulers became known, prepared for a long stay and sought to strengthen their position as well as their hold on the armed forces. Upon taking over, they immediately imposed martial law, suspended key sections of the constitution, detained scores of suspected citizens, froze all political activity, and took steps to purge the armed forces of officers suspected of insubordination and disloyalty. To this end the new rulers forced the retirement of some 400 of their senior colleagues, enlarged the army officer corps by adding 800 new slots, and promoted fellow officers closely aligned with the new regime. King Constantine, who in a belated and ill-prepared effort sought to bring down the Colonels in December 1973, found himself in exile. A general was appointed as regent to discharge the duties of the monarchy in the absence of its occupant.

The military rulers moved in other fronts as well to solidify their rule and prepare the ground for a sustained military presence in the political affairs of the country. In fact, the junta leaders made it plain that they had no intention of disengaging before a socio-political structure was in place, capable of safeguarding the long-range interests of the military institution. To realize this objective the praetorian rulers befriended many well known shipping tycoons such as Stavros Niarchos and Aristotle Onassis, and sought to gain the support of the conservative business community and the farmers by making available low-interest loans, grants, and other perquisites. In short, an effort was made to institutionalize the role of the military as the key political force in the country's future.

Central to a protracted stay in power is the ability of a regime to gain legitimacy, i.e., 'the capacity ... to develop and maintain a general belief that the existing social order and its main solutions are generally appropriate'.[19] Cloaking a regime with a mantle of legitimacy usually depends on its performance record. Performance denotes the attainment of 'those goals and exhibit operating features that are much desired by the population themselves and seen as intrinsically desirable to outside observers'.[20] Performance failure leads to 'deflation of governmental legitimacy',[21] and an illegitimate or non-legitimate government 'based on brute force alone is not long for this world'.[22] Military regimes are no exception to this rule.

In their effort to legitimize their rule, the Colonels complemented the measures outlined above with additional ones as well. At the institutional level, such steps included a constitutional framework (1968) with provisions for political parties, an elected parliament, freedom of speech and press, and other civil liberties. However, parts of the constitution pertaining to democratic processes were not to be implemented until the 'patient', as the Greek people were regarded, fully recovered. The 1968 constitution preserved the monarchy, although the throne remained empty due to Constantine's refusal to return before 'democratic processes were fully restored'.

Beneath this facade, the praetorian rulers sought a permanent and pervasive role for the armed forces in the future of the Greek polity. Law No. 58 designed to complement articles 129–32 of the 1968 constitution, pertaining to the organization and administration of the armed forces, stated that the military would be administered and led by the commander of the armed forces. Although the government would appoint the commander, it lacked the power to dismiss him. The law gave the armed forces chief control over the administrative bureaucracy of the Supreme Council of National Defence and, under special but not clearly delineated circumstances, jurisdiction over bureaux and agencies related to the nation's defence. Finally, the chief of the armed forces would have a decisive voice in matters of budgetary allocations and the power to establish special schools to train personnel for the needs of the defence establishment. These legal arrangements were conceived to elevate the military to the top of the state apparatus and transform the armed forces into the country's 'guiding political organization'.[23]

At social and economic levels, the regime sought to link its presence with ancient Hellenic values and Christian commands; portray the leader of the regime, Colonel George Papadopoulos, simultaneously as a dynamic visionary, a merciless smasher of the nation's enemies (internal and external), and a compassionate statesman striving to turn Greece into a modern, democratic but disciplined society; and, finally, lay the foundations for progress and prosperity, by bringing about economic development, bureaucratic modernization, educational reform, social harmony, and a 'healthy' political life. The regime dubbed these its modernization objectives.

A brief examination of the regime's capacity to obtain these goals shows there was a lot to be desired. A constitutional framework and appeal to Christian and ancient Hellenic values flew in the face of the martial law, torture, arbitrary arrests, and censorship associated with the Colonels' rule. Widespread corruption and nepotism marked the regime's tenure in office. Greece's notoriously mandarin and top-heavy bureaucracy[24] worsened as did the country's archaic education system. In the crucial areas of economic development and social reform, the regime's performance was also less than noteworthy. For example, there was a marked slow-down in agricultural production while industrial output fell below the projected levels. The rate of growth of investment in manufacturing declined, agricultural exports fell, the public deficit increased significantly as did tax exemptions for some of the country's more affluent groups. In 1973, the wholesale price index shot up by 48.3 per cent, while wages went up by only 16.4 per cent. The inflation rate rose from 4.2 per cent in 1972 to 15.5 in 1973 and a whopping 26.9 per cent in 1974.[25] From 1967 to 1974, the average annual deficit went up from 3.6 per cent of the gross domestic product to 7.4 per cent, a figure the Organization for Economic Cooperation and Development (OECD) called 'very high by historical standards'.[26] Finally, Greece's Agreement of Association with the EEC was frozen until democratic rule was restored.

Not only were the leaders of the regime unable to eradicate the ills of Greek society, as they perceived them, but they also failed to create a new political order capable of leading the country. Premier Papadopoulos tacitly recognized this when he told Sir Hugh Green that the 'absence of a party such as Hitler had had and Mussolini had had was a weakness of the regime', but in his characteristically erratic manner added that 'even the shadow of martial law is more effective than the normal process of law'.[27] By the end of 1972, the Colonels found themselves in a deep swamp. To go back to the pre-coup framework they had so vehemently denounced would have amounted to an admission of failure. This they were not prepared to do; but they had no viable successor scheme in mind.

Even though the international economic crisis of the early 1970s contributed to these difficulties, the lion's share of the blame lay with the Colonels' inexperience; their arbitrary and heavy-handed decision-making style; their lack of flexibility, political sophistication, clear-cut goals, and efficacious policies; and their failure to convince the populace that their regime was worthy of support. Such performance failures rendered the praetorian regime illegitimate in the eyes of the Greek people.[28] The ensuing malaise generated or rejuvenated opposition to the regime from a number of forces, both political and military. The support of the conservative Greek business community which reaped considerable profits during the first five years of the regime, in the form of low-interest loans and other perks, began to evaporate. The banned political parties showed little desire to cooperate with the regime, although the extreme right and a handful of other conservative elements lent their support to the junta.

Eventually, the armed forces themselves became the most potent force of opposition. The 1967 coup and the praetorian rule that followed was the affair of the army. The navy and the air force acquiesced but never really harboured feelings of affection towards the Colonels. However, the bankruptcy of the regime's governing efforts accentuated existing 'tendencies' within the nominally highest decision-making organ – the 'revolutionary council' – eventually factionalizing the once homogeneous military establishment. As time went by, these tendencies evolved into three distinct groups which differed regarding the future course of the 'revolution', as the 1967 intervention was referred to by the praetorian leaders. One group, the so-called 'parenthesis closers' advocated early return to civilian rule. A second faction, led by Papadopoulos himself, at first advocated protracted army rule but gradually favoured partial civilianization. Finally, a highly diverse assortment of hardliners, known as *Kadáfides*, believed in the indefinite continuation of military rule and pushed for radical, yet unspecified, social and economic reforms.

Of the three groups, the first appeared the smallest and was effectively neutralized rather early. The second and third groups joined forces and dominated the council as long as the former subscribed to the idea of maintaining the regime's military composition – though the hardliners objected to Papadopoulos' initial and very limited contacts with the 'political world' (meaning the politicians) beginning in 1970. The strongman sought to neutralize the *Kadáfides*. He gradually reduced council meetings, threatened his colleagues with resignation, and eventually elevated the other two members of the ruling triumvirate, Brigadier Patakos and Colonel Makarezos, to the honorific but powerless posts of vice premier. In so doing, Papadopoulos went a long way towards transforming the regime from 'corporatist' to 'personalistic', as is often the case in military-dominated governments.[29]

Of the other three services, the navy proved the least satisfied and apparently continually plotted the overthrow of the regime. Considered the most royal branch, the navy was an elitist-dominated institution with the highest number of educated officers. To navy officers the Colonels were an uneducated, power-hungry cabal whose failures and inconsistencies were damaging to the prestige, social standing, and even the careers of individual officers. But anti-regime feelings within the ranks of the navy did not come to fruition due to lack of effective leadership, the presence of a pervasive and often brutal security network under the control of the regime, Greece's geographic make up, the navy's smaller size compared to the much larger army, and American and NATO support of the junta. The navy's most determined effort to topple the Colonels took place in May 1973. But the regime uncovered the plot, tortured some of its leaders, and foiled it before it even had a chance to get under way.

The regime denounced the May mutiny as 'a piece of comic opera' and implicated King Constantine (exiled in Rome), former Prime Minister Karamanlis and other conservative politicians as ringleaders. Premier Papadopoulos and his colleagues seized the opportunity to issue a decree abolishing the monarchy, replacing it with a presidential republic. To show a semblance of legality, the government announced that the 1968 constitution – which the regime itself had put into effect – would be amended. Papadopoulos was proclaimed provisional president and a plebiscite would be held on 29 July to give the Greek people the chance to ratify the change. Denouncing the monarchy as 'an outdated left-over of past ages',[30] Papadopoulos urged his countrymen to vote 'yes', stating that a 'yes' vote would, at the same time, mean approval of the regime, and the automatic confirmation of himself as President of the Republic for an 8-year term. Papadopoulos also promised that following the successful outcome of the 29 July 1973 plebiscite, he would lift martial law, restore civil liberties and would appoint a new cabinet with a mandate to hold elections within 1974 to elect a parliament. In effect, he was promising a return to parliamentary rule, but of a very circumscribed type with the president holding almost exclusive authority in the areas of defence, internal security, and foreign policy.

Many elements within the 'revolutionary council', especially the hard-liners, wanted the monarchy abolished but disagreed as to the type and kind of governmental scheme that should follow it. None the less, replacing the monarchy with a presidential republic was seen by many officers as the 'drastic' move needed to salvage the 'revolution'. The plebiscite was held with Papadopoulos as the sole candidate. Under heavy one-sided propaganda and considerable ballot manipulation, the regime announced 78.4 per cent of the people endorsed the constitutional amendment and the confirmation of Papadopoulos as President of the Republic. In spite of opposition charges of fraud, Papadopoulos, with his characteristic penchant for exaggeration, proclaimed it 'the most genuine and uncoerced expression of the popular will ever given in the entire political history of Greece'.

Shortly after his confirmation, Papadopoulos secured the appointment of an 'all civilian' cabinet under Spyros Markezinis head of the tiny Progressive

Party – a conservative politician with considerable talent whose relentless pursuit of political power led him to span almost the entire ideological spectrum of Greek politics. Papadopoulos lifted martial law, partially restored civil liberties, and had installed a civilian government with a 'mandate' to hold parliamentary elections no later than December 1974. After over six years as first among equals, at long last, Papadopoulos became *primus solus*. But the moment he reached the pinnacle of power, Papadopoulos and his regime now appeared more vulnerable than ever. Less than four months after his confirmation as president, Papadopoulos and his 'civilian' cabinet were overthrown by the hardliners, and within a year praetorian rule in Greece came to an end.[31]

The results of the plebiscite were almost universally dismissed by the country's political elites as a sham.[32] They also rebuffed Markezinis' efforts to enlist their support in his plans to hold 'free and impeccable elections'. Even more threatening to Papadopoulos' supremacy were the deepening divisions within the armed forces. Hardliners and pro-royalist elements opposed the new situation created by the plebiscite for different reasons. As an experienced diplomat said a couple of days after the plebiscite: 'Sunday's vote simply solved nothing ... The regime failed to win credibility and still has all its headaches'.[33] Finally, Papadopoulos' refusal to allow American cargo planes to use Greece as a refuelling station en route to Israel during the October 1973 Arab-Israeli conflict deprived him of much-needed support. The political situation seemed more confused than ever and the regime appeared uncertain and tottering. The hitherto supportive *Wall Street Journal* in an article published in November 1973 remarked that 'the Athenian political and economic pot is [now] boiling in a fashion that has not been seen for many years'.[34]

Papadopoulos and his liberalization scheme were in trouble. The November 1973 student uprising, which the regime suppressed in a bloody confrontation, sealed his fate. The hardliners toppled the strongman and his government in a palace coup. The new set-up cancelled all liberalization efforts but had nothing new to offer and no solutions to the deepening problems. Under worsening circumstances the new strongman, the secretive and puritanical Ioannidis, resorted to a foreign policy adventure in an effort to create breathing space for what US Assistant Secretary Joseph Sisco described as 'the goddamnest government I have ever had to deal with'.[35] The Cyprus quagmire, a bone of contention between Greece and Turkey, seemed a tailor-made crisis candidate. In July 1974, the Cypriot National Guard supported by Greek military officers stationed on the island overthrew the President of Cyprus. The move provoked an invasion by Turkey which caught the Greek military totally unprepared. Instead of becoming the regime's saviour, the Cyprus quagmire became its epitaph. For days after the

Turkish invasion the Greek military hastily returned to the barracks and called back the very civilians they had overthrown to 'save the country from the abyss'. The cataclysmic outcome of the Cyprus affair hastened the inevitable.[36]

In other words, as in intervention, both ecological and institutional factors are responsible for military withdrawal or disengagement from the levers of authority. Societal or ecological dimensions, as well as economic social and political factors, determine whether there will be military withdrawal while organizational considerations, such as corporate interests, affect the disposition of the armed forces to withdraw and the methods it will employ. The socio-economic malaise that characterized the last period of the Colonels' rule, their inability to cloak their regime with a mantle of legitimacy, the devastating outcome of the Cyprus issue, and the corresponding damage to the professional image, social standing and corporate interests of the Greek military generated the need and disposition to return to the barracks and to allow for the return of civilian rule.[37]

RETURN TO THE BARRACKS

The national unity government headed by Constantine Karamanlis, once it weathered the immediate effects of the Cyprus crisis, moved expeditiously to solidify and institutionalize civilian rule and representative government. In less than a year's time, the ringleaders of the 1967 coup and subsequent 7-year rule found themselves behind bars, Greece had a democratically elected government, a new and fairly democratic constitution (1975), a vibrant parliament was back in business, a host of political parties (including the Communist Party [KKE] which was accorded legal status for the first time since the 1940s) emerged, and labour unions and other associations gained considerable influence. Since 1974 the country has gone through three successful presidential successions and four regular elections.[38] Political power has shifted from the conservative New Democracy party to Andreas Papandreou's Panhellenic Socialist Movement (PASOK), and back to the conservatives. The latter joined the Communists in what is billed as a short-duration, limited-purpose alliance following the inconclusive 18 June 1989 parliamentary elections – an unprecedented and highly controversial marriage. Post-1974 Greece, then, meets all the criteria of long-term disengagement and displays the characteristics of political democracy, i.e., secret balloting, universal adult suffrage, regular elections, partisan competition, associational recognition and access, and executive accountability – referred to by O'Donnell and Schmitter as 'procedural minimum'.[39] The military is back in the barracks and, in spite of some initial and feeble flirtations with golpism (interventionism), supports the democratic institutions and is devoted to its primary professional mission: protection of the nation's territorial integrity against outside threats.

What factors explain Greece's successful long-term military disengagement from politics which shows every sign of continuing? As in intervention and withdrawal, answers to sustained civilian rule and dominance can be found in societal and organizational dimensions. As in almost all cases, the factors that contributed to the re-civilianization of the Greek polity include the lessons and experiences drawn by the country's political and economic elites, the changing international environment, and internal professional military considerations and attitude changes. Let us analyse each one separately.

SOCIETAL CONSIDERATIONS

Though it occurred under chaotic and in a crisis-like atmosphere, the reintroduction of civilian rule in Greece was launched in auspicious circumstances from the point of view of the civilian leadership. The discredited military and the exiled king had little leverage to influence political events, leaving the country's political leadership an almost unprecedented range of freedom to chart the nation's political map and future. The Colonels' failure to create any viable political institutions left a void that pre-coup political parties rushed to fill. In this climate the Karamanlis National Unity cabinet threw the floodgates of political participation wide open and legalized the outlawed and crisis-ridden KKE, thus effectively bringing to an end the bitterness and divisions the civil war (1946–9) had left. The civil war was responsible for the anomalous situation that existed within the Greek armed forces in the post-war era and was certainly used by the Colonels as a pretext to launch the 1967 coup. The Communists now became direct and fully-fledged participants in the political process as opposed to excluded and exiled pariahs as they were in the pre-1974 period. Though deeply divided, they have shown every inclination to play the political game at the expense of achieving power through revolutionary means. Their recent decision to enter into an agreement with the New Democracy Party and subsequently to join the other two major parties in an 'ecumenical' government, are indicative of the changing nature of Greek politics and how political enemies of yesteryear can become political bedfellows of tomorrow.

The 7-year dictatorship discredited the extreme right wing using forces of the nation's political spectrum that had supported it. This made it possible for Karamanlis and his associates to distance their conservative New Democracy party from the 'unrepented' and 'antidemocratic' right,[40] and to present themselves as a right-of-centre force fully committed to the democratic process – an image the conservatives lacked in the pre-dictatorship era. The emergence of PASOK under the dynamic leadership of Andreas Papandreou and the eventual demise of the centre brought forward a political force committed to achieving social and economic reform along the principles of democratic socialism. PASOK's electoral victories in the 1981 and 1985 elections established an alternative political force acceptable to the military in sharp contrast to the pre-1967 era.[41]

The political adaptations just described were made possible by the dynamic and irreversible nature of socio-economic development that began in the post civil war era which not only generated reactions that gave rise to the Colonels' dictatorship, but also consumed and eventually overran it. Greece's economic elites benefited from the economic development and sought to tie their fortunes to the technologically advanced economies of Western Europe. A growing and largely urban class also emerged demanding greater participation in governance. These developments, in turn, created the basis for a social and political consensus, which, in spite of some rhetoric to the contrary, supported Greece's membership of the European Economic Community (EEC).

This newly found consensus is reflected in the broad agreement with respect to the nation's political institutions. In spite of some recent financial scandals, Greece's democratic institutions seem to have acquired legitimacy. Although public opinion polls show dissatisfaction with the inability of major political parties to provide magic solutions to the country's economic and social problems, the same polls indicate strong public support and confidence in the country's institutions. For example, a poll conducted in May 1986 showed that 90 per cent of the Greeks have trust in Parliament, 67 and 68 per cent trust in the President of the Republic and the Prime Minister respectively, 77 per cent have confidence in individual members of parliament, and 89 per cent in the future. The approval rate for the latter is far ahead of such traditionally strong competitors as priests (64 per cent), lawyers (55 per cent), and businessmen (58 per cent).[42] Another public opinion survey conducted by *Eurobarometer* revealed that the Greeks are generally satisfied with the way democracy works in their country. Surprisingly, this approval rate is higher than the corresponding rates in Belgium, France, the Netherlands, and even the United Kingdom.[43] The severe economic difficulties Greece is presently facing do not seem to have diminished public support for the nation's democratic institutions.

The leadership factor should not be left out, for Greece's political leaders displayed considerable imagination and skill in guiding the nation through the travails of transition from authoritarianism to democracy and after. Leadership, in the words of Thomas Cronin 'is about making things happen that otherwise might not happen and preventing things from happening that ordinarily would happen'.[44] The personalities of Constantine Karamanlis and Andreas Papandreou should be singled out. The former, with his prestige, experience, and pragmatism, was the ideal choice to succeed the fallen junta. He took the lead in dismantling the dictatorship, legalized the KKE, held an impartial plebiscite (December 1974) on the fate of the monarchy, and built a constitutional framework based on the principles of liberal democracy. Papandreou, a dynamic and charismatic leader who can be said to have been Greece's most powerful prime minister yet, managed single-handedly to create a socialist party which incorporated many positions advocated by the KKE. He presented them in the context of change through peaceful and democratic means, and led his party through two consecutive electoral victories. Thus not only was he able to steal the thunder and the potential appeal of the Communist party, but he also created an acceptable alternative to the conservatives who had been governing Greece for many decades. Ironically, Papandreou's most lasting contribution may yet prove his inability to magically solve all his country's problems, which many of his supporters believed. The latter may lead to a realization that there are no thaumaturges and there can be no wholesale and painless solutions to societal problems. Such attitudes, in turn, could strengthen the post-dictatorship democratic consensus and provide little support for would-be dictators.

While societal adaptations have helped the establishment and maintenance of civilian supremacy in Greece since 1974, disputes with neighbouring Turkey – a fellow NATO member – over Cyprus and the Aegean have been a contributing factor as well. Greeks blame the Atlantic Alliance and its leading member, the United States, for their unwillingness to prevent Turkey from invading and eventually occupying 40 per cent of Cyprus, and to check Ankara's expansionist designs in the Aegean.[45] Athens views Turkey and not the Eastern bloc as a threat to Greece's national security and territorial integrity. Under the circumstances the mission of the Greek military has evolved from essentially one of internal security to that of a truly professional one, i.e., protection of its client, the state, against outside encroachments – paths also adopted by the civilian regimes of Portugal[46] and Spain.[47]

Perceiving the Turkish threat as real, post-disengagement Greek governments have taken steps to improve the armed forces' state of preparedness. The latter includes sizeable increases in military budgets. Nearly 20 per cent of total government spending is devoted to defence, something that political parties of all ideological persuasions support.[48] As a result, the social standing of the military which had taken a nose dive during the 7-year rule has improved dramatically. For example, a public opinion survey showed that 81 per cent of the Greeks trust the armed forces' professional conduct, an approval rate 16 and 17 percentage points higher than that of the police and the Orthodox Church respectively.[49] This state of affairs has made it possible for the military to improve its professional standing and also to have an influence in charting Greece's security policies. And as Welch has correctly pointed out, the consistent but limited participation of the military in politics is one important factor that keeps the military in the barracks.[50]

Finally, successor civilian governments have moved carefully to limit the political role of the armed forces without antagonizing and provoking the officer corps. Act 660 places control over the military in the hands of the government through the minister of defence; yet a series of other laws – designed to complement article 18 of the 1975 constitution dealing with the role of the armed forces – allows the military, in cases of emergency, to assume direct responsibility in making policy without concretely defining 'emergency'. New Democracy governments (1974–81) punished the ringleaders of the 1967 coup but stopped short of an outright purge, continued the special benefits accorded to the military, (such as generous retirement allowances, medical care, and housing), and did little to intervene in the internal affairs of the military, save appointment and promotions to top posts.[51] At the same time military officers were reminded of the sanctity of civilian rule and the merits of democracy. In other words, in their handling of the military the conservatives adopted what Huntington calls 'subjective controls'. The socialists under Andreas Papandreou (1981–9), while praising the military, have supplemented these by 'objective controls'.[52] The latter included reforming the curricula of the service academies doing away with stringent anti-Communist propaganda, promoting the values of pluralism and ideological diversity, emphasis on merit and achievement as criteria for promotion and advancement, and stripping the military's control of its television and radio stations. Fellow socialists' regimes in Portugal under Mario Soáres and in Spain under Felipe González have adopted fairly similar paths.[53] Papandreou and his associates have desperately tried to diversify Greece's sources of arms procurement and to develop a domestic war industry – all in an effort to dampen the officer corps' excessive dependence on NATO and the United States that proved to be less than dependable in the past.

In sum, post-disengagement Greece displays few of the societal characteristics that lead to legitimacy deflation and provide a fertile background for military intervention and praetorianism.

THE INTERNATIONAL ENVIRONMENT

In an era of ever-increasing dependence and expanding communication capabilities the domestic social, political, economic and psychological developments can no longer be divorced from the international environment. Indeed never before have international developments influenced domestic developments, and vice-versa, as much as they do today. Civil–military relations and the role of the military are not immune from what is fast becoming a symbiotic relationship.[54] In this changing environment adaptations, experiences, attitudes, and problems involving the two superpowers have affected and continue to affect developments in their respective spheres of influence and the world; but the opposite is also increasingly true.

In the 1950s, 1960s and early 1970s, both the USA and the USSR, consumed by the Cold War, gave primacy to security interests, operating on the notion that a friendly regime, regardless of its nature, best served the security of their respective blocs. This was especially true in the USA where John Foster Dulles' slogan 'if you are not with us, you are against us' constituted the way Washington perceived the outside world. As a result, America supported oppressive regimes in many parts of the globe in the name of anti-Communism. Reform-oriented political leaders were perceived as dangerous and unacceptable. Washington used its influence to overthrow reform-oriented governments in Guatemala, the Dominican Republic, and Greece and to establish military dictatorships in these and other countries. The Kremlin was equally harsh vis à vis liberalization attempts within its bloc and moved ferociously against Hungary in 1956 and Czechoslovakia in 1968, although no Third World-type military dictatorships were imposed.

Events in Portugal, Spain, Greece and Ethiopia in the mid-1970s challenged the long-held view in Washington that a right-wing anti-Communist dictatorship of the Salazar, Franco, Haile Selassie, or Papadopoulos type would prevent the 'radicalization' of these countries and keep them firmly in the Western camp. The 1974–6 Portuguese Revolution showed that a right-wing dictatorship can plant the seeds of social discontent and radicalization in the ranks of the military and cause an upheaval which nearly delivered a NATO member into the arms of the Soviet Union. The botching of the Cyprus issue by the Greek junta created severe difficulties in the southern flank of the Atlantic alliance, and led to the rise of popular discontent and anti-Americanism in Greece. An even more discouraging outcome took place in Ethiopia, where the military overthrew Emperor Haile Selassie and installed a Soviet-type regime. Conversely, the Spanish experience revealed that reform, liberalization, and democratization are not synonymous with radicalization, instability, and a neutralist foreign policy. The thaw in Soviet–American relations under the spirit of détente, among other factors, led the Soviet Union also to allow a greater degree of independence in Eastern Europe.

Slowly and often selectively, starting with the mid-1970s, the USA began encouraging military regimes to withdraw or civilianize. President Carter's human rights policy was but a means designed to exert pressure on Latin

American, Middle Eastern, and Asian countries to move away from harsh praetorianism and opt for civilianization and democracy. Though not always consistently applied, and in spite of the problems it caused in American–Soviet relations, Carter's human rights policy gave considerable impetus towards military disengagement in Peru, Bolivia, El Salvador, Ecuador, and Honduras. This new American policy line reflected a new belief in Washington that US and Western interests can be best advanced by supporting political and social reform in changing societies. Vietnam, Watergate, and the catharsis that followed along with exposure and subsequent clipping of the CIA's wings also contributed towards this new climate.

In spite of the conservative and often militaristic rhetoric, the Reagan administration generally supported this new line. The proclaimed thrust of the so-called Reagan doctrine was to give American support to democratization movements, with disengagement and democratization being the direct beneficiaries. The Philippines was a clear example where the Reagan doctrine succeeded. In the South Korean case the State Department urged that country's military commanders 'to concentrate on the defence of Korea and allow the political process to develop in a manner agreeable to the Korean people'.[55] US acquiescence in the rise to power of Andreas Papandreou's socialists in 1981 and subsequent re-election contrast sharply with the posture adopted by the USA in the 1960s which, at least partially, led to the instigation of the 1967 coup. Finally, the National Endowment for Democracy, a quasi-governmental organization created by the Reagan administration in 1983 to promote democratic institutions around the world, announced in late May 1988 its decision to make available $600 million to opposition groups in Chile that contributed to the defeat of General Pinochet in the 1988 plebiscite – a move the US government endorsed 'enthusiastically'.[56] The Bush administration appears likely to continue with these policies and extend them to the East European context, but has yet to match the president's rhetoric with badly needed financial assistance.

One can also argue that the Soviet Union's heavy-handedness in Eastern Europe and elsewhere and the high cost Moscow incurred to keep friendly regimes in power, as well as stagnation of the Soviet economy and the emergence of *perestroika* and *glasnost* have encouraged a climate of liberalization and even democratization in that part of the world whose breathtaking nature has caught the entire world by surprise. Free elections and non-Communist governments in Poland, East Germany, Czechoslovakia and Hungary would not have been possible without Moscow's acquiescence. The dreaded Brezhnev doctrine – Moscow's right to come to the rescue of sister Communist regimes under pressure – has been replaced with what is emerging as the Gorbachev doctrine, i.e., abandoning the long-held view of Marxism–

Leninism as the only correct road to socialism and instead allow individual countries to follow their own path.[57]

As we have seen, the introduction of American military and economic aid transformed the Greek military into the most potent political force in the country, and provided the basis for a sophisticated mechanism that 'penetrated the Greek military and political policy-making process', encompassing such areas as trade, shipping, taxation, currency, and budget allocations.[58] Greece became one of the CIA's 'most important operations centres' for intelligence gathering in the Mediterranean, with the majority of the agency's operatives housed in the same building used by the Greek armed forces.[59] This rather close link prompted many observers to conclude that the Colonels' dictatorship was instigated and directed by the United States, with the CIA playing a prominent role. As evidence they cite the fact that Papadopoulos and some of his closest collaborators had been on the CIA's payroll throughout the 1960s and 1970s.[60]

While such charges can neither be proved nor disproved, since relevant documents are still classified, there is little question that 'the regime's main external prop was undoubtedly the United States'.[61] For America and NATO a friendly government in Athens was seen as vital to the strategic interests of the Western alliance. The rapid build-up of Soviet naval presence in the Mediterranean, coupled with the on-going Arab–Israeli conflict and America's commitment to protect Israel made the 'Pentagon particularly anxious to maintain good relations with Greece so as to continue to enjoy base facilities' there.[62] President Nixon made this plain in January 1972 when he stated that the defence of Israel was a primary concern of the United States and a friendly government in Athens would be of utmost importance towards the fulfilment of this goal.

In addition, in 1972 the USA managed to obtain 'Home Port' facilities in Greece providing permanent anchor facilities for the Sixth Fleet – something that previous civilian governments had consistently refused to sign. The USA rewarded the junta's good behaviour by providing abundant political support. American officials, including Vice President Spiro Agnew, streamed to Athens and voiced support and even admiration for the praetorian rulers. Maurice Stans, commerce secretary in the Nixon administration, on an official visit in 1971 conveyed the president's 'warmest love' for the Greek government – a statement the United States Embassy in Athens subsequently 'clarified' to 'warmth' and confidence. When the US Congress voted to suspend military aid to Greece, President Nixon quickly restored it, taking advantage of a clause in the law allowing the president to do so if he considered it essential to the strategic interests of the United States.

American support for the Colonels ultimately caused a strain in US–Greek relations in the post-disengagement era and stimulated the rise of anti-Americanism in Greece. Significant segments of public opinion have criticized the USA for meddling in Greece's internal affairs; supporting, if not instigating the dictatorship; and failing to check Turkey's expansionist designs against their country's territorial integrity. The latter includes inability or unwillingness on the part of the USA to side with Greece on the Cyprus issue, and subsequently to prevent Ankara's invasion and occupation of the island; and parallel disagreements between Greece and Turkey over the Aegean. A 1982 survey, for example, found that 48 per cent of the Greeks had no confidence at all in the USA and 39 per cent had very little.[63]

These developments coupled with a changing international environment, the Colonels' dismal failure and the experiences of the 1970s have prompted US policy-makers in the Bush administration to view a civilian Greek government – although often critical of the USA – preferable to an unpredictable, incompetent but friendly one dominated by the military. The US Ambassador to Athens, Edmund Keeley, expressed this feeling and, hopefully, the lessons drawn in a statement before the Senate Foreign Relations Committee during his confirmation hearing in July 1985:

> [The Greeks want] to get away from the past in their relationship with the U.S., and [want] to transform it into something where Greece is more independent and self-reliant. ... And I think we can perhaps establish a new basis for a different kind of friendship and different relationship of, let's say, more equal allies rather than the client–patron, which is what the history of our relations with Greece was for a couple of decades after World War II'.[64]

Prevailing thinking in Washington and in the international arena provides little support for praetorianism in Athens, and the Greek armed forces are cognizant of it.

THE ROLE OF THE MILITARY

Military thinking and attitudes are affected by societal considerations as well as the international environment. Moreover, officers are capable of drawing lessons and are not oblivious to recognizing and defending their institution's corporate interests. The Greek military is no exception and appears to have drawn its lessons. Direct political authority factionalized the once homogeneous Greek armed forces. The 1967 coup and the 7-year rule that followed were almost exclusively the affair of the army, led by a small band of conspiratorial officers. The other two services (navy and air force) tolerated the Colonels' regime but never harboured any warm feeling towards it. The many ill-fated efforts by the navy, including the May 1973 one, to topple the junta, can be seen in that light. Under the circumstances, Greek officers are no longer willing to tolerate factionalism within their ranks, especially when tense relations with Turkey militate in favour of unity and preparedness.

The student uprising of November 1973 and the Cyprus fiasco also strengthened these sentiments and caused a change of attitudes regarding the damage to the military's professional interests, prestige, and social standing praetorianism can generate. The student uprising and the brutal manner it was suppressed pitted the armed forces against the civilian population – something that the military is generally reluctant to do.[65] To many officers the disastrous handling of the Cyprus issue harmed Greece's interests and exposed the military's inability to carry out its professional mission of protecting the nation's physical integrity. All these lessons are not lost to today's military officers.

Largely because of Athens's continuing disputes with Turkey, the corporate interests of the Greek armed forces have never been better looked after. As mentioned, almost 20 per cent of total government spending is devoted to defence, one of the world's highest rates. More officers today are sent abroad for advanced training and the percentage of those conversant in foreign languages has reached an all-time high.[66] The Greek armed forces' state of preparedness and possession of tanks, ships, aircraft and other war material has never been better. The nation's political leadership has overwhelmingly supported those efforts as has the Greek public whose confidence in the armed forces' readiness to defend the homeland stands at over 80 per cent. Finally, the officer corps, through the military commanders, is in a position to influence Greece's defence policies, and, upon retirement, many officers enter Parliament as elected deputies. One such example is Tzannis Tzannetakis, a former submarine captain recently served as prime minister. He was chosen for the post because, as a Communist official put it, he 'has the honesty of an officer and the temperament of a gentleman'.[67] Under the conditions prevailing since 1974, the Greek military has so far had no reason to intervene.

THE FUTURE

At the beginning of this essay it was stated that the military return and stay in the barracks, and civilian supremacy is established and sustained when the factors and conditions that prompted intervention have passed. Welch develops this further, suggesting that military intervention does not occur when the following factors are present: institutionalization of civilian political values, the consistent but limited participation of the military in politics, and most important, the development of broad-based political institutions enjoying legitimacy and popular support.[68] The preceding narrative clearly suggests that post-1974 Greece meets all three conditions. Is civilian rule, then, likely to continue?

Writing on the same subject some years ago, this writer expressed only cautious optimism regarding the long-term viability of civilian rule and democracy in Greece. Five years later, and in spite of financial scandals involving some officials of Papandreou's last government, the future of civilian rule and democracy seem much brighter. Though louder and muddier than in recent memory, the last electoral campaigns (18 June, 5 November 1989 and 8 April 1990) revealed evidence that the post-dictatorship consensus is getting stronger. The leaders of the two major parties, New Democracy and PASOK, concentrated on blaming each other for past problems. This was in part due to the personal animosity between Mitsotakis and Papandreou, but also because the two parties differ little on most policy issues, foreign and domestic. Dwelling on the past is a method politicians use to obscure issues and conceal lack of real differences between themselves and their opponents, yet distinguish themselves from their rivals. Finally, the left seems to have joined the consensus. The KKE and other leftist groups that formed an electoral alliance presented a platform which emphasized individual initiative and restricted the role of the state in economic matters.

In sum, given the broad social pact that has emerged, absence of any real divisive issues, the incorporation of the left as a full participant, the virtual bitter disappearance of the extreme right, and the sorry lessons of praetorianism (for military and civilians alike) the future of civilian rule and democracy in Greece seem quite promising.

NOTES

1. This paper was presented at the 1990 conference of the Research Committee on Armed Forces and Society of the International Political Science Association. The meeting was held in Madrid, Spain, 6–7 July, and the paper was selected by the participants as the conference's 'Second Best Paper'.
2. Claude E. Welch, Jr, *No Farewell to Arms? Military Disengagement from Politics in Africa and Latin America* (Boulder: Westview Press, 1987), p. 20.
3. Talukder Maniruzzaman, *Military Withdrawal From Politics: A Comparative Study* (Cambridge, Mass: Bollinger Publishing Company, 1987), p. 29; S. E. Finer, *The Man on Horseback – The Role of the Military in Politics*, 2nd enlarged edition (Boulder: Westview Press, 1988), p. 305.
4. See, for example, Samuel P. Huntington, *Political Order in Changing Societies* (New Haven: Yale University Press, 1969); Finer, *The Man On Horseback*; and Amos Perlmutter, *The Military and Politics in Modern Times* (New Haven: Yale University Press, 1977).
5. Military professionalization is defined here in terms of (1) specialized theoretical knowledge accompanied by methods and devices for application; (2) responsibility, grounded on a set of ethical rules; and (3) a high degree of corporateness, deriving from common training and devotion to specific doctrines and customs.

See Bengt Abrahamsson, *Military Professionalization and Political Power* (Beverly Hills: Sage Publications), p. 15.

6. See, for example, Morris Janowitz, *Military Institutions and Coercion in the Developing Nations* (Chicago: The University of Chicago Press, 1977); Claude E. Welch, Jr, and Arthur K. Smith, *Military Role and Rule: Perspectives on Civil Military Relations* (North Scituate: Duxbury, 1974); and Eric A. Nordlinger, *Soldiers in Politics: Military Coups and Governments* (Englewood Cliffs: Prentice-Hall, 1977).

7. Janowitz, *Military Institutions*, pp. VIII and IX.

8. Nordlinger, *Soldiers in Politics*.

9. Welch and Smith, *Military Role and Rule*.

10. Nordlinger, *Soldiers in Politics*, pp. 65–78.

11. Yiannis Boulepsis and Pericles Rodakis, eds, *1943–1975: Ta Ellinika Istorika Dokumenta*, 9 vols. (Athens: Dimokratikoi Kairoi, 1978), 3: 129–291.

12. Nicos C. Alvizatos, 'The Greek Army in the Late Forties: Towards an Institutional Autonomy', *Journal of the Hellenic Diaspora*, vol. 5: 3 (Fall 1978), p. 37.

13. Lawrence S. Wittner, *American Intervention in Greece, 1943–1949* (New York: Columbia University Press, 1982), p. 53.

14. Yiannis P. Roubatis, 'The United States and the Operational Responsibilities of the Greek Armed Forces, 1947–1987', *Journal of the Hellenic Diaspora*, 6: 1 (Fall 1978), p. 55.

15. Nordlinger, *Soldiers in Politics*, p. 22.

16. For more details see my *Soldiers and Politicians in Modern Greece* (Chapel Hill: Documentary Publications, 1984), ch.2.

17. Nordlinger, *Soldiers in Politics*, p. 65.

18. Samuel P. Huntington and Joan M. Nelson, *No Easy Choice: Political Participation in Developing Countries* (Cambridge: Harvard University Press, 1976), pp. 43–5.

19. Jacques van Doorn, 'The Military and the Crisis of Legitimacy', in Gwyn Harries-Jenkins and Jacques van Doorn, eds, *The Military and the Problem of Legitimacy* (London: Sage Publications, 1976), p. 20.

20. Nordlinger, *Soldiers in Politics*, p. 7.

21. Ibid.

22. David Easton, 'The Analysis of Political Systems', in Roy C. Macridis and Bernard Brown, eds, *Comparative Politics: Notes and Readings*, 4th edn (Homewood: Dorsey Press, 1972), p. 80.

23. George Katiforis, *I Nomothesia ton Barbaron* (Athens: Themelio, 1975), p. 139.

24. For a more detailed analysis see my 'The Military and Bureaucracy in Greece, 1967–1974', *Public Administration and Development*, Vol. 8: 2 (April–June 1988).

25. A. F. Freris, *The Greek Economy in the Twentieth Century* (New York: St. Martin's Press, 1986), p. 191.

26. *OECD Economic Surveys: Greece* (Paris: Organization for Economic Cooperation and Development, 1975), pp. 21–2.

27. Sir Hugh Green quotes George Papadopoulos in a Hearing Before the Subcommittee on Europe of the Committee on Foreign Affairs, 92nd Cong., 1st sess., Washington, DC, 1971, p. 192.

28. For more details see my 'Military Professionalism and Regime Legitimacy in Greece, 1967–1974', *Political Science Quarterly*, 98: 3 (Fall 1983); and Constantine P. Danopoulos and Kant Patel, 'Military Professionals as Political

Governors: A Case Study of Contemporary Greece', *West European Politics* 3: 2 (May 1980).

29. Claude E. Welch, Jr, 'Personalism and Corporatism in African Armies', in Katherine McArdle Kelleher, ed., *Military Systems: Comparative Perspectives* (Beverly Hills: Sage, 1974), pp. 131–5.

30. *New York Times*, 2 June 1973, p. 1.

31. For more details see my 'From Military to Civilian Rule in Contemporary Greece', *Armed Forces and Society* 10: 2 (Winter 1984).

32. For more details on the impact of the Plebiscite see my 'Democratic Undercurrents in Praetorian Regimes: The Greek Military and the 1973 Plebiscite' *Journal of Strategic Studies* 12: 3 (September 1989); and Constantine P. Danopoulos and Larry N. Gerston, 'Democratic Undercurrents in Authoritarian Seas', *Armed Forces and Society* 16: 2 (Summer 1990).

33. *New York Times*, 1 August 1973, p. 8.

34. *Wall Street Journal*, 20 November 1973, p. 27.

35. Lawrence Stern, *The Wrong Horse: The Politics of Intervention and the Failure of American Diplomacy* (New York: The New York Times Books, 1977), p. 123.

36. For more detailed analysis see my 'The Greek Military Regime (1967–1974) and the Cyprus Question: Origins and Goals', *Journal of Political and Military Sociology* 10: 2 (Fall 1982).

37. For a more detailed information see my 'Beating a Hasty Retreat: The Greek Military Withdraws from Power', in Constantine P. Danopoulos, ed., *The Decline of Military Regimes: The Civilian Influence* (Boulder: Westview Press, 1988).

38. For more details regarding political parties and elections see: Howard R. Penniman, ed., *Greece at the Polls: The National Elections of 1974 and 1977* (Washington: American Enterprise Institute, 1981); and Richard Clogg, *Parties and Elections in Greece: The Search for Legitimacy* (Durham: Duke University Press, 1987).

39. Guillermo O'Donnell and Philippe C. Schmitter in their *Transitions from Authoritarian Rule: Tentative Conclusions about Uncertain Democracies* (Baltimore: Johns Hopkins University Press, 1986), p. 8.

40. For analysis of the transformation of New Democracy see J. C. Loulis, 'New Democracy: The New Face of Conservatism', in Penniman, ed., *Greece at the Polls;* and Clogg, *Parties and Elections in Greece*, ch.5.

41. For analyses of the emergence and philosophy of PASOK see: Angelos Elephantis, 'PASOK and the Elections of 1977: The Rise of the Populist Movement', in Penniman, ed., *Greece at the Polls;* Clogg, Parties and *Elections in Greece*, ch. 4; Michalis Spourdalakis, *The Rise of the Greek Socialist Party* (London: Routledge, 1988). For a more negative and controversial, if not outright biased picture, see a collection of essays by Nicalaos A. Stavrou, ed., *Greece Under Socialism: A NATO Ally Adrift* (New Rochelle: Orpheus Publishing, Inc., 1988).

42. 'Trust in Values/Political and Social Institutions (Greece)' in *World Opinion Update*, X: 5 (May 1986), pp. 52–3.

43. Cited in Jurg Steiner, *European Democracies* (New York: Longman, 1986), p. 247.

44. Thomas E. Cronin, 'Foreword' in William E. Rosenbach and Robert L. Taylor, eds, *Contemporary Issues in Leadership* (Boulder: Westview Press, 1989), p. xiii.

45. For an evaluation of Greece's membership in NATO see my 'Regional Security Organizations and National Interests: Analyzing the NATO–Greek Relationship', *Journal of Political and Military Sociology*, 16: 2 (Fall 1988).

46. For an analysis of the Portuguese military's withdrawal from political power see my 'Democratization by Golpe: The Experience of Modern Portugal' in Constantine P. Danopoulos, ed., *Military Disengagement From Politics* (London: Routledge, 1988).

47. For analyses regarding the Spanish military see: Fernando Rodrigo, 'A Democratic Strategy Towards the Military, Spain 1975–1979' in Constantine P. Danopoulos, ed., this volume; and Rafael Banón, 'The Spanish Military: Reform and Modernization for the New Strategic Thinking', and unpublished paper presented at the Institute for Defense Analyses, Washington, DC, 5 October 1988.

48. *World Military Expenditures and Arms Transfers 1986*, (Washington, DC : US Arms Control and Disarmament Agency, 1987).

49. 'Trust in Values', in *World Opinion Update*, pp. 52–3.

50. Welch, *No Farewell to Arms*, p. 13.

51. For more details see my 'From Balconies to Tanks'.

52. Samuel P. Huntington, 'Civilian Control of the Military: A Theoretical Statement', in Heinz Eulau, Samuel J. Eldersveld, and Morris Janowitz, eds, *Political Behavior – A Reader in Theory and Research* (Glencoe: The Free Press, 1956)., pp. 380–1.

53. For details on the Spanish case see Rodrigo's chapter in this volume; and Banón, 'The Spanish Military'.

54. Lawrence Whitehead, 'International Aspects of Democratization', in Guillermo O'Donnel, Philippe C. Schmitter and Lawrence Whitehead, eds, *Transitions from Authoritarian Rule: Corporative Perspectives* (Baltimore: Johns Hopkins University Press, 1986), pp. 3–46; and my 'Withdrawal and After: A One-Way Street or a Revolving Door?', in Danopoulos, ed., *The Decline of Military Regimes*.

55. Quoted in Tim Shorock, 'South Korea: Chun, the Kims and the Constitutional Struggle', *Third World Quarterly*, 10: 2 (January 1988), p. 109.

56. 'U.S. Group Channeling $600.000 to Pinochet's Foes in Chile', *New York Times*, 15 June 1988, p. A8.

57. 'Soviet Union and Eastern Europe: The Gorbachev Doctrine', *Economist*, 15–21 July 1989, pp. 40–41.

58. Michael Mark Amen, 'American Institutional Penetration into Greek Military and Policymaking Structures: June, 1946–October, 1949', *Journal of the Hellenic Diaspora*, 5: 3 (Fall 1978), p. 112.

59. Yiannis Roubatis and Karen Wynn, 'CIA Operations in Greece', in Philip Agee and Louis Wolf, eds, *The CIA in Western Europe* (Syracuse: Lyle Stuart, 1978), p. 147.

60. Andreas G. Papandreou, *Democracy at Gunpoint: The Greek Front* (Garden City: Doubleday and Company, 1970); and Stephen Rousseas, *The Death of a Democracy: Greece and the American Conscience* (New York: Grove Press 1968).

61. Richard Clogg, *A Short History of Modern Greece*, 2nd edn, (London: Cambridge University Press, 1987), p. 193.

62. Ibid.

63. Cited in George A. Kourvetaris and Betty A. Dobratz, *A Profile of Modern Greece in Search of Identity* (London: Oxford University Press, 1987), p. 442.

64. US Senate, Subcommittee on European Affairs of the Committee on Foreign Relations. Hearing on the Nomination of Robert Vossler Keeley to be Ambassador Extraordinary and Plenipotentiary to Greece. (Washington, DC : Alderson Reporting Company, Inc., 1985).

65. Janowitz, *Military Institutions*, p. 37.
66. Dimitrios Smokovitis reports that the Greek military employs today more specialists and people with advanced technical expertise. He also argues that the trend towards occupationalism and away from institutionalism is 'undeniable'. See his 'Greece', in Charles C. Moskos and Frank R. Wood, eds, *The Military: More than Just a Job?* (New York: Pergamon-Brassey's International Defence Publishers, Inc., 1988).
67. 'New Greek Coalition Sworn Into Office', *San Francisco Chronicle*, 3 July 1989.
68. Welch, *No Farewell*, p. 12.

4 A democratic strategy towards the military in post-Franco Spain

Fernando Rodrigo

The dismantling of the Francoist authoritarian regime in Spain and the establishment of a democratic one by peaceful, consensual and legal means has raised hopes of repeating this experience in other countries with similar backgrounds. In order to understand and appreciate how this transformation came about it is necessary to give a brief history of civil–military relations in that country before and during the tenure of the Franco regime.

In the early 1800s Spain entered a period of decline which was exacerbated by the loss of vast colonial holdings in Latin America. Regionalism, a fierce class struggle between the landed gentry and the landless peasantry, a non-productive economy, and foreign interference were some of the ills endured by Spanish society. Political divisions followed suit pitting the proponents of absolutism against advocates of a constitutional monarchy. The republican element soon made its début further complicating the nation's political landscape. Since none of these political forces was strong enough to prevail over the other, a political void was created which was filled by the armed forces, which came to occupy a privileged position in the nation's political spectrum Thus for almost a century (1820–3) a flurry of *pronunciamentos* occurred with the military playing the role of king maker. This interventionist, but no-direct-rule position, changed in 1923. Reacting to the *Cortes'* (Parliament) decision to investigate the army's dismal performance in the effort to annex Morocco, the Spanish military staged a *coup d'état* and imposed a six-year praetorian rule. It became known as the Primo de Rivera military dictatorship (1923–9) and is considered the first in Spanish history.

Faced with the same age-old problems of regionalism and class conflict, and under strong influence by the Catholic Church and reactionary elements within the armed forces, the Rivera dictatorship failed in its mission. The monarchy who supported the praetorian regime lost its legitimacy and was replaced in 1931 by the liberal Second Republic. But the internally divided Second Republic, who also encountered a less than favourable international environment, was unable to solve Spain's deepening social and economic wounds. The gulf between the republican forces (supported by the working classes) and the conservatives (representing the Church, the financial and industrial elites, and the landed aristocracy) intensified. On 17 July 1936, units of the Spanish army serving in Morocco staged a mutiny against the republican government in Madrid. A bloody civil war (1936–9) ensued which culminated in the defeat of the republican forces and paved the road for Franco's dictatorship which lasted until the general's death in 1975.

Although the Francoist regime was headed by General Francisco Franco himself, it was not exactly a military government. The armed forces supported but did not dominate the regime which was led by a coalition made up of the Church, the financial elites, monarchists and other conservative elements. The Spanish *caudillo* formed a close friendship with his colleagues in the armed forces and dismissed all those suspected of harbouring anti-Francoist feelings. Franco kept military appropriations low but made sure officers received hefty salaries, and kept each branch (army, navy, and air force) autonomous from the other two. During his rule Spain had no ministry of defence to coordinate security policy and make the military an independent political player.

Franco's eclipse in November 1975 deprived the Spanish military of political direction. In the past, the armed forces' participation in the regime had been determined by their relationship with General Franco in his capacity as Head of State and Commander-in-Chief. This relationship, which was based on the Generalissimo's charisma and reputation as the 'providential' military leader responsible for victory against the republican forces in the civil war, was not one his successor, King Juan Carlos I, could readily inherit.

Article 6 of the Francoist Organic Law of the State (1966) stated that the Head of State 'exercises supreme command of the Army, Navy and Air Force'. In spite of this, the Franco regime failed to institutionalize the means by which the head of state exercised this prerogative in practice. Franco's relationship with the military was purely personal. Furthermore, partly because the general did not appoint a head of the government other than himself until June 1973, the armed forces were unaccustomed to taking orders from the executive. Indeed the premier lacked the institutional and legal mechanisms necessary to exercise authority in this sphere.

The Franco regime, born of a military confrontation, gradually transferred the governing of the country to civilian politicians, often representing different elements of the founding coalition. Thus, in the final years of the regime the armed forces, while continuing to play an important role, were by no means at the centre of the decision-making process. The presence of military men in the government, for example, declined from 37 in 1969 to 18 at the time of the *caudillo*'s death in 1975.[1]

Qualitative factors, such as the nature of the posts held, must also be taken into account when measuring military participation in the regime. With the exception of Admiral Carrero Blanco, head of the government from June 1973 until his assassination in December of the same year, military men did not occupy key positions in the regime. The presidency of the Francoist Cortes and the Council of the Realm were always held by civilians. Military officers were never in a majority in either of these institutions, nor did they enjoy special veto powers. Indeed the only posts invariably reserved for the military were those associated with law enforcement. All of this was in marked contrast to other authoritarian regimes, such as Brazil or Chile, in which military influence was far greater.

This is not to say that the armed forces were entirely without political influence in the wake of Franco's death. Since the civil war, there had invariably been three military ministers in Franco's governments, representing the army, navy and air force – a tradition upheld in the immediate post-Franco era. There was also a small military presence in the Cortes, and in the Council of the Realm. The latter refers to a 16-man body responsible for assisting the new king in selecting candidates for key positions, including the presidencies of the government and the Cortes. In the immediate post-Franco era the armed forces continued to enjoy considerable political influence, but lacked leadership, organization and direction to translate it into political action. In other words, the military was a major social actor without a clear political role.

After Franco's death, the role of the armed forces in the political system underwent radical changes which resulted in the dismantlement of the *caudillo*'s authoritarian regime and the establishment of a democratic one. An analysis of the Spanish case would suggest that the characteristics of the dismantled regime, the role of the armed forces in it, and the path chosen to carry out the change were important elements determining the successful transition from authoritarism to democracy in Spain.[2]

A DEMOCRATIC STRATEGY TOWARDS THE MILITARY

There is a dimension to Spain's transition to democracy, which is essential for a fuller understanding of the behaviour of the armed forces, and which has received insufficient attention.[3] This is particularly true in light of what Alfred Stepan terms 'a democratic strategy towards the military';[4] in other words, a military policy. The difference between the mere withdrawal of the military to the barracks and the definitive neutrality of the armed forces often depends on the existence of a military policy which favours the professionalization of the military and facilitates the inclusion of the armed forces in the new political system. A comparison between the democratization of the armed forces in Spain and that of the other countries, such as Argentina, reveals the importance of a positive attitude towards the military on the part of the civilian political leadership, facilitating by every means available the integration of the armed forces in the new political system, instead of merely seeking their political neutralization.[5]

In order to formulate and carry out such a military policy, the civilian leadership requires the collaboration of certain elements within the armed forces. For after a prolonged period of military participation in politics, civilians lack the expertise necessary for this task. What was needed in the Spanish case was a promotions policy which would put reformist military elements in key positions replacing those reluctant to collaborate with the government. In Spain the civilian leadership was unable to initiate a reformist policy towards the military until the appointment of General Gutierrez Mellado as vice president responsible for defence affairs by Premier Adolfo Suárez in September 1976.

In order to carry out its military policy, the government sought the collaboration of prestigious military elements mainly concerned about the future of armed forces, rather than confirmed democrats. Such officers generally 'support the transition much more because of what they believe is good for the [a]rmed [f]orces than because of any enthusiasm for democracy'.[6]

The Spanish experience of civil–military collaboration would support the above view, as well as Rustow's criticism of some existing theories on democracy:

> Many of the current theories about democracy seem to imply that to promote democracy you must first foster democrats – perhaps by preachment, propaganda, education, or perhaps as an automatic by-product of growing prosperity. Instead, we should allow for the possibility that circumstances may force, trick, lure, or cajole non-democrats into democratic behavior and that their beliefs may adjust in due course by some process of rationalization or adaptation.[7]

In Spain the reforms were undertaken by military men who had taken part in the civil war on Franco's side and whose careers had prospered under the general's dictatorship.

WITHDRAWAL FROM POLITICS

A key aspect of the military policy implemented by the Suárez government was aimed at achieving the withdrawal of the military from all political activity, at a time when the emergence of new actors in the political scene was radically altering the rules of the game which had hitherto permitted military participation in politics. The military authorities themselves had already begun to establish a distinction between the political role the armed forces should enjoy as an institution and the direct involvement of the military in the political arena. According to one military minister:

> the [a]rmed [f]orces are not alien to politics in the most fundamental meaning of the word, that is to say, distanced from those activities designed to create and defend an order as a guarantee of the common good of the nation.[8]

Another military minister went a step further:

> It is not honest to belong to an institution which is beyond concrete political options, if one is convinced that he could better serve Spain through promoting or encouraging a particular political attitude. He who thinks thus will proceed honestly with himself, with the [a]rmy and with Spain if he departs from our ranks.[9]

These attitudes were embodied in a Royal Decree issued on 8 February 1977, which regulated the exercise of political and union activities by members of the armed forces. In its first article, the decree forbade political and union activities within the armed forces, while its second article categorically affirmed that those who in a professional capacity form part of the armed forces, regardless of their rank and status, may not:

> Be affiliated to, collaborate with or support any type of political or union organization, except the right of active suffrage;
> Express publicly, in any way, opinions of a political or union nature with respect to different party, group, institutional or organizational options;
> Attend any public meeting of a political or union nature organized or promoted by political or union parties, groups or associations;
> Hold public office or accept nomination for such office when this is elective and of a political or union nature;
> Accept and hold public office by direct designation, save those of military administration or which are appropriate to the military condition.[10]

Military officers wishing to run in electoral contests had first to request release from the army, which was granted automatically and was irreversible. On the other hand, the above-mentioned Royal Decree allowed six months for those military men who at that time held public office to leave the post, or request release from the army.

REMILITARIZING THE MILITARY

Another important matter to be determined when seeking the professionalization of the armed forces is whether they are to be involved exclusively in military affairs or whether they should be allowed to take part in civilian activities, such as economic and social development.[11] The Spanish case supports Huntington's view that: 'Objective civilian control achieves its end by militarizing the military, making them the tool of the state'.[12]

Huntington's hypothesis, to the effect that professionalization is the best means of achieving objective civilian control over the armed forces, is borne out by the Spanish case. The major issue here is the achievement of an adequate balance between military and civilian power: 'Civilian control in the objective sense, is that distribution of political power between military and civilian groups which is most conducive to the emergence of professional attitudes and behaviour among the members of the officer corps'.[13]

In Spain, this balance was obtained by seeking a new relationship between the armed forces and the nation's political institutions. Previously they only had contact through the head of state, who was also the commander-in-chief of the armed forces. This new relationship, which recognized defence matters as a problem concerning all Spaniards instead of the military alone, was positive for both the government and the services. It was positive for the government because it enabled it to establish mechanisms for the control of the military institution; as to the armed forces, it was advantageous because only through a close relationship with the other institutions of the state could they obtain the resources required to defend Spain against an external threat.

The first steps in this direction were taken by certain elements in the military high command some years before Franco's death. The armed forces sought this new relationship in order to overcome the stalemate reached in the modernization processes initiated independently by each of the services in the mid-1960s. But for this new relationship with the state to succeed it required political reform that the Francoist regime was not prepared to grant in the final days of its founder.[14]

In 1974, the Defence Law proposed by the head of the military high command to the government was exposed by the Francoist Cortes, the more hardline sectors of the regime, and the services.[15] Several months later, when general Diez Alegria ceased to be the head of the high command, the government withdrew the planned law from the Cortes for reconsideration. This experience convinced the reformist elements in the armed forces that military reorganization could not be accomplished without the support of a reformist government.

THE MINISTER OF DEFENCE

Military reform had to wait until the new head of government, Adolfo Suárez, could remove the Vice President for Defence Affairs, inherited from his predecessor. This did not occur until September 1976. With the appointment of Lieutenant General Gutierrez Melládo as the new Vice Premier for Defence Affairs, Gutierrez Melládo had been second in command to General Diez Alegria in the high command. With him in charge changes in the armed forces took place rapidly.

The method chosen by Gutierrez Melládo to achieve a balance between the civilian and military authorities aimed at encouraging the flourishing of professional attitudes and conduct among the officer corps, and the removal of the military chain of command from the political–administrative sphere. This allowed him to consolidate the three military ministries (air force, navy and army) under a single Ministry of Defence and incorporate the latter into the administrative apparatus of the state.[16]

The consolidation of the three ministries, however, did not entail any loss of authority for the military institution over its own affairs, since the military, in collaboration with the government, was made responsible for implementing the planned reforms. Prior to the creation of the Ministry of Defence, the powers of the chiefs of staff of the three services were significantly increased. The chiefs were given overall responsibility for organization, logistics and personnel which the minister had previously possessed. The chain of command was completed with the creation of a Joint Chiefs of Staff, designed as a collegiate body to guarantee coordination between the three services and advise the government on further reforms.[17]

The creation of the Ministry of Defence in July 1977, took place a few days after the first democratic elections which brought to power a centrist coalition government led by Adolfo Suárez. The creation of the ministry reinforced the government's authority and enhanced the professional autonomy of the armed forces.[18]

GUTIERREZ MELLÁDO'S INVESTMENT POLICY

The institutional arrangements provided Gutierrez Melládo with the necessary legal instrument to set reforms in motion. It was nevertheless necessary to guarantee their economic viability. For as Claude Welch states:

> officers urging returns to the barracks do so in part in the expectation that the successor civilian governments will treat the armed forces well, both as gestures of will and as insurance against further intervention. Specifically, the decision to disengage and subsequent achievement of

neutrality in politics are eased by increases in armed forces' budget allocation[19]

The experience of the armed forces under the Franco regime had not been a happy one in the economic field. Indeed one could say the military had been left behind other sectors of the regime, if not actually abandoned.[20] By contrast, the newly established democratic government committed itself to provide adequate budgetary support for the armed forces at a time of acute economic difficulties – a commitment honoured by successor civilian cabinets.

The government's budgetary decision was taken on 21 January 1977, immediately following the dissolution of the Francoist regime approved by the Cortes and not long before the calling of the first democratic election. The cabinet approved a 5-year programme designed to modernize the forces' war-fighting capability.[21] This decision, apart from providing the civil authorities with valuable means of influencing the future organization of the armed forces paved the way for General Gutierrez Melládo to begin implementing the policy of military reform.

GUTIERREZ MELLÁDO'S PAY POLICY

The professionalization of the Spanish armed forces would not have been possible without the dedication and the professional mission of many officers. The loss of officers' purchasing power during the 1970s, relative to that of other state employees, had forced many military men to resort, like many other Spaniards at the time, to having more than one job in order to make ends meet. General Gutierrez Melládo made reference to this issue in his first appearance before the Defence Commission of the newly elected Congress:

> What is happening is that at the moment the multi-job situation, in use for many years, cannot be suddenly stopped. [Officers] must be convinced, as the majority of us are, that it cannot persist, that it must come to an end, albeit gradually and respecting people's rights, for we could be faced with critical situations, extraordinarily difficult, and there must be absolute dedication.[22]

In an attempt to overcome this situation the government passed in April 1977 a new pay law for civil servants, which, for the first time, included the professional military, thereby equalizing the earnings of both civilian and military state employees. A final article in the law pointed the way along the lines previously set out by Gutierrez Melládo:

At the suggestion of the Army, Navy and Air Force Ministers, the government, in keeping with the principle of sole dedication to the military professions, will determine, before 1 June 1977, activities deemed incompatible with full dedication to a military career.[23]

THE DEMILITARIZATION OF LAW ENFORCEMENT

The professionalization of the armed forces, which Huntington describes as the best way to remove the military from politics,

> is rooted in the assumption that armies develop their professional skills for conventional warfare against foreign armies. ... [if] the focus shifts from interstate conflict to domestic war it will encourage a different pattern of civil–military relations[24]

The Spanish case demonstrates the importance of this aspect of civil–military relations. The dismantling of an authoritarian regime and the transition to a democratic system of government required eliminating the source of conflict between political and military forces which arose from the involvement of the army in the administration of justice and police-related activities. For most of the Franco period, the military was used to maintain curbs on civil liberties and suppress acts of terrorism. For example, as late as 1970, 407 civilians were condemned by military courts.[25]

One principal reason behind the existence of military courts was the military character of the national police and the civil guard. Since their members were considered part of the armed forces any contact with strikers, demonstrators, and violators amounted to war since the Code of Military Justice was responsible for the punishment of 'insults' against the armed forces' and 'offences against the army'.

It was not possible to reform satisfactorily the Code of Military Justice until the second half of the 1980s, [26] even though the first governments under King Juan Carlos sought to reduce military jurisdiction in the punishment of political offences. The latter considerably reduced the activity of military courts. In November 1980, a bill for the partial reform of the Code of Military Justice was passed following the guidelines laid down in the Moncloa Pact which was signed in September 1977, and in the new constitution which was approved in December 1978.[27] Certain aspects of this reform bill, in spite of its subtlety, raised angry complaints among military jurists:

> Two changes were made to Article 84–1. ... The second of these was more important, for it involved the suppression of the term 'highest' when describing the authority of the Supreme Military Court ... this might mean that the Court would cease to be 'Supreme,' both because it would no

longer be 'the highest,' and because some of its decisions might in the future be referred to the Supreme Court.[28]

The elimination of the military nature of the police forces did not become effective until the Law of State Security Forces was passed in 1986. The Civil Guard has yet to be stripped of its connection with the military which dates back to the middle of the nineteenth century.[29] Moreover, the guard is jointly administered by the Ministries of Defence and Interior, a practice which allows it considerable autonomy. Nevertheless some progress towards the solution of this problem was made when the Police Law passed by the first freely elected Parliament in December 1978, stated that ordinary jurisdiction will always be competent to cope with the offences committed against members of the National Police; and the Civil Guard will have a special military legal status, but not for those crimes committed against its members during the performance of the duties stated in this law, these crimes come under ordinary jurisdiction.[30]

Throughout the 1975–7 period the intervention of the national police and the civil guard, under orders from army officers, was customary in the repression of political and labour demonstrations. Consequently, one of the chief objectives of the reformist government was to safeguard political rights by law and thus render intervention of the security forces in this area illegal.

The appointment of civilians to head law enforcement departments, positions traditionally held by military men, made it easier for the government to control the activities of these bodies.[31] Finally, the 1978 Constitution separated the security forces from the three military services, placed responsibility for law enforcement exclusively in the hands of the former, and restricted military jurisdiction solely to defence-related matters.[32]

THE INTERNATIONAL CONTEXT

The professionalization of the armed forces brought about added emphasis on the external defence mission of the Spanish military and weakened its traditional concern for the 'enemy from within'. As Claude Welch has observed,

> The roles armed forces are called upon to play directly and clearly affect their political involvement. ... The initial decision and process of disengagement are thus eased by a redirection of military mission towards classic defence duties[33]

In Spain perceptions of the external threat had been perpetuated almost exclusively by the army, the most numerous, worst equipped and politically most influential of the three services. Traditionally, the army had mainly perceived a threat from the south, where it had been engaged in several colonial wars. This threat was still considered relevant in the mid-1970s due to Spain's military presence in the Sahara.

Franco's death in November 1975 coincided with the signing of the Madrid Agreement in which Spain agreed to withdraw from the Sahara and put an end to its century-old colonial experience in Africa.[34] The withdrawal brought about a major change in the military's strategic perceptions and strengthened the importance of the navy and the air force at the expense of the army.

It was necessary to reconsider the question of the conflict outside Spain and this could only happen if Spain were included in the machinery for the defence of the West: NATO. From the beginning of the transition period the possibility of Spain's entry into NATO had emerged as one of the benefits which the armed forces would obtain from the establishment of a democratic regime.

Incorporation into NATO became more necessary as the military relationship with the United States had long since exhausted the modernizing potential it had once represented. Spain's entry into NATO was not widely discussed outside military circles during the transition, however. This was largely because the priorities of the reformist governments were with the left whose cooperation was making the elaboration of a democratic constitution possible. Spain's formal entry into NATO had to wait until February 1981, when the government which was formed the day after the abortive *coup d'état* of 23 February 1981, proposed the attachment of Spain to the Washington Treaty.

The integration of Spain into a multilateral defensive organization provided the Spanish armed forces with a new impetus to modernize. It also allowed the government to justify many of the pending reforms arguing that NATO membership required the technical upgrading of the three services. Similarly, it has contributed to the improvement of civilian expertise in military affairs, thanks to the presence of Spanish representatives in NATO headquarters, thereby providing the government with an alternative source of information.

Spain's entry into NATO has been of great importance in this second phase of military reform, initiated with the advent to power of the Socialist Party (PSOE) in December 1982. This phase could be characterized as that of the establishment of the necessary mechanism guaranteeing the supremacy of the elected government over the armed forces. During the first phase, the reformist governments had endeavoured to respect the external status quo, keeping relations between the Spanish military and their counterparts abroad beyond the realm of reform. The Defence Agreement with the United States, in force since 1953, was renewed in 1976 and upgraded by the United States

Senate to the category of treaty. The latter was meant to show support for Spanish democratization, but with practically no alteration in the military relationship.[35] This treaty was only revised by the PSOE government, once Spain's democracy was fully consolidated and her entry into NATO had been completed.

THE LIMITS OF REFORM

Changes in military organization, budgetary and personnel policies would be of no use without parallel and fundamental internal reform in the services. In the mid–1970s the Spanish armed forces were singularly top-heavy. Suffice to say that in 1975, 71.4 per cent of the army budget was spent on personnel, leaving only 28.6 per cent for maintenance and procurement.[36]

Gutierrez Melládo's attempts to reduce personnel were to no avail, and illustrated the limits of reform. The attack against Gutierrez Melládo for his plans in this area were so vehement that the general himself saw fit to reassure his colleagues on more than one occasion:

> The other point on which I wish to insist, maybe because I am told there is a certain uneasiness is this: when the replacement of commanding officers by younger men is mentioned – and I believe this should be done – it is not going to be me who in an 'inspired moment' is going to withdraw three lots of officers duly elected – according to some – by me, to be surprisingly eliminated from the Army. Anything important which is done to the [a]rmy and this is one of them, will be done with the collaboration, study and analysis of the headquarters of the [a]rmy, the High Command, Captain Generals ... but there will be no unpleasant surprises for anybody.[37]

It would be difficult to find a better explanation of how the reform was carried out and also what its limits were. The Ministry of Defence, employed by Gutierrez Melládo as an instrument to advance reforms consisted by the end of 1978 of little more than a group of officials and the heads of the three services, organized in a rudimentary manner and without its own headquarters. Consequently, the capacity for influencing the behaviour of the officer corps depended more on the personal relationships between the leading military connected authorities than anything else. The mission of the Defence Ministry employees, in the words of Gutierrez Melládo, would be:

> to harmonize appropriate military activities in such a manner as to prevent incompatibility and unnecessary grievances;
> to coordinate and harmonize activities that complement one another and minimize outside interferences;

to not pursue consolidation of the three services at all cost, except in those cases in which it can be demonstrated to be beneficial to overall preparedness and professional duty;

to accept inevitable differences deriving from the distinct nature of the three services;

to introduce no modifications without first demonstrating that such changes would have positive results;

to respect tradition in everything which does not jeopardize professional efficacy.[38]

Given this cautious tone, it is hardly surprising that the Defence Ministry's first achievements were the consolidation of military prisons and of social security provisions for all members of the armed forces. This cautious approach, together with the need to negotiate the implementation of every reform with the general staff of each of the three services, meant that changes were implemented at a far slower rate than that at which they were announced, thereby undermining the reformist team headed by Gutierrez Mellado.

In April 1979, Gutierrez Mellado was succeeded by a civilian minister of defence. By then the broad outlines of the reform had already been drawn, but the delicate balance between the military and the government created during the previous years had deteriorated. The government still lacked the necessary resources to fully control the armed forces, as the events of 23 February 1981 revealed.[39] The latter refers to a failed attempt by a group of reactionary officers to seize power.

It was not until late 1982, with the advent of the first socialist government, that the military reform entered its final phase. By then, the political system was sufficiently consolidated for the democratic institutions to alter the unstable balance in Spain's civil–military relations inherited from the earlier transition period.[40]

Today Spain's democratic political system is well rooted and enjoys strong popular support from all social classes and groups, save ultra-reactionary but isolated elements. The nation's military appears to feel content with its new, more professional role and shows little interest in golpist (interventionist) activities.

NOTES

1   These statistics come from a data-bank established by the Instituto Nacional de Administracíon Pública.

2   For a detailed account of Spain's transition to democracy, see Charles T. Powell, 'Reform versus "Ruptura" in Spain's Transition to Democracy', D. Phil., Oxford University, 1989. For a sociological approach see José Maria Maravall and Julian

76 From military to civilian rule

Santamaria, 'Political Change in Spain and the Prospects for Democracy', which forms part of the collective work directed by G. O'Donnell, P. C. Schmitter and L. Whitehead, *Transition from Authoritarian Rule* (London: The Johns Hopkins University Press, 1986.)

3 For an analysis of the role the armed forces have played during the transition in Spain, see Fernando Rodrigo, 'El papel de las Fuerzas Armadasespañolas durante la transicion politica: algunas hipotesis basicas', *Revista Internacional de Sociologia*, 43(2), 1985; and Felipe Aguero, 'La afirmacionde la supremacia civil en la democratizacion española', paper presented at the workshop, 'Fuerzas Armadas y consolidacion democratica', Instituto Universitario Ortega y Gasset, Madrid, 1988.

4 Alfred Stepan, *Rethinking Military Politics* (Princeton, NJ: Princeton University Press, 1988), p. x.

5 Ibid, p. 139.

6 Guillermo O'Donnell and Philippe C. Schmitter, Tentative Conclusions about Uncertain Democracies', in O'Donnell, Schmitter and Whitehead, *Transitions*, p. 25.

7 Dankwart A. Rustow, 'Transitions to Democracy', *Comparative Politics* (April 1970).

8 For the statements by the Minister of the Army issued on 5 January 1975, see Granados, '1975. El ano e la restauracion', TEBAS, Madrid 1977.

9 For the Navy Minister's statement, see ibid.

10 *Boletin Oficial el Estado*, no. 34, 9 February.

11 This subject is discussed rather clinically by O'Donnell and Schmitter, in O'Donnell, Schmitter, Whitehead, ed., *Transitions*, p. 32.

12 Samuel P. Huntington, *The Soldier and the State* (Cambridge: Harvard University Press, 1957), p. 83.

13 Ibid, p. 83.

14 For the distinction between modernization and reform, see Aguero, 'La afirmacionde', p. 7.

15 The proposed Defense Law appeared in the *Boletin Oficial de las Cortes*, 23 April 1974. Its withdrawal by the government was announced in the same publication of 9 January 1975.

16 For Gutierrez Melládo's military reform project see his own account, 'Al servicio de la Corona', Iberico Europea de Ediciones SA, Madrid, 1981.

17 The Real Decreto 3.026/1976, of 23 December, regula las atribuciones, funciones y responsabilidades del Jefe del Estado Mayor del Ejercito. The Real Decreto 241/1977, de 13 de enero, se reorganiza el Ministerio del ejercito. The Real decreto 8/1977, de 8 de febrero, reestructura el Consejo Superior del Ejercito de Tierra. The Real decreto 11/1977, de 8 de febrero, institucionaliza la Junta de Jefes de Estado Mayor. These changes took place in rapid succession, and virtually unnoticed.

18 The Ministry of Defence was created after the general elections of 15 June 1977 by Adolfo Suárez' new government. Its internal structure was not determined until November by Real Decreto 1.558/1977, de 4 de julio por el que se reestructuran determinados organos de la Administracion Cenral del Estado y Real Decreto 2.723/1977, de 2 de noviembre, por el que se estructura organica y funcionalmente el Ministrio de Defensa.

19 Claude E. Welch, *No Farewell to Arms?* (Boulder: Westview Press, 1987), p. 22.

20 The budgetary aspects are discussed in J. A. Olmeda, 'las Fuerzas Armadas en el Estado Franquista', ediciones el arguero, Madrid, 1988.

21 Real Decreto, 5/1977, de 25 de enero, por el que se modifica y prorroga la vigencia de la Ley 32/1971, de 21 de junio, sobre dotaciones presupuestarias para la Defensa Nacional.

22 Manuel Gutierrez Melládo, 'Al Servicio', p. 216.

23 Real Decreto 22/1977, de 30 de marzo, de reforma de la legislacion sobre funcionarios de la Administracion Civil del Estado y personal militar de los Ejercitos de Tierra, Mar y Aire.

24 Alfred Stepan, 'The New Professionalism of Internal Warfare and Military Role Expansion', in Alfred Stepan, ed., *Authoritarian Brazil*, ed. (Yale University Press, 1973).

25 For the relation between military intervention in politics and law enforcement see Manuel Ballbe, 'Orden publico y militarismo en la Espana constitucional (1821–1983)', Alianza Editorial, Madrid, 1983.

26 The reform has subdivided the previous Code of Military Justice into four laws: El Codigo Penal Militar, la Ley de Regimen Disciplinario de las Fuerzas Armadas, Ley de Competencia y Organization de los Tribunales Militares y la Ley Organica Procesal Militar.

27 Ley Organica 9/1980, de 6 de noviembre, de Reforma del Codigo de Justicia Militar.

28 Jesus Valenciano Almoyna, 'La reforma del Codigo de Justicia Militar', p. 71, Madrid, 1980.

29 The historical background to the Civil Guard is dealt with by Diego Lopez Garrido, 'La Guardia Civil y los origenes del Estado centralista', *Editorial Critica*, Madrid, 1982.

30 Ley 55/1978, de 4 de diciembre, de la Policia.

31 For the government's views on law enforcement during the transition see the account by Suárez' Minister of the Interior, Rodolfo Martin Villa, 'Al servicio del Estado', *Editorial Planeta*, Barcelona, 1984.

32 For a good account of the change in military affairs brought about by the Constitution of 1978 see Roberto Blanco Valdes, 'La ordenacion Constitucional de la Defensa', *Editorial Tecnos*, Madrid, 1988.

33 Welch, *No Farewell to Arms*, p. 22.

34 For a study of the Madrid Agreements see Francisco Villar, 'El proceso de autodeterminacion del Sahara', Fernando Torres Editor, Valencia, 1982.

35 For the political background to the renovation of the Defence Agreement with the USA see the account by then Spanish Foreign Minister, Jose Maria de Areilza, 'Diario de un ministro de la Monarquia', *Editorial Planeta*, Barcelona, 1977.

36 See 'Los gastos de Defensa', a study carried out in July 1979 by a work team under vice-admiral Jaime Diaz Deus, for the Ministry of Defence.

37 Gutierrez Melládo, 'Al Servicio', p. 172.

38 Almirante Liberal Lucini, paper presented at the seminar on 'Fuerzas Armadas y Consolidacion Democratica', Instituto Universitario Ortega y Gasset, Madrid, 1988.

39 For a journalistic account of the February 1981 coup, see Pilar Urbano, 'Con la venia ... yo indague el 23 F', Editorial Argos Vergara, Barcelona, 1982.

40 On the military reform carried out by the socialist government since 1982, see 'Memoria de la Legislatura (1982–1986)', Ministerio de Defensa, Madrid, 1986.

5 Costa Rica: the crisis of demilitarization

N. Patrick Peritore

Costa Rica has its own *leyenda blanca*; born of egalitarian yeoman farmers, politics *a la Tico* is based on compromise and strong respect for electoral democracy and human rights and has created a welfare state which gives it the highest living standard, life expectancy, and educational rate in the region. Much of this legend is true. A country of 51,022 square kilometres in the semi-tropical isthmus of Central America, Costa Rica has a population of 2,811,650, and a high annual population growth rate of 2.7 per cent. A predominantly Hispanic population (96 per cent) enjoys a life expectancy of 67/72 years, a caloric intake of 118 per cent the United Nations minimum, 93 per cent literacy, and a per capita income of $1467 within a GNP of $3.7 billion.[1]

The country is also unique in having no army and in maintaining official neutrality in international relations. Costa Rica is demilitarized in the sense that the armed elements of the state are confined to the specific functions of maintaining domestic order and national defence, and play no active role in political decision-making. This demilitarized status, a result of specific Costa Rican historical conditions, is under constant challenge by international political pressures which the ruling elites are increasingly unable to resist due to an on-going fiscal crisis, massive indebtedness, and increasing structural dependency on United States capital.

Costa Rica is beset by serious contradictions which could nullify the social welfare state and relative social stability which the country has enjoyed since 1948. A sophisticated welfare state apparatus providing a relatively high level of social benefits in a small dependent heavily indebted agro-export economy, a populist social democratic policy run by a fragmented and weak state apparatus, redistributional programmes which created a new privileged bureaucratic middle class, a demilitarized state subject to dangerous US pressures to remilitarize and corrupted by the inroads of the drug trade, a country in socio-economic crisis and under debt pressures which cancel possibilities of further economic development, and finally a relatively clean democratic system which perpetuates the rule of a narrow ruling class; these are the contradictions which beset Costa Rica's experiment in democracy. These contradictions open the possibility of increasing class polarization and a cycle of violence and remilitarization within a troubled social experiment. The question of Costa Rica's demilitarization can only be considered within the matrix of these interlocking crises.

This essay will address the issue of *Tico* (Costa Rican) demilitarization within the framework of four interlocking crises: the crisis in its political structure and processes. the crisis of indebtedness and subsequent foreign leverage; the crisis of its international relations wherein it is forced to struggle for autonomy and a regional solution to central American problems against US pressures; and the crisis of foreign-induced remilitarization.

THE POLITICAL CRISIS

Costa Rica has a compact political elite whose genealogies can be traced back to the colonial epoch. Three political families (Acosta, Gonzales, and Vasquez) have produced 34 of the 48 Presidents of the Republic, and a small interlocking group of families still provides the leadership for all tendencies of the political spectrum.

Costa Rica was an impoverished and isolated backwater of the Viceroyalty of Guatemala with a minuscule Indian population and not enough production to justify the import of expensive black slaves. Thus both the *hidalgos* (nobles) and *plebeyos* (commoners) worked the land. Class differences were reflected in access to political office and not in broad economic differentials. Much of the *hidalgo* class were Sephardic Jews, forcibly converted to Catholicism (*marranos*) fleeing the Inquisition and anti-semitism of Spanish society. For this reason they welcomed the socio-economic isolation of the Meseta Central, and were industrious and hard working without the usual aristocratic disdain of manual labour, and also proved peculiarly tolerant and pluralistic.

By the early 1700s, an incipient cacao boom, which created minor plantation slave production in the Caribbean coast, exhausted itself and reduced the elite to genteel poverty. Equal division of land among heirs speeded this process of wealth reduction. However, the elite never gave up its monopoly of political positions. The elite divided into liberal and conservative tendencies over the question of contraband; a pattern of class division not unusual in Central America. Illegal importers of goods tended towards liberal free trade politics and were centred in San José and Alaluela, while conservative, bureaucratic and clerical fractions remained centred in the towns of Cartago and Heredia.[2]

Receiving independence from Spain in 1821, without mobilizing a national military, and later seceding from the Central American Federation, the elite 'dynasty of the *conquistadors*' continued with the presidency of the liberal Braulio Carillo, who encouraged a free press, education, and incipient social legislation, as well as assisting the coffee boom begun by the German immigrant Jórge Stiepel's diffusion of coffee production techniques in the 1830s. The coffee boom led to engrossment of land; by 1883 landless peasants comprised 71per cent of the rural population. The coffee oligarchy was liberal – that is, positivist, rationalist, and anti-clerical – and stressed political, economic, and religious freedoms.

Political rivalries between the Mora and Montealegre families led to a coup and military rule by Colonel Tomás Guardia (1870–82), whose Comteian positivism (parallel to the Porfiriato in Mexico) led to implantation of a banana enclave economy, a railroad to the port, and importation of Jamaican workers. Management of this complex fell to Minor Keith, the founder of United Fruit. The coffee oligarchy preserved its landholdings intact through primogeniture. The less favoured descendants of this elite became urban liberal professionals, the Generation of 1888, which enacted the Liberal Laws of 1884 separating church and state, expelling the Jesuits and closing their University of Santo Tomás (until 1940), and presiding over the first openly contested elections in 1889.

Two men, Cleto González and Ricardo Jiménez, held the presidency for 20 out of the 30 years between 1906 and 1936, and consistently pursued liberal laissez-faire policies in accord with Costa Rica's position as a primary product exporter. However, declining coffee prices, and the fall in imports from developed nations embroiled in World War I, led to fiscal and monetary crises because customs duties were the main source of government revenue. A coup d'état by the Tinoco brothers in January 1917 created a police state, with domestic spying and the use of violence to suppress dissent. Pressures from Woodrow Wilson and *Tico* émigré resistance movements based in Nicaragua, led to the Tinocos' resignation in August 1919. This was to be Costa Rica's last military government.

Restored to power, the liberal coffee oligarchy resumed its paternalistic laissez-faire policies. The Great Depression ended their Victorian reign. Coffee prices fell from 60 to 27 cents per kilo (representing the loss of 70 per cent of exports), fungus attacked the banana plantations, and racial strife and economic dislocation led to the successful implantation of radical unions and a Communist Party in the banana zone in 1931. It is interesting to note that even the founder of the Communist Party (PCCR), Manuél Mora Valverde, was a descendant of the *conquistadors*.

The oligarchy's reaction to this crisis was to take refuge in an authoritarian government in 1936. Because German immigrants were important coffee entrepreneurs, and because Germany provided the principal market for coffee exports, the government of the National Republican Party under President León Cortés demonstrated pro-Nazi tendencies. In the election of 1940, Cortés choose Rafael Angel Calderón Guardia as a pliable successor, but was disappointed when Calderón revealed himself a serious social Catholic influenced by Leo XIII's corporatist welfare-state ideology. Once in the presidency, Calderón thrust aside Nazi influences and established an office of social security in 1941 to administer sophisticated social guarantees including an 8-hour day, minimum wage, legalization of unions, cooperatives, unemployment benefits, and hospitals. The progressive 1943 Labour Code brought Calderón's government into alliance with the Communists, giving him control of labour in the banana enclave, and support for seizure of German properties in December 1941, when Costa Rica entered World War II on the side of the Allies. Following the Popular Front line, the PCCR dissolved itself and merged with the National Republican Party, creating a strange alliance of liberal elites, Communists and social Catholics. Despite his liberal policies, Calderón's government at times used excessive violence against opponents and the PC provided shock troops for use against rightist parties.

Opposition to Calderón grouped itself around the figure of José Figueres (b. 1906) and took the form of a coalition of social democratic intellectuals, centrist liberals, and Cortéz's conservative Democratic Action Party. This coalition became the forerunner of the National Liberation Party (PLN, 1951), a social democratic party with quasi-corporatist national and sectoral organization, which is currently a member of the Socialist International. The PLN is quite similar to Mexico's Institutional Revolutionary Party (PRI) but for the fact that it alternates in power with unstable coalitions of its opponents.

The opposition won the 1948 election, but Calderón annulled the result. Figueres raised a volunteer army and fought a six week long civil war, defeating the small national army and Communist militia by 24 April 1948. For eighteen months Figueres ruled through a junta, advancing his programme of social democratic legislation, overseeing the drafting of the 1949 Constitution, and creating a government with strong checks and balances, autonomous agencies, and a supreme electoral tribunal to provide impartial oversight of future elections.

Figueres officially abolished the army on 1 December 1948, and made Costa Rica formally neutral in international relations, but he always manifested strong pro-United States leanings (the price of this friendship being abolition of the Communist Party). Strongly influenced by the New Deal and abhorring Communism and class struggle, Figueres also opposed the Caribbean dictatorships currently in place and aided Fidel Castro in 1959 as well as the Sandinistas in 1979 in their struggles. However, at the same time he maintained close ties with the US right wing and CIA, while openly criticizing US foreign policy for not combating the economic basis of revolution in Central America with social welfare policies. Although tainted by various economic scandals, and by his association with fugitive financier Robert Vesco during his 1970–4 presidency, Figueres remained the grand old man of *Tico* politics. A strong personalist charismatic leader, the late Figueres was the centre-piece of Costa Rican politics during the post-war era and has left an interesting if ambiguous legacy.

Intending to secure the welfare state apparatus from oligarchical attack, Figueres' constitution provided for an extremely weak executive, and a bureaucracy comprised of 182 autonomous institutions each with a guaranteed budget line.[3] The president shares power with the Council of Ministers, at least one of whom must countersign his acts. The 57 member Legislative Assembly must approve his budget and his conduct of war, treaty, and foreign relations, and can subject his ministers to censure.

The president may appoint the heads of administrative agencies but all other appointments are subject to civil service rules, and these agencies, autonomous both in budget and personnel decisions have legislative and executive powers beyond his control. These agencies include the national bank and a host of planning agencies and ministries of research and development, social security, electricity, tourism, ports, cooperatives, housing, colonization, agriculture, culture, economics and trade, education, treasury, health, justice, foreign relations, labour affairs, state oil, parks and the university. As is to be expected, the fragmentation of the government apparatus leads to undue influence on the part of powerful interest groups and elite power brokers.

The public sector employs over 18 per cent of the workforce and has led to technocratization of the traditional elites and their accession to privileged positions in the state apparatus through a sophisticated spoils system. Educated in the constricted-access national university system or abroad, privileged members of elite families become part of the state bourgeoisie. Their powerful unions and extensive welfare benefits give them the interest and capacity to paralyse the nation through public-service strikes in order to protect their income base. Entry into this privileged circle requires not only passing the formal exams and procedures of civil service, but also the right surname, personal contacts, and militancy in the PLN which guarantees continued career development.

Having created enormous bureaucratic inertia in support of the *Tico* welfare state, the PLN must confront the increasing immobilism and conservatism of its own apparatus, and must face the fiscal crisis of the state and extreme indebtedness without being able to trim the bureaucracy to match its constricted resource base. The PLN expanded government service to co-opt elite youth and intellectuals, but is being forced to pay an excessive price for the increasingly conservative and consumerist orientation of the state bourgeoisie.

Costa Rica's shifting political parties are personalistic and unstable elite coalitions constructed in opposition to the PLN's national apparatus. The PLN and its opponent coalitions alternate peacefully in power, and policy differences are usually subordinated to individual clientele network spoilsmanship. Critics argue that the parties all represent a narrow elite, and centre-right status-quo thinking. Despite the liveliness and relative honesty of *Tico* democratic processes, the party's leadership is derived from so narrow a social base that the parties do not represent serious emergent class conflicts and do not address the need for profound readjustment of the dominant model, a model which has reached the limits of its developmental capacity and is no longer fiscally viable. Costa Rica is a successful but highly unrepresentative democracy.

The revolution of 1948 broadened the elite base but did not include popular strata in the process of governance. The class structure of Costa Rica remains that of a society structurally, economically, and politically dependent on the USA. Socio-economic status is strongly conditioned by politics, and an actor's class position is affected by his or her position in the political system.[4] The class system in Costa Rica approximates the following strata:

At the top of the class hierarchy lies the agro-export bourgeoisie, the 1 per cent of farmers that own 36 per cent of the arable land, and devote it to export cash commodities such as: coffee, bananas, and cattle.

Immediately below this stratum lies the dependent industrial bourgeoisie, heading some three thousand medium industries, but also highly dependent on state subsidies and foreign association and uninterested in import substitution. This dependent capitalist class is anti-nationalist, monopolistic, reactionary and authoritarian, and through its professional associations is becoming aggressively influential in government.

The next stratum is the state bourgeoisie, 18.6 per cent of the workforce endowed with influence and a high degree of welfare, powerful in government, controlling the PLN, tied to elite families, and influential unions.

The service middle class, about 40 per cent of the economically active population in the urban sectors, to which can be added a declining rural middle class, represent a group which is rapidly being marginalized by the on-going economic crisis.

The lower classes are made up of the 25 per cent of the population that lives in poverty. Three-quarters of peasants are landless workers. Some 16.8 per cent of the active population works in industry, but there is growing structural unemployment. Costa Rica has suffered massive deforestation and soil erosion because of its colonization programme, which, combined with its excessive birthrate, may engender future ecological collapse. Only recently has the government committed itself to reafforestation, and to allowing foreign ecological movements to purchase forest reserve lands with debt-equity bonds to preserve the tropical forest biome, which was reduced from 71 per cent to 15 per cent between 1955 and 1981.[5]

In summary, Costa Rica suffers the defects of its virtues. The PLN's dependent welfare state has engendered the growth of industrial capitalist and state bureaucratic classes which expanded the ruling bloc but did not include the majority of increasingly marginalized rural, urban, and service workers. The fragmented government is losing its agility, is increasingly penetrated by interest-group demands, and is susceptible to the ugly corruption of the heavy drug traffic now transiting the country. Allegations regarding former Presidents Oduber and Monge's corruption and involvement in the cocaine trade must be taken seriously given that the drug cartels are much more financially powerful than the entire national economy of Costa Rica.[6] The indebted government cannot modernize its structure nor re-start the industrial growth necessary to continuation of its social commitments. The party system offers little hope of creative solutions to serious structural problems and to the growing economic marginalization of large portions of the population. A sophisticated but largely bankrupt welfare state cannot re-establish class harmony, lost to growing polarization and marginalization, without embracing the worst expedient: the implantation of a boom economy based on the cocaine trade, the long-term cost of which will be violence, social decay, and massive deculturation.[7]

THE ECONOMIC CRISIS

As Tom Buckley relates his interview with José Figueres: 'I agreed that he [Figueres] had brought forth a miracle. How, I asked, had he done it? He gazed at me for a long moment, and folded his face into that beatific U-shaped smile. "That's easy," he replied, "by borrowing"'.[8]

A sophisticated welfare state apparatus erected on debt must eventually suffer from its own artificiality. In the 1980s Costa Rica reached the point of bankruptcy. The country's $4 billion debt represents over 13 months of national production and a crushing $1585 per capita. Debt service, or the amount of exports used to pay the debt, equals 106.4 per cent, for a total of $568 million per annum, about 60 per cent of which is at variable (commercial) interest rates.

The external debt tripled by 1982 due to both the oil crisis and a precipitous drop in coffee prices. Capital flight equalled 75 per cent of reserves. A 60 per cent inflation rate, and 20 per cent un- and under-employment, led the Carazo administration (1978–82) to renege on its agreement with the International Monetary Fund (IMF) and unilaterally suspend debt payments in July 1981. The Monge administration (1982–6), which campaigned on a pro-labour platform, addressed the crisis with an opportunistic Reaganite monetarism. Costa Rica won a $100 million stand-by credit from the IMF by committing itself to elimination of import substitution and adoption of export of non-traditional industrial and agro-industrial products to US-controlled markets, as well as accepting the policy of dismantling the welfare state and holding wages below inflation to stabilize the currency so as to better repay the international bankers.

The effects of this stabilization programme were anything but stabilizing. During the Monge administration, Gross Domestic Product (GDP) fell 7.3 per cent, while per capita GDP fell 9.8 per cent. Consumer prices rose 80 per cent, the number of families given as 'poor' rose from 25 per cent to 51 per cent, and low-income families came to represent 71 per cent of the population. However, the foreign banks were profiting. Debt repayments in 1983 equalled 85 per cent of export income, and the interest payments alone represented 65 per cent of gross domestic production. The IMF and US Agency for International Development (USAID) supervised preparation of the 1984 national budget and demanded adoption of the following measures; abolition of all import taxes and controls on foreign exchange, debt interest repayment at commercial exchange rates, privatization of banking and state corporations, devaluation of national currency, creation of a new Central American Common Market, (about which Costa Rica was never enthusiastic), and creation of more free trade zones to attract multinational corporations (MNCs). A substantial North American expatriate community settled in real estate developments in Costa Rica.

The flow of debt payments and new loans is not purely an economic question, but is strongly conditioned by US political expectations. Thus, the IMF and AID cut lines of credit in March 1987 when President Arias launched his peace plan, calling for a diplomatic solution to the Contra war in Nicaragua. Costa Rica's debt makes it a net exporter of developmental capital: capital outflows exceed inflows by $120.2 million in 1983, $24.4 million in 1984, and $239.7 million in 1985. Between 1979 and 1984 capital flight has grown from $203 million to $528 million. Along with interest and principal, Costa Rica is losing a large portion of the domestic capital it needs to develop.

The continued emphasis on agricultural export production concentrates land in the hands of a few companies and has devastating long-term ecological effects. Peasants are driven into urban slums, increasing infrastructural and public safety costs. Foreign industrial enclaves (*maquilas*), based on state subsidies and tax holidays, add only low-paying jobs and generally create more debt than revenue. Opening the economy to multinational capital causes high state expenditures on infrastructural support which increases debt without generating revenue. Most of the profits generated by foreign businesses are repatriated to their mother countries and do not help capital accumulation in Costa Rica, which incurs foreign debt to attract and service these industries.

Such debt makes Costa Rica vulnerable to US political leverage. As the price of further loans to help repay interest on the debt, Costa Rica must denationalize its industries, open its markets, and drastically cut public services and welfare. It must forego the opportunity of developing its bauxite, geothermal (volcanic), and hydroelectric resources, which can only be done through state investment. The state must play the passive role of protecting 'free contract' by gearing up to repress its own working class.

The influx of foreign industries Americanizes culture, creating demand for conspicuous consumption of imported luxury goods thus worsening the balance of payments picture. Costa Rican capitalists have become heavily dependent on foreign capital goods; to produce $100 in output values, domestic manufacturing requires $80 in imported inputs. The only point of optimism is the agreement between the European Community and the Central American Common Market countries, along with Mexico, Venezuela, and Colombia, to disburse Euro-money credits (ECU) 300 million between 1985 and 1989 to encourage economic integration. Costa Rica's economy is thus becoming denationalized by the debt crisis. The country is virtually a neocolony of the USA. As José Figueres admitted, 'Costa Rica is not a country. It is a pilot project'.[9]

THE DIPLOMATIC CRISIS

Costa Rica is officially a neutral and disarmed state, an advocate of regional peace and international law solutions to political problems. However, this demilitarized and neutral status is beset by contradictions. Figueres and the PLN have privately pursued an aggressively anti-dictatorial programme, actively intervening financially, politically, and militarily to hasten the downfall of regional tyrants such as Somoza and Trujillo. Also, because of its demilitarized status, Costa Rica has developed into a stopover flight base for the drug trade from Colombia to the USA. It has also become a base for undesirable elements like arms smugglers, mercenary armies, right-wing paramilitary groups, criminal gangs, rancher's private 'security services', and private 'urban vigilantes' who shake down rich homeowners. Finally, Costa Rica's positive attempt at international legality is constantly thwarted by US pressures. USAID and the CIA have disproportionate power in domestic politics as agents of international banking and US foreign policy.

Costa Ricans feel a sense of detachment from world or regional politics growing as much from relative geographic isolation as from cultural provincialism. Despite continually strained relations with Nicaragua and Panama, its turbulent neighbours, Costa Rica settled its border disputes with these countries through treaty and arbitration. In foreign policy, Costa Rica has usually followed the political lead of its dominant export partner, first England, later Germany whose citizens became a major part of the planting class until World War II, and finally the US with which it shares ideological affinities and a culturally conservative democracy.

Tico foreign policy has shown the ambivalence of a weak political actor. In the late 1940s, José Figueres helped create a ragtag exile army, the Caribbean Legion, dedicated to overthrowing the regional dictatorships which proliferated under the terms of US generosity. His private army helped him overthrow Calderón and make profound social changes during the junta of 1948, but was finally exiled to Guatemala as part of a deal with the Organization of American States and Rio Treaty forces which defended Costa Rica from two *Calderonista* invasions sponsored by Somoza. The Cold War made such 'filibustering' expeditions irrelevant in the face of international security considerations.

José Figueres embraced the Cold War because of his avid anti-Communism, a legacy of his war with the Calderón government and its Communist Party shock troops. As a close friend of John Foster Dulles and Richard Nixon, he supported the suppression of domestic Communist movements, but opposed the emplacement of dictatorships for that purpose on the grounds that social programmes and structural reform were more lasting means to the creation of social stability than state terror. Perhaps for these reasons the CIA tried to destabilize his 1953 presidency.[10]

Figueres aided Fidel Castro's 1959 revolution with arms and money, but later disagreed with Cuba's growing militancy. To Figueres's credit, he opposed the 1961 Bay of Pigs invasion as unrealistic and hypocritical (given the continuance in power of Trujillo and Somoza). Under the cover of the Alliance for Progress, the CIA assisted Figueres and the social democratic parties of the region to block the spread of guerilla movements. CIA money was used to create the Inter-American Institute of Political Education, a training centre for social democrats. Later, after a 1967 scandal, the CIA pulled out and the European social democratic Ebert Foundation provided operating funds.

Figueres was also intent on overthrowing the Somoza dynasty in Nicaragua. He materially aided the ill-fated guerilla movement of Pédro Joaquím Chamórro in May 1959, and later aided the Sandinista National Liberation Front (FSLN) in its successful revolution of July 1979, by supporting *Los Doce*, the moderate leaders of the future revolutionary coalition, and harbouring Edén Pastóra Comandante Cero, who kidnapped the Nicaraguan National Assembly in 1978. Pastóra had business ventures in Costa Rica and good relations with PLN elites, but is also said to have been on the CIA payroll even during the revolution.[11] After breaking with the revolution, Pastóra opened the southern Contra front (ARDE) in Guanacaste Province in conjunction with Alfonso Robélo. On refusing to work with the ex-national guardsmen of the Honduran Contras, Edén Pastóra was wounded in a CIA bomb attempt on his life, and withdrew from the counter-revolution.

Unlike Figueres, President Carazo's PLN government was decidedly ambiguous towards assistance to the FSLN. Anxious to remove Somoza, the government was also concerned with a leftist state on its border, and thus offered to mediate in the crisis on several occasions, a move that would have left the National Guard structure intact and which corresponded to Carter's policy of '*Somocismo* without Somoza'. A 1979 opinion poll reported by Seligson and Carroll shows 96.2 per cent thought the FSLN a just cause, but only 54 per cent supported direct government aid, and 40 per cent maintained that violence was not the solution. Thirty-two per cent feared that the Sandinista movement would lead to Communism in Nicaragua.[12] Opinions divided along class lines, with 79 per cent of the poor opting for governmental aid to the FSLN and 41 per cent of rich *Ticos* opposing such aid. This popular ambiguity was faithfully reflected in the Carazo administration's policy vacillations.

The flux of revolution and counter-revolution across the face of Costa Rica is profoundly destabilizing. There is an influx of refugees from Nicaragua, El Salvador, and Guatemala. Exile politics are heated and disruptive. The northern frontier is militarized and contested territory. Charges were heard that Carazo received some $30 million dollars from the gunrunning attendant on supporting the Nicaraguan cause.[13] US pressure to remilitarize is constant and multi-channelled. President Monge accepted Green Beret advisers to begin counter-insurgency training of *Tico* forces in 1982 close to the Contra bases in Murcielago. Overt US military aid reached $18 million in 1984. The Costa Rican Civil Guard even aided the Contras in cattle rustling across the Nicaragua border.[14]

Part of the Iran–Contra scandal was played out in Costa Rica. John Hull, an Indiana rancher with 8000 acres in northern Costa Rica is linked to the CIA and to Contra resupply operations. US mercenaries and convicted drug smugglers have testified that Hull coordinated guns-for-cocaine deals to supply the Contras, and coordinated their training by Miami Cubans. Robert Owen, Vice President Quayle's adviser when the latter was a Senator, was Oliver North's courier to Hull.[15] US Ambassador Lewis Tambs testified before Congress that he was ordered 'to open a southern front'. Oliver

North's operations in the area are the subject of continuing investigations and trials.

Costa Rica was in a poor position to respond to this unremitting US diplomatic pressure. President Monge, elected in 1982, strongly allied himself with the Reagan administration, gaining in the process $64.5 million in credit to local businesses, $110 million in aid, and $70 million in Caribbean Basin Initiative monies, making Costa Rica the second recipient of US largesse in the hemisphere after El Salvador. In 1981, US aid to Costa Rica was $15.3 million, in 1982 $52 million (almost all in loans), but in 1983 Costa Rica was rewarded for its compliant posture with $200 million, one quarter of which was grant money. In 1984 US aid delivered $179 million, two-thirds in grants, plus $9 million for security assistance. Costa Rica became the largest per capita aid recipient in the world after Israel, with US aid equal to 5 per cent of GDP, 25 per cent of government expenditure, and 20 per cent of import financing.

This aid caused Costa Rica to vacillate on regional efforts to stop the US war against Nicaragua. In 1982 Costa Rica hosted the Central American Democratic Community a club of US client states, and the Forum for Peace and Democracy, both used to denounce the Sandinistas, and legitimize the regimes of El Salvador and Honduras.[16] In January 1983, the foreign ministers of Colombia, Panama, Mexico, and Venezuela met to originate negotiations towards a regional peace plan, the Contadora Treaty, which was signed on 7 September 1983. The Contadora Treaty called for the elimination of all foreign military involvement in the region, electoral democratic regimes in all countries, the end of arms trafficking and support for groups seeking to destabilize sitting governments, and negotiations for on-site verification mechanisms for the accord.

Costa Rica was initially enthusiastic about the accord, and strove to regain its neutrality by openly voicing reservations about the US invasion of Granada and US manoeuvres in the region. In November 1983, President Monge reasserted legal national neutrality; however, in retaliation the IMF held back the last payment in the 1983 loan programme. Costa Rica then switched its position, joining with Honduras and El Salvador, US neocolonies, in blocking further progress in the Contadora programme.[17]

When the other Central American countries signed the treaty, Nicaragua accepted it 'in its totality, immediately, and without modifications'.[18] However, the USA put immediate pressure upon the countries of the region to renege on the agreement, which would have halted its military exercises, Contra programme and military/police training in the region. A National Security Council document said 'We have effectively blocked Contadora group efforts to impose the second draft of the Revised Contadora Act'.[19]

On 19 October 1984 Costa Rica, Honduras, and El Salvador created a new unauthorized Contadora draft agreement which favoured continued US military presence in the area, but which was unacceptable to the other Contadora countries. A revised authorized draft of the treaty incorporated an option for US military exercises. But without a bilateral non-aggression pact with the USA, Nicaragua refused to sign the new accord. Costa Rica missed Contadora meetings in January 1985, withdrew its ambassador to Managua, and supported the Reagan administration's alternative peace plan. The Costa Rican government set up a northern frontier camp where US advisers could train civil and rural guardsmen in counter-insurgency, and a large airstrip that was used for Contra supply during 1985.[20] Costa Rica maintained 26 radio stations penetrating Nicaraguan airspace, one large facility, a powerful transmitter and information centre built under a $3.2 million grant from *Voice of America* and nominally run by a rightwing business group, violating Costa Rican neutrality. Radio Colombia and Radio Impacto are considered by some observers to be vehicles of CIA disinformation.[21]

In January 1986 in Caraballeda, Venezuela, the Contadora support group, Argentina, Brazil, Peru, and Uruguay, reaffirmed the original Contadora Treaty as the basis for renewed negotiations. In subsequent Contadora meetings, Costa Rica acted with El Salvador, and Honduras to block Mexico's proposal that the US suspend consideration of Contra aid legislation then in Congress in order to facilitate negotiations. A final draft was proposed, which Nicaragua reluctantly agreed to sign. However, President Reagan clearly opposed 'any lousy, fake, sham Contadora treaty' which 'sells out the Nicaraguan people's right to be free'.[22] Honduras and El Salvador rejected the draft. Costa Rica criticized the draft and put off signing. Congressional votes for $100 million in Contra aid effectively killed the Contadora process.

The February 1986 election was won by Oscar Arias of the PLN on a peace and neutrality platform. Polls showed 70 per cent support for peace with Nicaragua, and Arias began diplomatic initiatives to that end. But when President Arias called a press conference to denounce the Contra airstrip near the Guard base at Murcielago, Oliver North called him to insist the conference be cancelled, and threatened to block $80 million in AID money.[23] The conference was not held. Edén Pastóra's withdrawal from the Contras left the movement isolated in the south, but still in receipt of $10 million of US aid money.

Arias' neutral and regionalist posture was not acceptable to the US. Payments to Costa Rica were held up by the World Bank, IMF and USAID. Arias' programme of growth was stopped by IMF pressures to sign a new letter of intent abolishing import duties, reducing government deficits to 1 per cent of GDP, increasing service costs, ending grain subsidies, and further privatizing banking. Farmer demonstrations against these measures on 17

September, were violently suppressed by US trained riot police. Public outrage led to re-establishment of farm subsidies, but this action in turn led to cancellation of World Bank payments of $26 million.

Since mid–1986 Costa Rica has not repaid debt principal, and has cut interest payments to 4 per cent of exports ($5 million per month). Arias, as an opponent of Reagan administration policies, increasingly felt the leverage of international banking. Between 1986 and 1987 Costa Rica's portion of total Central American aid dropped from 29.6 per cent to 19.1 per cent. The March 1987 Peace Plan, which won Oscar Arias the Nobel Prize, and was endorsed on August 1987 by all the presidents of the region, cost his country $120 million in lost USAID money and $55 million in IMF funds. The Peace Plan called for amnesties for belligerents, human rights policies and elections, an end to all external aid for insurrectional movements, repatriation of refugees, prevention of hostile groups from using national territories for attacks on neighbouring states, and international mediation and verification mechanisms. Essentially, the plan represents a reworked Contadora proposal.

Costa Rica is shifting from import substitution to non-traditional exports and MNC assembly plants, and is losing control of its own economy because of IMF, USAID, and US governmental debt leverage. The country is a net capital exporter, and in 1984 known private Costa Rican deposits in US banks were $528 million, while 1985 capital outflow data indicated a loss of $239.7 million.[24] The economic crisis increases political vulnerability to US pressure in international relations.

Tico foreign policy, once neutral, disarmed, and legalist, has thus fallen hostage to US diplomatic pressures backed by an increasingly hostile use of international finance. Peace in Central America is the sine qua non of Costa Rican recovery, but is not a sufficient condition of economic growth and the continuing exercise of its political sovereignty. Limits on national sovereignty in economic and foreign policy undermine the preconditions for maintaining a demilitarized condition, and increasingly draw Costa Rica into the vortex of Central American armed conflict and US intervention.

THE CRISIS OF DEMILITARIZATION

On 1 December 1948 José Figueres declared, 'Costa Rica, her people and her government, always have been devoted to democracy and now practice their belief by dissolving the army because we believe a national police force is sufficient for the security of the country'.[25] Many factors led to the dissolution of the Costa Rican army. Figueres, victorious in the civil war of 1948, (and maintaining his own private army just in case) found it easy to abolish a national army – unpopular because it had looted shops during the fighting and had been so handily defeated by his invading forces.

Costa Rica signed the Rio Treaty three days later, de facto putting the country into the US sphere of influence. In December 1945, a US Military Group was assigned to the country by treaty, so US influence was evident, and its intervention in border disputes constant. Not only the US security umbrella, but internal social programmes which lowered the level of social conflict, served to strip the armed forces of any real function. The PLN offered an active social welfare state as the alternative to repression.

PLN ideology dictated the abolition of the armed forces. The draft constitution, written by social democrats, argued,

> In our opinion, war, being banished as an instrument in national and international politics, and obligatory arbitration as a means of solving conflicts accepted by all the countries on the continent, with Costa Rica, fortunately lacking all military tradition, and observing the grave damages militarism has caused in all our countries, we have come to the conclusion that there exists no reason to maintain an army.[26]

And it came to pass. Article 12 of the 1949 Constitution states, 'The army as a permanent institution is proscribed. For vigilance and the preservation of the public order, there will be the necessary police forces. Only through continental agreement for the national defence may military forces be organized; in either case they shall always be subordinate to the civil power; they may not deliberate, nor make manifestations or declarations in individual or collective terms'.[27]

The army Figueres abolished was not very impressive. It consisted of some 1000 men, some light equipment, and an officer corps of amateurs drawn from the oligarchy and rotated at the whim of incoming administrations. From 1824 to 1899, 19 per cent of the presidents were deposed by the military. One-half of the period 1835–99 was controlled by the military, although the coffee oligarchy held the presidency, so it is incorrect to assert that Costa Rica does not have a military tradition. However, the military was a weak and politicized institution, and had steadily shrunk, even during the dictatorship of 1871–1889, falling from 10 per cent of the population in 1874 to 8 per cent in 1887. During the war of 1984 it was outmanned by the irregular Communist militia of 3000 men which fought along with it, and which also went down to defeat at the hands of Figueres' ragged army of 800 mercenaries.[28]

The armed forces were, in effect, transmuted into a police force, which is really what they were all along. A Civil Guard of 1200 police and 700 coastal guards, grew to 4500 men by 1978, organized in companies of 80 to 350 men. The Rural Assistance Guard created in 1970 grew to 3500 men by 1978 and was brought under the control of the Ministry of the Interior. In 1985, the Civil Guard totalled 8000 men and had one armoured car, 3 helicopters, 5 patrol craft and 6 81mm mortars.[29] Constant officer training at Fort Gulick in Panama, sophisticated radio and computer facilities, a handful of aircraft and small patrol boats, and high salaries make the force quite professional. But constant turnover of the officer corps based on the political spoils system ensures that the force remains divided and politically weak.[30]

More efficient are the Judicial Police with some 647 men trained in security functions in the USA, and more ominously, in Taiwan, and Chile. The National Security Agency, Intelligence and Security Directorate (DIS) of some 100 men, and the Military Police with some 250 men provide specialized security services.[31]

Unremitting US pressure to remilitarize and coordinate with Contra pressure against the Sandinistas has led to a partial militarization of Costa Rica Civil Guard. US pressure to remilitarize Costa Rica began before the Reagan administration. Since the 1960s the Guard and intelligence services have been centralized under AID pressure and through US training programmes. Between 1950 and 1968, the US trained 529 officers in police techniques and an estimated 1639 in counter-insurgency and the ideology of 'national security'.[32]

After the Sandinista revolution, Costa Rica began receiving a massive influx of US military aid, jumping from zero in 1980 to $21 million by 1983. In 1981 police training resumed, and by 1985 104 Ticos were in US military schools, and an additional 34 were receiving training in Honduras. In May 1985 Special Forces began training in counter-insurgency and the ideology of national security (*Communist bueno, Comunista muerto*) at the Guard camp at Murcielago. US helicopters, light aircraft, rocket launchers, machine guns and M16s, anti-tank weapons and mortars, the excessively high-tech and high-security *Voice of America* radio station, and *Tico* participation in 1986 exercises and 'civic action programmes' involving the building of military roads in the north, all indicated a threatening military posture towards the Sandinistas which correlated to *Tico* diplomatic attitudes.

CIA presence became heavy and constant and its influence was said to stretch to cabinet-level personnel, and certainly encompassed the various security police forces mentioned above, many of which have their salaries paid by AID.[33] Taiwanese and Israeli military trainers also play a shadowy role in *Tico* military affairs.

Rightist paramilitary movements made their appearance. The Organization for National Emergencies (OPEN) claims 10,000 trained men, and although designed as a legal Guard auxiliary it is heavily rightist and has been used to break strikes and demonstrations. The secret and neofascist Free Costa Rica Movement (MCRL) works within OPEN. Most political parties, including the PLN, are said to have private militias, and neighbourhood security companies are becoming ubiquitous, all of these activities providing employment for military men transferred from active status because of a change of administration. In fact, the effect of massive US ideological and military training, combined with a four-year turnover of military officers, is to pepper organizations in civil society with a cadre of rightist military who are closely interlinked and politically powerful. Costa Rica in effect has a hidden reserve army of ideologically committed and militarily trained individuals which may some day prove to be politically dangerous.[34]

US aid to Costa Rica, motivated by anti-Sandinista policy as well as by the *Tico*'s need for immediate assistance to stabilize their economy, has grown steadily and plateaued at a high level. US Security assistance rose between 1982 and 1985, from $22.1 million, to $161.6 million, $140.1 million, and $170 million year by year. From 1986 to 1988 military assistance was $123 million, $144 million, and over $90 million.[35]

The most corrosive and dangerous long-term trend is the use of Costa Rica as a refuelling point for Colombian drug flights to the USA. Costa Rica is peppered with some 2400 landing strips, and its rough terrain provides an ideal cover for transfers and staging. The Contras, and Oliver North's resupply operation, were implicated in this traffic, which has also corrupted the highest levels of Costa Rica's party and government. This new 'boom economy' crop is making the continuance of democracy impossible by creating a powerful, violent, and infinitely wealthy government within the government. There are strong allegations linking former Presidents Oduber and Monge directly to the narcotraffic, and it is difficult to estimate the extent of drug-related corruption.

CONCLUSIONS

Given US influence, which has lessened the PLN's capacity to govern its own society or to pursue its welfare state commitments on an expanding economic base, and given the corrosive corruption emanating from the drug trade and the indirect militarization of *Tico* society, it is hard to be optimistic about the future of this noble experiment in demilitarization. Neutrality, legality, and demilitarization function only in a diversified civil society and with a skilled political party elite that can channel structural social conflict into institutional resolutions possible within the economic limits of the society.

Given Costa Rica's indebtedness and virtual economic collapse, social issues become zero-sum conflicts among social classes and strata. Governing, to the extent that native and not foreign forces are in control, requires increasing repression of popular alternatives to maintain power for an increasingly illegitimate ruling class. The functions of repression can be done by a military, police, or in the worst scenario, by paramilitary 'death squads'.

The tragedy of Costa Rica is that increasing immobilism in the government and political structure, and US and international bank mismanagement of the *Tico* debt, as well as unreasonable US pressure to coordinate with the Contra programme, have led Costa Rica into a socio-economic and political impasse which may stretch its tolerant democratic culture to a violent breaking point. The Switzerland of Central America has enough mercenary, paramilitary, and criminal elements to become another Beirut. If this happens, it will not have been entirely her fault.

NOTES

1. Paul Goodwin, *Global Studies: Latin America* 3rd edition (Guilford, Co. : Dushkin, 1988), p. 24. Tom Barry, and Deb Preusch, *The Central America Fact Book* (New York: Grove Press, 1986). Jenny Pearce, *Under the Eagle* (Boston: South End Press, 1982).

2. This and the following historical and sociological account is based on Charles Ameringer, *Democracy in Costa Rica* (New York: Praeger, 1982); Charles F. Denton, *Patterns of Costa Rican Politics* (Boston: Allyn and Bacon, 1971); Lowell Gudmunson, *Costa Rica Before Coffee* (Baton Rouge: Louisiana State University Press, 1986) Mario Ramirez Boza, 'Notas para el estudio de las politicas estatales en Costa Rica', *Ciencias Sociales* 31: 9–37, 1986; Samuel Stone, 'Costa Rica: sobre la clase dirigente y la sociedad nacional', *Revista de Ciencias Sociales*, 41–69, April 1976; Olivier Dabene, 'Las bases sociales y culturales de lo politico en Costa Rica', *Ciencias Sociales* 31: 67–83, 1986; Ana Sojo Martinez 'La democracia politica y la democracia social: una vision desde Costa Rica', *Ciencias Sociales* 31: 39–48, 1986; José Véga Cárballo, 'Democrácia y dominación en Costa Rica', *Foro Internacional*, 20.4: 646–72, April 1980; Burt English, *Liberación Nacional in Costa Rica* (Gainesville: University of Florida Press, 1971); Oscar Aguilar Bulgarelli, *Costa Rica y sus héchos politicos de 1948* (San José: Universidad de Costa Rica, 1969); and the journal *Mesoamerica*.

3. *Constitution of the Republic of Costa Rica 1949*, (Washington DC: Pan American Union, 1961).

4. Stone, 'Costa Rica', pp. 62–3.

5. James R. Gosz *et al.*, 'The Flow of Energy in a Forest Ecosystem', 238.3 *Scientific American*, 1978: 92–10; James Nations and Daniel Komer, 'Rainforests and the Hamburger Society', *Ecologist* 17.4, 1987: 161–7; Barbara Bramble, 'The Debt Crisis: The opportunities', *The Ecologist* 17.4, 1987: 192–7; Julie McGhie 'Reclaiming a Natural Legacy', *The Ecologist* 17.4, 1987: 200–3. On social class see James D. Cockroft, *Neighbors in Turmoil: Latin America* (New York: Harper and Row, 1989), p. 204, Dabene, 'Las bases', pp. 69–70; Stone, 'Costa Rica', pp. 62–9; Daniel Goldrich, *Sons of the Establishment* (Chicago: Rand McNally, 1966).

6. Interview 26 April 1989 with prominent editor of national paper in Costa Rica.

7. Deborah Pacini and Christine Franquemont, eds, *Coca and Cocaine*, Cultural Survival, Rept. 23, (Cambridge Ma., 1986); Scott MacDonald, *Dancing on a Volcano* (New York: Praeger, 1989).

8. Tom Buckley, *Violent Neighbors* (New York: Times Books, 1985), p. 183.

9. Cockcroft, *Neighbors*, p. 205, ch. 6, Jackie Roddick, *The Dance of the Millions* (England: Russel Press, 1988), Ch. 9; Robert G. Williams, *Export Agriculture and the Crisis in Central America* (Chapel Hill: University of North Carolina Press, 1986); Mitchell A. Seligson, *Peasants of Costa Rica and the Development of Agrarian Capitalism* (Madison: University of Wisconsin Press, 1980); J. Edward Taylor, 'Peripheral Capitalism and Rural Urban Migration: A Study of Population Movement in Costa Rica', *Latin American Perspectives*, 7.2 1980: 75–90; Carlos Mackinlay, 'Estructura productiva y tamaño de las economias: el caso de las pequeñas economias Latinoamericanas', *Economia de America Latina*, 15, 1986: 136–210; Dennis Gayle, *The Small Developing State* (Aldershot: Gower,1986); Royce Shaw, *Central America: Regional Integration and National Political Development* (Boulder: Westview, 1978); Jeffrey Nugent, *Economic Integration in Central America* (Baltimore: Johns Hopkins, 1974); Jorge Perez-Lopez, 'Central America's External Debt in the 1970s and Prospects for the 1980s' (Florida Int. Univ.: LACC, 1983); Bruce Herrick and Barclay Hudson, *Urban Poverty and Economic Development: A Case Study of Costa Rica* (New York: St Martin, 1981); Victor Brajer, 'An Analysis of Inflation in the Small, Open Economy of Costa Rica' (University of New Mexico Research Paper 18, June 1986).
10. Cockcroft, *Neighbors*, p. 204, Ameringer, *Democracy*, p. 85. David Wise and Thomas Ross, *The Invisible Government* (New York: Vintage, 1964), pp. 119–20, Steve Ropp and James Morris, *Central America: Crisis and Adaptation* (Albuquerque: University of New Mexico Press, 1984), p. 180.
11. Author interview with Edgar Chamorro 30 March 1989, see his book, *Packaging the Contras: A Case of CIA Disinformation* (New York: Inst. for Media Analysis, 1987).
12. Thomas Walker, ed., *Nicaragua in Revolution* (New York: Praeger, 1982), pp. 331–44.
13. Ameringer, *Democracy*, p. 91.
14. Cockcroft, *Neighbors*, p. 208.
15. V. Bielski and D. Bernstein in *Covert Action Information Bulletin* 28, Summer 1987: 13–16; Jonathan Kwitny, *The Crimes of Patriots* (New York: Norton, 1987), pp. 378–81; Daniel K. Inouye et al., *Report of the Congressional Committees Investigation of the Iran–Contra Affair* (US Govt Printing Office, 1987), p. 338.
16. Marc Edelman, 'Costa Rica: See Saw Diplomacy', *NACLA Report on the Americas*, 17.6, November 1983, pp. 40–3.
17. Roddick, *Dance*, p. 203.
18. William Goodfellow in Thomas Walker, ed., *Reagan Versus the Sandinistas* (Boulder: Westview, 1987), pp. 148–55.
19. Ibid., p. 150.
20. Roddick, *Dance*, p. 206.
21. Howard Frederick in Walker, ed., *Nicaragua*, pp. 139, 130–5; Tom Barry and Deb Preusch, *The Soft War* (New York: Grove Press, 1988), pp. 210–12.
22. Walker, *Reagan*, p. 154, Nina Serafino, 'Contra Aid 1981–March 1987' (Congressional Research Service, 1987), Jonathan Sanford, 'Major Trends in US Foreign Assistance to Central America: 1978–86' (Congressional Research Service 1986), Peggy Ann James, 'The Impact of US Aid on the Nicaraguan Peace Talks 1987–1988', paper presented at Midwest Political Science Assn Chicago, 14 April 1989; Timothy Birch, 'The US, Nicaragua, and Low Intensity Conflict:

Proinsurgency Warfare in Lieu of Overt Military Intervention', Masters Thesis University of Missouri–Columbia, April 1989. Michael Klare and Peter Kornbluh, *Low Intensity Warfare* (New York: Pantheon, 1988).

23. Roddick, *Dance*, p. 206.
24. Roddick, *Dance*, pp. 212–14.
25. Tord Hoivik and Solveig Aas, 'Demilitarization in Costa Rica: A Farewell to Arms?', *Journal of Peace Research*, 18.4, 1981: 333–51., p. 334.
26. Hoivik 'Arms', p. 342. Leonard Bird, *Costa Rica: The Unarmed Democracy* (London: Sheppard Press, 1984), chs 8, 11, 12.
27. *Constitution*, p. 2.
28. Ropp, *Central America*, p. 159–60.
29. Bruce Bagley, ed., *Contadora and the Diplomacy of Peace in Central America* (Boulder, Westview, 1987), p. 29; Nina Serafino, 'The Contadora Initiative: Implications for Congress' (Congressional Research Service, June 1987); PACCA, *Changing Course* (Washington DC: Inst. for Policy Studies, 1984), p. 114. For US military aid figures, also Sanford, 'Trends', Appendix 2; also Richard Allen White, *The Morass* (New York: Harper,1984), p. 234–5; and Jonathan Sanford, 'Costa Rica: US Foreign Assistance Facts' (Congressional Research Service, July 1987). Tom Barry *et al.*, *Dollars and Dictators* (New York: Grove Press, 1983), pp. 208–13 for list of US corporations operating in Costa Rica. For the Eurosocialist perspective on the question see, Eusebio Mujal-Leon and Herman Gutierrez B., 'Central America and the New International Political Order: the Eurosocialist dimension', *International Journal*, 43, Summer 1988: 446–72.
30. Hoivik, 'Arms', pp. 347–8.
31. Marc Edelman and Jayne Hutchcroft, 'Costa Rica: Modernizing the Army', *NACLA Report on the Americas*, March 1984:, pp. 9–11.
32. John Saxe Fernandez, 'The Militarization of Costa Rica', *Monthly Review* May 1972, 61–70, pp. 65–6; Elena de la Souchere, 'Costa Rica: Citadel of Democracy', *Monthly Review* June 1955: 58–67. Sheppard, *Unarmed*, ch.12.
33. Cockcroft, *Neighbors*, pp. 47–8, Sherman, *NACLA*, pp. 9–11.
34. Sherman, *NACLA*, pp. 9–11.
35. Richard Alan White, *The Morass* (New York: Harper and Row, 1984), pp. 234–5; PAACA, *Changing Course*, p. 114, Jonathan E. Sanford, 'Costa Rica: US Foreign Assistance Facts', (Congressional Research Service, July 1987); Sanford, 'Major Trends', pp. 59–60, *Congressional Quarterly* vols 37–44 data compiled by Timothy Birch.

6   The politics of civilian rule in Colombia

Daniel L. Premo

INTRODUCTION

A work published several years ago on liberal democracy in Latin America listed Colombia, Costa Rica, and Venezuela in its subtitle, currently the three countries in the region with the longest tradition of continuous democratic rule.[1] Prior to 1973, Colombia and Venezuela would undoubtedly have been pre-empted by Uruguay and Chile in any ranking of democracies in Latin America, a not so subtle reminder that even the most democratic polities in the region are subject to sudden, radical shifts in their civil–military relations.

The present chapter focuses on civil–military relations in Colombia, the largest of the aforementioned democracies, but in many respects the least understood. For the purpose of this study, we have accepted the definition of a civilian-dominated regime used by the editor of this volume, which basically assumes that the military is willing to carry out the policies of the civilian authorities and only seeks to influence policy in relevant areas through 'normative, group, or institutional processes'.[2]

The political significance of the Colombian military has been considerably less than any other Latin American country except Costa Rica. Except for a period of military rule from 1953 to 1957, Colombia has maintained a tradition of civilian supremacy throughout the twentieth century. Therefore, many of the assumptions and stereotypes concerning the military's interventionist role in Latin America are not applicable.

Democratic rule has survived in Colombia since 1958. Various factors of violence have affected Colombian society since that time, including the longest on-going guerrilla emergence of Colombia as a major drug supplier. Mounting violence and the deterioration of public order in recent years has once again called into question the ability of democracy to survive there.

This chapter provides a brief history of civil–military relations in Colombia leading up to the military's intervention in 1953, and then examines the role of the armed forces in the personalist dictatorship of General Rojas Pinilla. Major emphasis is given to the role of the armed forces since 1958 and the reasons for their continued acceptance of civilian rule. The study concludes with speculation on prospects for the future.

HISTORICAL BACKGROUND

The role of the armed forces as a political force has varied considerably throughout Colombia's history. However, the basic pattern of civil–military relations was established during New Granada's protracted war for independence. The Colombian elite basically distrusted the independence armies dominated by Venezuelans and openly expressed their anti-military biases. After the dissolution of the Gran Colombia federation in 1830, the army was reduced in size and influence.[3] The Constitution of 1832 clearly defined the military's primary duty as 'obedience to civilian leaders' and placed the armed forces under the control of Congress. The civilian elite's low regard for the military has persisted, in varying degrees, throughout the history of the republic and is a central factor in understanding the place of the military in national life.

Throughout the nineteenth century the power of the civilian elite was largely unquestioned in Colombia. From the time of the formal establishment of the present Conservative and Liberal parties in the late 1840s, men with military titles were actively engaged in political life. However, they were essentially civilians who took up arms in the country's numerous civil wars rather than professional soldiers. After the major constitutional revision of 1886, the number of generals who came to occupy the presidency markedly declined. Since that time only three generals have been elected president, and only one achieved power by means of a military coup, Gustavo Rojas Pinilla in 1953.

During the nineteenth century the Colombian army, which seldom exceeded 3000 men, was led mostly by part-time officers with little interest or professional ability in military matters. The small standing army was used as a political tool by rival Conservative and Liberal politicians. Early attempts to imbue the armed forces with a sense of nonpolitical involvement invariably failed in the face of bitter political factionalism. The creation of a professional Colombian military began in the wake of the War of the Thousand Days during the dictatorial rule of General Rafael Reyes (1904–9).[4] Reyes enlisted the services of two Prussian-trained Chilean officers to assist in the establishment of a military academy, which officially opened on 1 June 1907. With the restoration of constitutional government in 1909, Colombia returned to a basically civilian-oriented national policy. Political partisanship remained acute among the officer corps, but violence in support of it was largely absent. Although the military's status gradually improved, Colombia's army in 1932 was still proportionately the smallest in Latin America and had not yet achieved a high degree of professionalism.

The clashes between Peruvian and Colombian forces at Leticia in 1932–3 did much to awaken Colombian public opinion to the inadequate preparation of the army. The military budget was increased, albeit temporarily, and for the first time in its history the military gained in popular prestige. Colombia further enlarged its military establishment as an ally of the United States in World War II. By 1946 the military had succeeded in staying out of active politics for over forty years; for the most part, it had avoided being used for political ends by civilian administrations during that time. Its gradual development and acceptance as a national force, as opposed to political or regional, and its abstention from direct intervention, had firmly established the military's tradition as a nonpolitical institutional force in Colombian society and its subordination to civilian authority.[5]

When the Conservative Party returned to power in 1946 after sixteen years of Liberal administration, the military had no official political role. The armed forces were assigned by charter the tasks common to all national militaries, namely defending the national territory from external threat and assisting in the maintenance of public order when called upon. Primary responsibility for the preservation of internal security lay with the national police, who were separate from the military and functioned under the authority of the Minister of the Interior.

The breakdown in Colombia's social and political order after 1946 led to the growing involvement of the military in political affairs. The Conservative administration of Mariano Ospina Pérez (1946–50) made increasing use of the army and the national police as partisan political instruments. On 9 April 1948, the assassination of popular Liberal leader Jorge Gaitán sparked an explosion of mob violence in the capital known as the *bogotazo*. The military drew largely upon its reputation and a modicum of force to restore order. Extremist elements within both traditional parties undermined collaborative efforts and led to unprecedented levels of partisan rural violence during the presidency of Laureano Gómez (1950–53). Although the number of military personnel remained relatively stable at 15,000, the military budget more than doubled in size as Gómez intensified the effort to convert the armed forces into a repressive instrument of the central government. Discrimination against liberal officers in the army resulted in many of them deserting to the rural areas, where they undertook partisan warfare against the government. Gómez skilfully courted the military by raising salaries and by partially reorganizing its internal structure. He created the post of Commanding General of the Armed Forces and then appointed Lt General Gustavo Rojas Pinilla, an avowed conservative sympathizer, to the office. The military's position became increasingly uncertain in the face of Gómez's proposed constitutional reforms, the enactment of which would have increased the powers of the presidency to a considerable degree and threatened the institutional autonomy of the military. Gómez further alienated some officers when he appointed a civilian to the post of minister of war, thereby depriving the military of institutional representation. Ultimately, the military could not escape the consequences of the deteriorating political situation. With Colombia's political party system at a point of almost complete collapse, on 13 June 1953, the armed forces assumed direct power for the first and only time during this century.

It is difficult to assess the degree to which the military's tradition of nonpolitical intervention dissuaded members of the officer corps from taking direct action earlier, especially when one contemplates the dimensions of the violence that brought virtual civil war to Colombia's rural areas between 1946 and 1953. Certainly 40 years of uninterrupted civilian rule had contributed to the observance of political non-intervention, although partisanship within the officer corps was never effectively eliminated. Even so, the military's concern did not result in unified action against the government until the corporate survival of the military itself was threatened and its principal leader faced with dismissal. On balance, the military's deviation from its time-honoured tradition was not actively sought by the institution itself. Conservative leaders, especially former President Ospina, conspired with the military against Gómez. The military clearly acted beyond the constitution in removing Gómez, but, to use Morris Janowitz's term, it was scarcely a 'designed' grab for power, especially when considering the circumstances and the reluctance with which Rojas finally accepted the chief executive's role.[6] Most observers have concluded that the military had no other choice.

THE 'GOVERNMENT OF THE ARMED FORCES', 1953–8

Rojas' government was military in name only. The armed forces at this time had neither the capability nor the inclination to govern without civilian assistance. The National Constituent Assembly legitimized the provisional government by naming Rojas to complete Gómez's elected term. Although Rojas appointed three officers to his cabinet, the principal architects of his government from the beginning were civilians. The office of the chief executive under Rojas and the armed forces under the active duty military elite became and remained distinct entities.

The literature dealing with Rojas' 'Government of the Armed Forces' is consistent in the general condemnation of the man and of the military institution that backed his rise to power but ultimately deposed him.[7] Rojas' abortive attempts to establish an independent political movement and his subsequent efforts to perpetuate himself in office attest to his shortcomings as a politician. His transformation from the role of national saviour in 1953 to that of demagogue in 1954–5, and, finally, to that of military dictator during the final years of his rule also underscores his inability to comprehend the resilience and adaptability of Colombia's political elite, who reaffirmed civilian distrust and bitterness towards the military as an institution.

In view of the political instability that preceded the 1953 coup, the military was justified at the outset in not returning the government to civilian control. There is little doubt that immediate national elections would have returned the country to the old conditions of party strife and violence. While most officers probably neither wanted nor expected the military to become a prolonged alternative to normal political life, there existed the proviso, both expressed and accepted, that the termination of military rule was dependent on the restoration of internal order. The resurgence of violence in the countryside, which was easily traceable to partisan agitation, convinced a majority of the officer corps that the continuation of military rule was a political necessity. However, as Rojas continued to postpone the expression of popular will through elections, an increasing number of officers viewed with alarm his attempts to convert the military into a political force. With no organized base of political support, Rojas sought to harness the prestige and unique power potential of the military into a political base to confront the Liberal–Conservative coalition forming against him. His announcement in 1956 that the military would be a 'Third Force' in the government jeopardized once again the military's respected tradition of nonpolitical involvement. To the officers who were not an integral part of Rojas' palace coterie, the prospect of the armed forces being placed in the forefront of political action and in direct confrontation with the principal leaders of the traditional political parties must have appeared professionally distasteful. Indeed, the emergence of a 'Civic-Front' coalition in 1956 paved the way for the military's withdrawal from its political role.

Erosion of the military's support for Rojas began as early as 1955 with a breakdown in the hierarchy of command within the officer corps. Internal discipline and morale suffered from the practice of favouritism and largesse displayed towards many of the higher-ranking officers. A growing number of officers were displeased that the military had become associated in the public mind with widespread accusations of graft and corruption involving Rojas and his closest followers. The military's inability to eliminate partisan violence and banditry made officers more sensitive to public charges that the armed forces, traditionally the 'saviours and guardians' of national honour, were benefiting unduly while the country was still in crisis. Finally, as economic difficulties began to undermine the regime's support, the armed forces found themselves once again being used as an instrument of repression.

Although Rojas' political ineptness was as apparent to the military leadership as it was to the general population, military opposition to his rule was not sufficiently organized before 1957 to ensure that his removal would not create serious divisions within the officer corps. Consequently, the armed forces did not take the initiative in his overthrow. It was not until Rojas attempted to manoeuvre himself into another four-year term that the military concluded it was in its corporate interests to dissociate themselves institutionally with his government. Even then, the military's role, although ultimately decisive, favoured the preservation of institutional principles and internal unity above political expediency. The officers who confronted Rojas allowed him the face-saving gesture of appointing the members of the military junta who relieved him on 10 May 1957.

The actions of the military junta that supervised the return to civilian constitutional government did much to restore public confidence in the armed forces. Among its first acts was to order the withdrawal of military units from Bogotá and restore freedom of the press. The new military leaders lost little time in making it clear to leaders of both the Conservative and Liberal parties that the time was ripe for disengagement provided that satisfactory institutional mechanisms for the development of national political consensus could be re-established. It reassured the citizenry of the neutrality of the armed forces and pledged that free elections would be held to elect a civilian president in 1958. As Jonathan Hartlyn notes, the military facilitated the transition process by successfully 'de-linking' the Rojas regime from the armed forces as an institution, and blaming all excesses on him and his immediate advisers. The military's central concerns of institutional autonomy and of regaining prestige were respected by the party leaders who recognized they would need to rely on the armed forces in the future.[8]

Although faced with continued violence in the countryside and serious economic problems, the junta's actions clearly revealed the desire of the armed forces' high command to get the military out of politics and back to its more traditional nonpartisan role. Once the Liberal and Conservative parties agreed to share power in the unique experiment in 'controlled democracy' known as the National Front, the major conflict area between them ceased to exist, as did most of the causes around which the military had unified for intervention in 1953.[9]

CIVIL–MILITARY RELATIONS DURING THE NATIONAL FRONT, 1958–74

With the creation of the National Front in 1958, the role of the military in internal affairs came under scrutiny. During the presidency of Alberto Lleras Camargo (1958–62) the functions of the military, the police, and civilian authorities were clarified, and important changes in organizational structure were carried out. From the beginning, the protagonists agreed upon a classical model of civil–military relations which established civilian supremacy and reaffirmed a non-deliberative role for the armed forces. At the same time, the military was provided with sufficient autonomy to protect it from the debilitating effects of Colombian politics. Subsequently, when the emergence of revolutionary guerrilla movements created additional national security problems in the early 1960s, political and military leaders amended their concepts of military professionalism and national defence and agreed upon an expanded role for the army into extra-military affairs, principally military civic action programmes, to counter new threats.

President Lleras Camargo set the tone of future civil–military relations early in his presidency. In a speech to assembled military elite, he outlined the relationship he expected to obtain between himself and the military. He stressed that by nature and training the military was poorly equipped to govern a complex civil society.

> Yours is a radically different type of command from what is required in civil life. Politics embraces the art of controversy; the military, the art of discipline. Maintaining the military apart from political deliberation is no mere caprice of the Constitution, but a necessity to the military's function.

According to Lleras, the military's involvement in politics would not only distort the democratic governing process but also corrupt the military organization itself. At the same time, he reaffirmed his awareness of another salient principle of the professional military ethic, the 'civilian toleration of the autonomous development of military influence within the military sphere'.[10] Although Lleras' remarks reflect the historical antimilitaristic bias of Colombia's political leaders since independence, they also recognize the requirements for a professional military. Together with increased reliance on the army in developmental projects, the attitudes articulated by Lleras and other civilian leaders characterize the basic civil–military perspectives of the traditional political elite during the National Front period.

Organizational changes after 1958 also affected the institutional role of the military. The Ministry of War was restructured in 1960 to ensure a higher degree of unity within the internal command and to provide for a more efficient separation between administrative and technical functions. Two high-level advisory councils were created to improve civil–military relations within the formal governmental apparatus. The more important of the two, the Superior Council of National Defence, was charged with directing the overall policies of the Ministry of War, and included the commander-in-chief of the armed forces, in addition to the minister of war, who since 1958 has been the senior ranking army general. These revisions provided the military high command a position within the government from which it could protect its institutional integrity.[11]

By 1958 it had become obvious to authorities that the national police were incapable of coping with the problems of internal security and public order on a scale associated with *la violencia*. As a result, the army was given primary responsibility for the planning and implementation of counter-insurgency. The national police were legally designated members of the armed forces, placed directly under the command of the minister of war, and given a defensive, supportive role to the army in internal security affairs.[12] In a military sense the change was intended to minimize political influence within police ranks and to assign primary responsibility to the specific armed force that was best organized, trained, and equipped to carry out counter-insurgency activities. Politically, however, the shift marked a significant change in the definition of the military's traditional role. In effect, the armed forces became a legitimate political instrument responsible for defending the National Front coalition.

The historic change of the military's mission was also influenced by the decision of the United States to shift the basis for its military assistance programme in Latin American from hemispheric defence to internal security. By mid–1962 evidence of the shift in US policy can be seen in the Colombian military's approach towards the control of guerrilla activity, which still existed in certain areas of the country. With technical assistance from US officials, a counter-insurgency plan was conceived and implemented under the direction of the minister of war, Major General Alberto Ruiz Novoa. 'Plan Lazo' provided for special training in antiguerrilla operations, intelligence techniques, and the development of military civic action programmes.[13] Military civic action became an integral part of the army's mission, especially after the emergence of the pro-Castro National Liberation Army (ELN) in 1964 and the Communist-dominated Revolutionary Armed Forces of Colombia (FARC) in 1966.[14]

The military's initial involvement in a developmental role appears to have been well received within the officer corps, despite some concern that civic action programmes were incompatible with the military's primary tasks and its professional status. Most Colombian officers writing on the topic in the mid–1960s assumed that the country's economic and social development were essential ingredients in a successful internal security mission. Indeed, it was Ruiz Novoa's insistence on a larger role for the armed forces in Colombia's socio-economic development that precipitated the most significant civil–military confrontation of the early National Front period. His criticism of the lack of development under President Guillermo León Valencia (1962–6) and the government's failure to use fully the military's potential as a modernizing force aroused civilian apprehension that the military might be considering an independent course of action. By making public his disagreement with the president, Ruiz rekindled long-standing antimilitarist sentiments among Colombia's civilian political elite. After consulting with senior officers, President Valencia demanded Ruiz' resignation on 27 January 1965. In doing so, he reaffirmed the principle of civilian supremacy and, at least for the moment, discouraged further politicking within the military. Significantly, Ruiz's dismissal produced no public protest by the officer corps. The military's firm rejection of the political opportunity, found in Ruiz's activism, did much to reassert the corps' traditional adherence to its function as a non-deliberative body.

During the presidency of Carlos Lleras Restrepo (1966–70) the principal function of the military continued to be internal security. Although a few civic action programmes were maintained by the army, most of the responsibility in this area passed to a rapidly expanding government bureaucracy and private institutions. Like Valencia, Lleras Restrepo did not hesitate to act decisively in settling differences of opinion with his military commanders. In February 1969 he summarily removed the commanding general of the army, Guillermo Pinzón Caicedo, ostensibly for openly rejecting a governmental decree. Unlike Ruiz Novoa, Pinzón was immensely popular with younger officers, prompting both the local and international press to speculate on the likelihood of a coup. However, the military hierarchy demonstrated once again its basic civilist character and deferred to civilian political authority without serious dissent.

The military's role remained essentially unchanged during the final National Front presidency of Misael Pastrana Borrero (1970–4). In addition to its counter-insurgency priority, special military units continued to work in conjunction with the national police to suppress occasional urban disorders involving students and workers and to eliminate networks of urban support for the various guerrilla movements.

In retrospect, the National Front arrangement provided the framework for a stable civil–military relationship under which civilian rule was restored while preserving the military's institutional integrity. The support of the armed forces was essential in preserving the stability of the political system, especially during the years when the populist movement organized by Rojas Pinilla, the National Popular Alliance (ANAPO), mounted a serious electoral challenge that almost captured the presidency in 1970. Presidents allowed the military a greater role in national security and in the direction of military affairs, but they denied them a voice in political matters. While the military was hardly apolitical during this time, it should be recognized that the military hierarchy ignored various opportunities for political involvement in moments of institutional crisis and uncertainty, such as the dismissals of Ruiz Novoa and Pinzón Caicedo. By doing so, the military enhanced its reputation for professionalism and improved its prestige with the general populace.

By the end of the National Front era, the military had developed an institutional self-conception independent from the two traditional parties.

The movement away from identification with either of the traditional parties fostered generalized support for the National Front regimes, permitting them to use the military as an instrument to confront guerrilla threats or contain popular demands.[15] There existed considerable agreement in the civil–military outlooks of the traditional elite and military leaders in terms of fundamental structure, basic mission, and the military's role as a major pressure group in Colombian politics. However, since the mid–1970s the line between civilian and security matters has become more blurred. The resurgence of guerrilla activity in 1975, Colombia's emergence as the principal supplier of drugs in the hemisphere, the appearance of paramilitary groups, and an increase in criminal activity, have produced spiralling levels of violence in the 1980s and resulted in new strains on civil–military relations.

THE MILITARY'S ROLE SINCE THE NATIONAL FRONT

Under Liberal President Alfonso López Michelsen (1974–8), the military once again became deeply involved in counter-insurgency. The rise of the M–19, a new revolutionary group claiming to be the armed branch of ANAPO, and the continued operations of the ELN and the FARC, spurred renewed debate within the officer corps over the most appropriate means of dealing with the guerrilla problem. One faction, headed by Army Commander General Alvaro Valencia Tovar, advocated widespread social reforms as the best means of eliminating popular resistance to the government. A second tendency, represented by Defence Minister General Abrahám Varón, perceived the solution to popular discontent in military terms through the repression of 'subversive' groups. As the leader of the military reformists, Valencia Tovar believed that the guerrillas could be contained militarily but could only be defeated through political action. Like Ruiz Novoa a decade earlier, he became openly critical of the civilian administration and his military superiors for relying on new antiguerrilla offensives rather than addressing basic social problems. Amidst widespread rumours of a coup attempt, President Lopez and his defence minister dismissed Valencia Tovar and several of his supporters in May 1975.[16]

Once again the military failed to offer any opposition to civilian interference in the armed forces' hierarchy, this time against a general considered to be the most popular officer in the army. The incident presaged the restiveness over policy, promotions, and careers that have become part of the military's professional internal adjustment to the more openly partisan political manipulations of civilian administrations since the formal expiration of the National Front agreement in 1974.[17]

The growing number of relatively young officers forced into early retirement during López's presidency became a focal point of political agitation and criticism directed against the government and particularly Defence Minister Varón. López's efforts to remove the more politically inclined officers from top military positions reached a climax in December 1977 with the involuntary retirement of five generals, including General Matallana Bermúdez, the chief of the joint general staff. Although the military high command publicly endorsed the President's action, 53 high-ranking retired officers published a communique claiming that the dismissals since 1975 were 'gravely threatening the republic's institutions' and represented 'a threat to the discipline, future and morale of the military forces with consequences difficult to foresee'.[18] A group of 33 generals and admirals headed by General Camacho Leyva subsequently issued its own communique expressing 'deep concern' over the state of insecurity prevailing throughout the country and condemning elements of the mass media and the civilian judicial system for their attempts to 'dishonour the chief of the armed forces' and to disrupt the unity of the institution. The officers reaffirmed their duty to 'uphold the honour and prestige of the military' and called upon President López to implement emergency measures to improve the country's internal security and to guarantee the armed forces 'the respect they deserve'.[19] Their demands prompted an official rebuke from Defence Minister Varón who reminded them that 'the military's regulations on discipline prohibit any collective request or demand'. He termed their action a 'serious violation of military ethics' which, if left uncensored, would establish a precedent for pressuring officers of lower grade and coercing government personnel.[20]

The military expanded its political role dramatically during the presidency of Julio César Turbay Ayala (1978–82) through increased responsibility in the area of internal security and the assumption of broader jurisdiction in the administration of justice. On 6 September 1978, Turbay invoked a controversial 'statute on security' that substantially augmented the powers of arrest of the armed forces, increased the kinds of 'political crimes' connected with terrorism and subversion, and transferred their jurisdiction from civil to military courts. The military thus was assigned the dual task of maintaining public order and prosecuting those charged with crimes broadly defined as 'subversive activities'.

Serious security problems tested severely the tenuous relationship between civil and military authority during Turbay's term in office. The arbitrary application of the security statute left the military vulnerable to widespread charges of human rights abuses and intensified concern over the role of the armed forces in Colombia's democracy. A vigorous campaign by the army against the M-19 in early 1979 led to the arrest of thousands, many of whom charged they were subjected to torture.[21] The M-19's seizure of diplomatic hostages at the Dominican Republic embassy in February 1980 exposed an on-going struggle between Turbay and the military high command over the formulation of antiguerrilla policy. While Turbay worked through Congress to secure a limited amnesty for guerrillas, the hardliners headed by General Camacho continued to pursue a military solution.

In the late 1970s many high-ranking Colombian officers indulged openly in the rhetoric of the national security doctrine popularized by their Argentine and Chilean counterparts. They spoke and wrote frequently about a 'third world war' being waged in Latin America in which Colombia's strategic geopolitical location makes it a prime target for 'internal subversion'. The military has developed and maintained a strident anti-Communist position, claiming that Colombian guerrillas receive tactical and financial support from Cuba and the Soviet Union.[22] Cuba's alleged training of Colombian guerrillas involved in an aborted invasion attempt in southern Colombia in early 1981 precipitated a break in diplomatic relations on 23 March. Shortly thereafter, Army Commander General Landazábal called for socio-economic and political changes to wipe out subversion and predicted worse days ahead for the country. Reviving political and developmental concerns previously articulated by Ruiz Novoa and Valencia Tovar, Landazábal expressed his conviction that the army could militarily 'destroy the guerrillas', but subversion would continue 'as long as the objective and subjective conditions in the economic, social and political fields, which daily impair and disrupt stability, are not modified'.[23] Landazábal's views received extensive press coverage and focused attention on the fears of 'creeping militarism' expressed by such public figures as novelist Gabriel García Márquez and former Foreign Minister Alfredo Vásquez Carrizosa, one of the country's leading human rights activists. It is a measure of the military's increased political influence under Turbay that Landazábal was not officially reprimanded, much less dismissed, for espousing a position that previous presidents had found politically unacceptable.

The disruptive effects of the escalating drug trade in Colombia also contributed to the prominent political role assumed by the military under Turbay. Prior to August 1978, the military had resisted its direct involvement in antinarcotics operations. However, as part of Turbay's 'crusade' against drug trafficking, the Colombian army was given responsibility for combating marijuana production in the Guajira Peninsula and narcotics control in general. Despite early claims of success, evidence of troop demoralization and front-line exposure to corruption prompted General Camacho to reassess the military's assignment. In May 1980, at the military's urging, special units of the national police once again assumed primary responsibility for drug interdiction, and in June 1981 the Colombian army was officially relieved of its antinarcotics role. Although no longer directly responsible for drug interdiction, the military remains involved through its organizational link to the national police and continues to provide 'auxiliary support' in the war against drugs.[24]

Senior military commanders since the early 1980s have remained fearful of the corrupting influence of the drug mafia and until recently were reluctant to take part in anticocaine operations. Some, like former Defence Minister General Rafael Samudio Molina, concluded that the military should not be deployed in the war against drugs because it diverts them from their central mission of 'fighting the guerrillas'.[25] However, widespread corruption in the national police, along with domestic and international pressure to curb the power of Colombia's drug cartels, has led the government of President Virgilio Barco (1986–90) to overrule the military and once again involve it directly in the antidrug war.[26]

Conservative President Belisario Betancur's (1982–6) conciliatory policy towards Nicaragua and his determination to negotiate an end to Colombia's long-standing insurgency problem led to frequent disputes with senior military commanders over the extent of military influence in the formulation of foreign and internal security policy. Military leaders opposed his attempt at rapprochement with Cuba ('a moral impossibility', according to the army commander), and his promise to investigate charges of human rights abuses by the military during Turbay's presidency. Above all, they opposed his decision to negotiate a ceasefire with the country's major guerrilla organizations, with a view towards their incorporation into legal political activity.

Military leaders made no secret of their displeasure with the government's initial amnesty initiative, particularly after it became evident that several score of the guerrillas amnestied after November 1982 had rejoined guerrilla ranks.[27] By November 1983 military spokesmen were openly contradicting the President's policies. During congressional testimony, Defence Minister General Landazábal Reyes stated emphatically that the military would not yield to guerrilla demands that the army withdraw from the main areas of guerrilla conflict, nor would it agree to dialogue with the rebels. In a New Year's message to the Colombian people, he indicated that the military 'respected' the government's efforts to establish peace talks with the guerrillas, but it did not support a ceasefire. In a document delivered to Betancur in early January 1984, the top commanders of the armed forces expressed their support for Landazábal's position on the need to take stronger action against the guerrillas.

Betancur responded to the military's challenge to his authority by reprimanding the high command for criticizing the efforts of his Peace Commission. He 'persuaded' Landazábal to resign, thereby reaffirming the government's policy of pursuing a negotiated settlement and, more important, effectively reminding the armed forces to adhere to their constitutional role as a non-deliberative body.[28] With military opposition muted, Betancur's peace negotiations culminated in 1984 in historic truce agreements with three of Colombia's four major guerrilla movements.[29]

When the M-19 decided in June 1985 to abandon Betancur's peace initiative, the military announced a 'total war' against the movement.[30] After M-19 guerrillas seized the Palace of Justice on 6 November 1985, the military acted on its own to end the siege and left the President to assume responsibility for the outcome.[31] The incident further eroded public support for Betancur's peace proposals and allowed the military to recover some of the initiative it had lost in the formulation of antiguerrilla policy during his presidency.

CIVIL–MILITARY RELATIONS SINCE 1986

Since the inauguration of Liberal President Virgilio Barco in August 1986, Colombia's political leaders have become increasingly nervous about the escalation of guerrilla, paramilitary, and drug-related violence. The hope generated by former President Betancur's commitment to peace was replaced during Barco's first year in office by apparent resignation to a period of intense conflict between the armed forces and insurgents. From the beginning Barco's administration showed itself to be less tolerant of ceasefire abuses than his predecessor and inclined to coordinate its policy more closely with the military.

The country's major guerrilla organizations intensified their attacks on government forces shortly after Barco's inauguration, prompting the army to launch its most impressive counter-insurgency offensive of the decade.[32] Violations on both sides threatened the government's fragile truce agreement with the FARC, which was further eroded by mounting evidence of cooperation between the guerrillas and Colombia's powerful drug rings.

Guerrilla attacks on military patrols in early 1988 resulted in heavy troop losses, prompting Defence Minister Rafael Samudio Molina to report that the army's antiguerrilla war had reached a stalemate. Military frustration increased in May when the M-19 kidnapped former Conservative presidential candidate Alvaro Gómez Hurtado as part of its strategy to force the government to promote peace talks. When the government agreed to make concessions in exchange for Gómez's release, Samudio and other members of the military high command ruled out any participation by the armed forces in a national dialogue with guerrilla groups 'as long as soldiers continue to be killed'. According to Samudio, it had been a mistake before to enter negotiations on the basis of unilateral guerrilla demands and without a time limit. He warned that the country could not afford to continue to make such mistakes.[33]

In September 1988, President Barco announced a new peace initiative.

Unlike Betancur's plan, which offered immediate negotiations with guerrillas, Barco's offer required that rebels demonstrate concrete signs of renouncing armed struggle before engaging in dialogue with the government.[34] Following an upsurge in guerrilla activity, Army Commander General Guerrero Paz publicly stated that only a military solution could put an end to violence in Colombia. At the funeral services for eleven soldiers killed in a guerrilla ambush on 31 October, Defence Minister Samudio called for the armed forces to end their 'martyrdom' and wage 'an all-out offensive' to destroy the guerrillas.[35]

President Barco moved quickly to reaffirm presidential authority by rejecting Samudio's mandate and reiterating his support for a policy of reconciliation towards the guerrillas. Without directly mentioning his defence minister, Barco recalled that during Army Day celebrations three months earlier, he had warned about 'the risk of assuming extreme positions'. Quoting from parts of that speech, he said:

> The adherents of an all-out war or unconditional amnesty do not bear in mind the complexity of public-order problems, which must be dealt with within the context of an overall reconciliation policy. We must prevent restricting our options to either a strategy of total destruction or to a complete political surrender by the state. We will not be tempted by simplistic solutions.[36]

Once again Colombia's president emerged the winner in a policy dispute with the military. In a sweeping reshuffle of the military hierarchy, Barco replaced Defence Minister Samudio and ten other generals, including the commanders of the army, navy and air force. At his first news conference, Samudio's replacement, General Guerrero Paz, reassured the nation that the armed forces respected the civilian government and supported the President's policy.[37]

Despite Guerrero Paz's assurances, the military adopted a cautious stance towards Barco's subsequent negotiations with guerrilla groups. Although spokesmen for the military high command declared they would abide by the government's agreement in March 1989 to dialogue with the M-19, Army Commander General Oscar Botero stated that the army would only become an active party to the peace initiative during its final phase when guerrilla groups are expected to demobilize.[38] It is clear that many members of the military remain opposed to any peace plan. Previous attempts to end Colombia's 25-year guerrilla war by negotiation have failed, in part because the armed forces have chosen to remain on the sidelines in the peace process. As long as the military's attitude remains unchanged, hostilities are likely to continue even if the M-19 agrees to lay down its arms.

The guerrilla conflict during Barco's presidency has been accompanied and, to a degree, overshadowed by a dramatic increase in violence attributed to paramilitary groups, death squads, self-defence groups, and bands of assassins organized by drug interests. Human rights organizations contend that drug traffickers, large landowners, and members of the military and regional civilian elite are often allied to protect their interests, making it increasingly difficult to determine culpability for any given act. Criminal activity, for example, is often falsely labelled as anti-Communist or anti-guerrilla. In addition, death squads sponsored by drug traffickers have proliferated in recent years and are responsible for an alarming number of murders and attacks on high-level military and government officials, as well as leftist political leaders.

According to various human rights organizations, the Colombian military has reacted to increased guerrilla activity with a policy of terror designed to intimidate and eliminate its opponents. Amnesty International has reported on 'disappearances' and deliberate killings in Colombia since the early 1980s, but since mid-1987 the range of victims has extended far beyond left-wing opponents of the government to include 'people who criticize the government or armed forces or fail to actively support them'.[39] Although there is no proof that the military high command is organizing paramilitary actions, Colombian legal officials have found evidence that officers in positions of responsibility at mid-levels of the police and armed forces have participated in death squad activity in some regions of the country.

Until recently, the Colombian government has been slow to confront the existence of paramilitary groups. The minister of government provided the Congress in October 1987 with a list of 140 groups operating in the country, with names and headquarters. Yet, it appeared to many observers that the high command of the armed and security forces not only did little to investigate and punish such abuses, but in some cases they were accused by Colombian officials of actually obstructing legitimate judicial action.

There is little doubt that the impunity with which paramilitary and so-called 'self-defence' groups have operated in the past has contributed to the citizenry's loss of confidence in public authority in general, and in the military and police forces in particular. The massacre on 18 January 1989 of twelve members of a judicial commission investigating paramilitary activity in rural Santander marked a qualitative leap in the activities of the extreme right. What many officers saw in the beginning as a means of defence against subversion has become a no less serious threat. There is growing realization among members of the military high command that tacit support for the ends, if not always the means, of the various paramilitary groups threatens to undermine the moral and ethical basis of the institution. The unity the officer corps demonstrated when one of its members was singled out for criticism has led to a more realistic and self-critical attitude. There is now great concern both within the national government and the armed forces that part of the army and the national police, however small it may be, is losing its professional military ethics due to paramilitarism and narcotics trafficking.[40]

THE MAINTENANCE OF CIVILIAN RULE

The preceding narrative suggests a number of reasons why Colombia has avoided military rule throughout much of its history, particularly since 1958. The social and regional antipathies that led to an early, profound condescension on the part of Colombia's civilian elites towards the military and the depth of Colombians' attachment to the traditional Conservative and Liberal parties have provided a historical context to civil–military relations unique to the region.[41]

A number of factors help to explain the restoration of civilian control over the military in the first years following the junta's departure in 1958. First, the civilian population massively displayed its rejection of the military's support for the Rojas regime.[42] Secondly, several clumsy conspiracies by lower ranking officers to restore Rojas to power failed to draw enough popular support or military cooperation to succeed. There was no support within the upper echelons of military leadership for renewed intervention by the armed forces. They seem to have concluded that the institutional costs of their political role in the latter stages of Rojas' dictatorship had been too great in terms of weakened internal unity, loss of prestige, and threats to their long-term corporate interests. The military also accommodated itself readily to its responsibility for defending the National Front. Finally, there is the all-important question of the unity and prestige of Colombia's political elite.

The strength and persistence of Colombia's civilian elites and the pattern of hegemonic party rule prior to 1953 meet one of Talukder Maniruzzaman's criteria for lasting military disengagement from politics – the rise of a hegemonic class or coalition of classes. According to Maniruzzaman, the role played by talented and imaginative politicians in establishing civilian supremacy is crucial.[43] In the case of Colombia, it is apparent that political elites have been able to reach a consensus for sharing power at critical junctures in the country's history, most recently in the period of the National Front.

For the most part, Colombia's presidents since 1958 have demonstrated considerable skill in promoting the cause of civilian government through a combination of flexibility and force. Since the reorganization of the armed forces under López, presidents have maintained communication with the military high command through the Defence Ministry and the Superior Council of National Defence, seeking their advice, but tolerating no ultimatums on political matters. Indeed, presidential assertion of civilian authority has been a recurring feature of singular importance to any understanding of civil–military relations in Colombia. Military subordination has been reinforced by a continuous purge of disaffected elements. Those members of the high command unwilling to accept presidential policy unquestioningly have been cashiered. The list of dismissals over the past 25 years is impressive, with Generals Ruiz Novoa (1964), Pinzón Caicedo (1969), Valencia Tovar (1975), Matallana Bermúdez (1979), Landazábal Reyes (1984), and Samudio Molina (1988) representing the more prominent cases. It is both a measure of the military's historic predisposition towards civilian authority and an indication of its low self-esteem that, with the exception of General Matallana's removal, such sudden shifts in personnel produced little overt negative reaction within the officer corps. The military's behaviour is hardly a mark of professionalism in the sense that Nordlinger and others have defined it, whereby the military, as it becomes more professional, acquires the ability and the will to intervene, if necessary, in order to protect its corporate interests.[44]

Retired officers have been less reluctant to criticize government policy, either individually or through the Colombian Association of Retired Officers (ACORE). Articles and commentary by retired officers appear frequently in the media. A few like Ruiz Novoa, Valencia Tovar, and Landazábal Reyes have tested the political waters, but none has attracted serious support.[45]

Colombian presidents have not been insensitive to the institutional concerns of the military. Presidents frequently praise the loyalty, patriotism and self-denial of the armed forces, especially at significant military ceremonies. Over the years, improved benefits and training have gradually raised the prestige of a military career from its low point at the end of the Rojas period, although it still suffers in comparison with civilian professions. For the most part, chief executives have been careful not to tamper with the military's hierarchical structure, basing promotions on rank and seniority, rather than political connections. They have also displayed considerable skill in assuaging the military's demands for sophisticated equipment, providing the basic resources required to carry out their mission but exhorting against 'an unbridled arms race'. By providing institutionalized access for the military to pursue its interests, civilian leaders have reduced the risk of more direct intervention.

Although size alone is not a reliable indicator to the political behaviour of any military organization, an analysis of defence expenditures and the size of the armed forces can tell us something about the bargaining power of the military relative to civilian demands. Adequate budgetary support ranks prominently among the military's corporate interests since it is the means to achieving the manpower, equipment, and status necessary to fulfil its mission. Table 6.1 presents data on the size of the armed forces and percentages of the total national budget Colombia spent on its military in selected years from 1948 to 1988.

Table 6.1   Selected data on military size and budget, 1948–88

Year	Military Expenses as % of Government Budget	Military Expenses as % of GNP	Size of Armed Forces	Size of National Police
1948	14.3	n.a.	12–15,000	10,000
1953	25.4	2.0	"	"
1955	18.7	2.1	"	"
1958	17.1	1.5	"	"
1960	15.9	1.2	"	"
1963	14.5	2.3	"	"
1965	13.4	2.0	15–20,000	"
1968	13.1	2.3	20–25,000	12,000
1970	10.3	1.4	50,000	35,000
1975	9.2	1.2	50,000	35,000
1977	6.5	0.7	60,000	35,000
1980	7.7	1.1	66,700	50,000
1981	6.9	1.0	65,000	50,000
1982	8.0	1.2	70,000	50,000
1983	9.3	1.3	70,000	50,000
1984	10.0	1.4	70,000	50,000
1985	7.8	1.2	66,000	50,000
1986	n.a.	n.a.	64,400	50,000
1988	n.a.	n.a.	68,400	55,000

Source: Adapted from data presented in Joseph E. Loftus, *Latin American Defense Expenditures*, 1938–65, (Santa Monica, Calif.: Rand Corporation, RM-5310-PR/ISA, 1968); US Arms Control and Disarmament Agency, *World Military Expenditures and Arms Transfers, 1987*, (Washington, DC: US Government Printing Office, 1987); *Statistical Abstract of Latin America*, Volume 26 (Los Angeles: UCLA Latin American Center Publications, University of California, 1988); and *The New Statesman's Yearbook*, (London: Macmillan, 1986 and 1989).

Given the widespread discrepancy in data, it is precarious to infer more than the most general trends from the figures presented in Table 6.1. With that caveat in mind, it is clear that the armed forces have shown a steady increase in size, with the most dramatic growth occurring in the late 1960s. In absolute terms, the more than 68,000 personnel in Colombia's armed forces in 1988 might well be considered a sizeable force, especially for a country with no serious external threat.[46] However, in relative terms, both the size and the cost of maintaining Colombia's armed forces have been historically below the levels of most other Latin American countries. The navy and air force are small in comparison with the army with an estimated 7200 and 4200 members, respectively.

With the restoration of civilian government in 1958, a declining trend developed in the military's portion of the national budget that was sustained through the formal expiration of the National Front. Military expenditures since 1974, while not insignificant, likewise have not been overwhelmingly large. Fluctuations in military expenditures for the periods 1963–8 and since 1980, especially when reflected as a percentage of GNP, coincide with renewed threats to internal security and Colombia's expanding role in hemispheric affairs.[47] In one important respect, the latter data tend to confirm the assessment in mid-1988 by then Defence Minister General Samudio that military appropriations remained 'almost the same' during the period from 1978 to 1988. In a letter to President Barco, he complained that after 'many years of minimal appropriations' the armed forces and the national police were facing a budgetary deficit in the critical areas of overhead and investment.[48]

President Barco responded to growing demands within the military for increased budgetary support by approving supplementary appropriations and proposing an increase in the military's share of the budget by US $300 million a year for a period of five years. During a visit to Washington in May 1989, he called for increased security assistance from the United States to provide improved training and equipment for Colombia's armed forces and special police units as part of his antidrug initiative. Although some politicians have criticized certain aspects of the military build-up, for example, the purchase of Israeli Kfir jets, which are of no use in the antiguerrilla war, there is growing acceptance within the civilian sector that substantial increases in the defence budget are justifiable. Indeed, the rapid increase of resources for the military since 1986 is an indication of the growing political strength of the armed forces.

Colombia's preoccupation with organized guerrilla activity since the early 1960s has had a twofold effect on the military's role in the political system. On the one hand, the threat posed by guerrilla movements has enabled the military to develop a clearer sense of mission and made it easier to justify demands for greater autonomy in areas of professional concern affecting personnel, budget, and organization. Doubtless, the military would not play such a major role in matters of internal security in Colombia today were it not for the persistent threat of armed subversion. On the other hand, the military's inability to eliminate that threat after almost three decades of fighting has contributed to a lack of corporate self-confidence and reflected poorly on the overall prestige of the institution. For most of that period guerrillas have not been a dominant factor in Colombian politics except in the eyes of the military. In fact, one author has cited the absence of a sustained revolutionary challenge as a compelling factor in explaining Colombia's failure to follow the political path of authoritarianism elsewhere in the region.[49]

Finally, favourable economic conditions for much of the period under study is another factor that has undoubtedly aided Colombia's political leaders in maintaining civilian control. Despite its on-going guerrilla war and increased political violence, Colombia has enjoyed one of the region's most buoyant economies. Its foreign debt of $16.5 billion is modest by Latin American criteria. For the most part, the country has avoided the overwhelming economic crises that have contributed to political discontent and interventionist proclivities by the military elsewhere in the region.

PROSPECTS FOR CONTINUED CIVILIAN RULE IN COLOMBIA

It is ironic that in the decade of the 1980s the military's role in Colombian politics appeared to be moving towards increased involvement at a time when the military elsewhere in Latin America actively sought disengagement. One of the anomalies of civil–military relations in Colombia is that despite having experienced only two coups since 1901, there is a tendency within the country to perceive the political situation as 'crisis-laden and on the verge of military takeover'.[50] This perception has been exacerbated in recent years by the emphasis given to drug-related violence in the domestic and international press.

To be sure, Colombia today ranks among the most violent nations in the world in terms of homicide rates, kidnappings, and other forms of criminal activity. The US State Department estimates that more than 16,000 Colombians were murdered in 1988, 10 per cent of them in politically-motivated killings. Colombia's minister of justice, the seventh since President Barco took office, readily conceded that Colombia's legal system is in a shambles. According to the President's adviser on human rights, 90 per cent of the crimes committed in Colombia go unpunished. At a forum on Constitutional Reform and Human Rights held in Bogotá in February 1989, he concluded that the state's inability to consolidate democratic processes leaves open the prospect of 'totalitarian solutions' in the near future.[51] Government officials openly admit that the consolidation of large landholdings by drug barons who create private 'armies' to protect their investments from guerrilla harassment has led to an alarming loss of government control in many rural areas. The continued assassination of political leaders, predominantly from the leftist Patriotic Union, and the recent massacres of peasants are disturbingly reminiscent of the lawlessness associated with *la violencia*. One suspects that it will be as difficult for the military to bring paramilitary groups under control as it has been to defeat the guerrillas.

There is concern among political commentators that the country is rapidly becoming ungovernable. In the absence of inspired leadership, the traditional two-party system is languishing. Newspaper editorials criticized the Barco administration for 'nonaction' and the further disintegration of the judicial system. Charges of cover-ups within government circles and the military are reported routinely by the media, leading to further erosion of confidence in government institutions. In short, Colombians appear to be losing faith in Congress, in their presidents, and in those responsible for their security.[52]

Recent economic indicators for Colombia are likewise not encouraging. According to the National Council for Economic and Social Policy (CON-PES), the Colombian economy grew by only 3.7 per cent in 1988, compared to 5.8 per cent in 1986, and 5.3 per cent in 1987. Continued attacks by the ELN on the country's major oil pipeline and a decline in international coffee prices are expected to limit the country's potential for economic growth in the short run.[53]

In almost any other Latin American country faced with similar problems of mounting violence, institutional crises, and restricted economic outlook a military coup would be a formality. However, military rule is not seen as a viable substitute to democratic rule in Colombia – at least not at the present time. Despite the many problems facing the country, civilian rule retains the legitimacy and support of the armed forces. Even the strongest critics of the military doubt that Colombia's top military leaders want to take power. For the most part, the military has refrained from making forceful or threatening pronouncements to the nation. In responding to a US firm's prediction of a 30 per cent chance that the armed forces will intervene in the next five years to restore order, Air Force Commander General Alfredo Ortega replied tersely: 'Versions on the probability of a military coup are baseless. The armed forces are in favour of democracy, and they are fighting to defend it'.[54]

If there is a dominant theme throughout the history of civil–military relations in Colombia, it is the degree to which civilian authority has maintained its supremacy over the military. The military has undeniably gained a degree of autonomy in matters of internal security over the past decade, especially in the formulation of antiguerrilla policy. Yet, civilians still appear to be firmly in control. The Colombian armed forces clearly have the size and the organizational capacity to intervene, but it is doubtful that they possess the requisite political and administrative skills, or the technical expertise, to conduct efficiently the complex affairs of government. Moreover, from the stand-point of motivation there is little incentive for them to displace civilian rule. With the political influence the military already enjoys, the armed forces would have little to gain and a great deal to lose in any calculated seizure of power.

In the final analysis, the military, given its tradition of nonpolitical involvement, is only apt to intervene if Colombia's civilian elites fail to provide the inspired moral and political leadership needed to halt the present deterioration of public order. The paradox, and perhaps the danger, is that to succeed, they will have to rely even further on the coercive powers of the state, which portends an expanded political role for the armed forces, at least in the short run.

Apocalyptic predictions about Colombia's future tend to ignore its past. Colombians, civilian and military alike, have displayed a remarkable ability 'to muddle through' during previous periods of social and institutional crisis. While the challenges facing the country today are formidable, the most probable scenario is that barring a major economic crisis or the emergence of a genuinely mass-based revolutionary movement, neither of which appears likely, civilian rule will continue uninterrupted in Colombia.

NOTES

1. John A. Peeler, *Latin American Democracies: Colombia, Costa Rica, Venezuela* (Chapel Hill: University of North Carolina Press, 1985).
2. Constantine P. Danopoulos, 'Military Dictatorships in Retreat', in C. P. Dano-poulos, ed., *The Decline of Military Regimes: The Civilian Influence*, (Boulder: Westview Press, 1988), 22.
3. Mark J. Ruhl, 'The Military', in Albert Berry, Ronald Hellman and Mauricio Solaun, eds, *Politics of Compromise: Coalition Government in Colombia* (New Brunswick: Transaction Books, 1980), 180. Ruhl provides a more extended treatment in *Colombia: Armed Forces and Society* (Syracuse, NY : Syracuse University, 1980). Also recommended for general background are Anthony P. Maingot, 'Colombia', in Lyle N. McAlister, Anthony P. Maingot, and Robert Potash, eds, *The Military in Latin American Sociopolitical Evolution: Four Case Studies* (Washington: Center for Research in Social Systems, 1970), 127–97, and the author's 'The Colombian Armed Forces in Search of a Mission', in Robert Wesson, ed., *New Military Politics in Latin America*, (New York: Praeger, 1982), 151–73.
4. The War of the Thousand Days (1899–1902) was occasioned by a Liberal revolt that divided the officer corps as it divided the nation. This bloody civil war, which cost Colombia some 100,000 lives, conclusively demonstrated the incompetence of the military and persuaded Reyes of the need for institutional reforms and a formally trained officer cadre.
5. The most flagrant deviation from this tradition was the abortive coup against Liberal president Alfonso López Pumarejo (1942–6) by a small group of army officers on 10 July 1944. The conspirators resented López's attempts to interfere with promotions in the largely Conservative army, the build up of the national police as a counterforce, and his generally condescending attitude towards the military. Fluharty presents the interesting thesis that reaction to the coup effectively prevented military intervention on a larger scale until 1953, despite the chaotic political situation and violence that developed after 1946. See Vernon Lee Fluharty, *Dance of the Millions* (Pittsburgh: University of Pittsburgh Press, 1957), 74–5.

6. Janowitz makes the distinction between 'designed militarism', the premeditated search for political power, and 'reactive militarism', the expansion of military power that results from the weakness of civilian institutions and the pressures of civilians to co-opt and expand the role of the military. Morris Janowitz, *The Military in the Development of New Nations* (Chicago: University of Chicago Press, 1964), 16.

7. Fluharty's work is the major exception. The most balanced treatment of Rojas' rule remains Robert H. Dix, *Colombia: The Political Dimensions of Change* (New Haven: Yale University Press, 1967). For an excellent analysis of the transition to civilian rule in 1953, see Jonathan Hartlyn, 'Military Governments and the Transition to Civilian Rule: The Colombian Experience of 1957–8', *Journal of Interamerican Studies and World Affairs* 26 (May 1984): 245–81.

8. Hartlyn, 'Military Governments', 274.

9. Under the terms of the National Front agreement, ratified by a national plebiscite on 1 December 1957, political participation in elections was explicitly limited to the Conservative and Liberal parties. The presidency alternated every four years between the two parties, and both shared equal representation in all legislative, executive, and judicial bodies, extending to the municipal level, regardless of electoral strength. Under this system of absolute parity, no new political parties were permitted. Since neither presidential nor legislative elections were actually contested between opposing parties – equal representation was assured regardless of the outcome – programmatic differences between the traditional parties became obscured and one of the dominant issues in politics during the period became the question of the National Front's survival. For an historical perspective and overview of the National Front, including modifications to the original agreement, see Harvey F. Kline, 'The National Front', in Berry *et al.*, eds, *Politics of Compromise*, 59–83.

10. Alberto Lleras Camargo, *Conferencia a los miembros de las fuerzas armadas* (Bogotá: Imprenta FFMM, 1958), 12. Lleras' observations are expressed in more theoretical terms by Eric Nordlinger who postulates that civilian rule is more likely to last when two conditions prevail: 1 when civilians do not interfere with the military's corporate interests; and 2 the military concludes that politics has a negative effect on the internal unity, prestige, and long-term professional interests of the armed forces. Eric A. Nordlinger, *Soldiers in Politics: Military Coups and Governments,* (Englewood Cliffs, NJ: Prentice-Hall, Inc., 1977), 207–10.

11. The Council is responsible for advising the president in the formulation and implementation of national security and defence policy. In January 1987, President Barco assigned the functions of permanent executive secretary to the office of the General Commander of the Armed Forces, which is certain to enhance the military's influence within the Council. For a military perspective of the Council's function, see the speech by General Samudio in the *Revista de las Fuerzas Armadas*, vol. 42, no. 122 (January–March 1987): 5–6. The military also has important access to political authority at lower levels, particularly through army brigade commanders who exercise considerable influence on departmental governors who are appointed by the president. Note: the Ministry of War was renamed the Ministry of National Defence in 1966.

12. Colombian officers distinguish between the 'armed forces' and the 'military' with respect to their composition. The former includes the national police, while the latter refers only to the traditional services. The distinction is of no small consequence in determining such basic data as the size of the military estab-

lishment, defence expenditures, and troop casualties. For the purpose of this study the terms are used interchangeably, with the national police treated as a separate entity.

13. Under these programmes the armed forces were cast as agents of social and economic change intended to eliminate guerrilla violence and rural banditry. For a detailed discussion of the counter-insurgency activities of Colombia's armed forces during the National Front period, see Richard L. Maullin, *Soldiers, Guerrillas, and Politics in Colombia* (Lexington, Massachusetts: Lexington Books, D. C. Heath, 1973). For an early evaluation of Colombia's civic action programme, see Edward Glick, 'The Nonmilitary Use of the Latin American Military', *Background*, 8 (November 1964): 161–73.

14. The new guerrilla threat resulted in a quantum jump in military manpower. According to Maullin, between 1964 and 1966 the army more than doubled in size from under 23,000 to an estimated 53,500. *Soldiers, Guerrillas, and Politics in Colombia*, 82. The national police also grew, tripling in size between 1966 and 1970 to a force of approximately 35,000. *The Statesman's Yearbook* (New York: St. Martin's Press, 1965–6 and 1970–1).

15. Jonathan Hartlyn, *The Politics of Coalition Rule in Colombia* (Cambridge University Press, 1988), 83–4.

16. In a revealing letter published in the *New York Times*, Valencia Tovar wrote: 'In any country afflicted by 'objective conditions' favoring armed revolution, guerrillas taking advantage of extremely adequate geographical environment cannot be destroyed by force alone. Social and economic changes ... are more suitable tools for strategic victory than costly and bloody armed efforts. Perhaps the latter could yield some measure of tactical success but will never uproot a sickness which lies in the depths of an unbalanced society' (*New York Times*, 20 July 1975).

17. The forced retirement of four senior officers in December 1975, including the commander-in-chief of the armed forces, allowed for the promotion of several of the more impatient hardliners, among them Luis Carlos Camacho Leyva, who moved up from army commander to commander-in-chief, and Fernando Landazábal Reyes, the ambitious head of the Military Institutes Brigade (BIM) who was promoted to major general.

18. *El Tiempo*, 16 December 1977, 1(A).

19. *El Espectador*, 10 December 1977, 1(A), 8(A).

20. Ibid., 22 December 1977, 1(A).

21. Amnesty International produced in April 1980 the first in a series of documents by international human rights agencies over the past decade reporting evidence of torture, disappearances, and other abuses by the Colombian military in the name of national security.

22. The Colombian Communist Party (PCC) has been a favourite target of attack since it regained legal status in 1972 and began participating in elections under its own banner. Military spokesmen routinely charge the PCC with promoting subversion through its links with the FARC and its participation in the Patriotic Union (UP), a coalition of the PCC, amnestied FARC guerrillas, and independent leftists organized in early 1985. Civilian authorities tend to be less concerned than their military counterparts with the threat of international communism in Colombia. As one Colombian observer recently stated: 'There are those among retired officers like Generals Valencia Tovar and Landazábal Reyes and the entire slate of generals on active duty who believe themselves to be engaged in a holy war

against communist subversion and who therefore do little to reduce the even greater threat represented by paramilitary groups' (Jorge Child, 'Soy libre', *El Espectador*, 11 February 1989, 3(A)).

23. *Revista Militar del Ejército* (April 1981), as cited in FBIS *Daily Report: Latin America*, 3 April 1981, VI.

24. Colombian Military Attaché, interview by author, 15 June 1989, Washington, DC For a discussion of the negative impact of drug trafficking on the military from an officer's perspective, see the article by Major Fredy Padilla, 'Víctimas del Narcotráfico', *Revista de las Fuerzas Armadas*, vol. 42, no. 124 (July–September 1987): 310–30. For an excellent overview of the drug problem, see Bruce M. Bagley, 'Colombia and the War on Drugs', *Foreign Affairs*, 67 (Fall 1988): 70–92.

25. *Washington Post*, 11 April 1988.

26. Alan Riding, 'Military Involvement in Anti-Drug Campaign', *New York Times*, 5 May 1988. Barco's decision to involve the military more directly is still being debated by members of the high command. In a recent speech before newly commissioned army officers, Army Commander General Nelson Mejía Henao, after conceding that some soldiers have been corrupted by the drug traffic, affirmed that 'As long as the army exists, its mission is to prepare for war. We are not going to concern ourselves in other areas'. *El Espectador*, 1 March 1989, 14(A).

27. *El Siglo*, 5 January 1984, 4(A).

28. *El Espectador*, 19 January 1984, 1(A), 8(A). Although there was some speculation that Betancur would have preferred to appoint a civilian as Landazábal's successor, his selection of General Gustavo Matamorros preserved the existing seniority within the high command and, in effect, replaced one hardliner with another. Betancur's admonition provoked the resignation of four other senior generals, including Army Commander General Bernardo Lema Henao. Lema was among those officers who later bitterly contended that the army was on the verge of eliminating the guerrilla movement at the time the 1984 peace agreements were signed.

29. The FARC agreed to a one-year ceasefire, effective 28 May, while the M–19, the People's Liberation Army (EPL), and the small Workers Self-Defence Movement (ADO), agreed to suspend armed activity indefinitely after August 30. The National Liberation Army (ELN) was the only major guerrilla group to reject the government's peace initiative. Neither accord required the guerrillas to surrender their weapons, nor did the government make any explicit commitment to withdraw troops from guerrilla strongholds. For a study of the pacification process in Colombia prior to 1986, see the author's 'Coping with Insurgency: The Politics of Pacification in Colombia and Venezuela', in Donald L. Herman, ed., *Democracy in Latin America: Colombia and Venezuela*, (New York: Praeger Publishers, 1988), 219–44.

30. *El Tiempo*, 9 August 1985, 7(A). President Barco's first defence minister, General Rafael Samudio Molina, reaffirmed the military's hard line on 11 August 1986, declaring that Colombia's pacification requires 'fighting with the full vigor of the law those who refuse to return to normal life' (*El Espectador*, 14 August 1986, 6(A)).

31. *Latin America Regional Report, Andean Group*, 13 December 1985, 1. Although Betancur later insisted it was his decision not to negotiate with the guerrillas, there is much to suggest that he was not given much choice by the military high

command. The M–19's mediation attempts were rejected outright. The military's assault on the palace left 95 people dead, including 11 supreme court justices.

32. A reported 10,000 troops participated in the offensive, mainly in Cauca, Valle, and Northern Santander departments (*El Tiempo*, 27 August 1986, 1(A)).

33. *El Espectador*, 14 July 1988, 1(A). From the military's perspective, open-ended peace negotiations are incompatible with its counter-insurgency strategy. While commander of the armed forces, General Jaime Guerrero Paz wrote that in order to defeat the guerrillas, the military must adopt the tactic of 'permanent offensive'. According to Guerrero, subversion's greatest political success in Colombia was to bring the government to the bargaining table for an unlimited dialogue, without demanding concessions on the guerrillas' part. The military resents the guerrillas' success in persuading the government, the traditional parties, the Church, and public opinion in general to support another dialogue exercise, without their having done anything to merit one. Guerrero also feels that subversives have succeeded in exploiting the banner of human rights to discredit the military and police forces. See 'Colombia: objetivo estratégico y los conflictos de baja intensidad', *Revista de las Fuerzas Armadas*, vol. 43, no. 128 (July–September 1988): 319–32.

34. The plan is intended primarily to facilitate the M–19's transition to a legal political movement. The precedent for such a move is not encouraging, however. The Patriotic Union is an example of what was supposed to happen under Betancur's 'democratic opening'. Since the UP became an active political party and the country's only significant leftist opposition, some 900 of their members have been murdered, including their president, Jaime Pardo Leal, two senators, two congressmen, and scores of elected state assembly and municipal council officials. There is no reason to believe the government will be any more successful in guaranteeing the personal safety of M–19 activists who accept the option of operating within the legal system.

35. *El Espectador*, 4 November 1988, 1(A).

36. *El Tiempo*, 5 November 1988, 1(A). Ironically, Barco's speech celebrating Army Day was reproduced in *Revista de las Fuerzas Armadas*, vol. 43, no. 128 (July–September 1988): 269–77. In another revealing passage from the same speech, Barco acknowledged that the military has been delegated responsibilities that more properly fall under civilian jurisdiction: 'This practice has diverted the military from its primary functions and occasionally placed it in difficult situations that have reflected poorly on the institution's integrity. One such case has been to assign civil crimes to military courts'. Barco's remarks seem to have been motivated in part by Samudio's earlier assertion that the only solution to the breakdown in Colombia's criminal justice system is to permit the prosecution of private individuals by military tribunals and grant special judicial police powers to the military and the national police. See Samudio's letter to President Barco published in *El Tiempo*, 13 June 1988, 1(A), 13(A).

37. *El Espectador*, 11 November 1988, 1(A). Although the Defence Ministry refused to comment on reports of discontent and low morale within the armed forces, a spokesman conceded that changes in the military high command had been 'accelerated' following Samudio's resignation. Retired officers were less restrained in their criticism. General Landazábal termed the events a 'victory' for Colombia's guerrillas and said that the civilian government had acted 'in a spirit of unconditional surrender' to the rebels. He added that under the circumstances, the only thing left for the army to do was to 'remain in its barracks to avoid being

further weakened and losing its prestige' (Andres Oppenheimer, 'Colombia Military Shuffle Spurs Ill Will', *Miami Herald*, 13 November 1988).

38. *El Espectador*, 18 March 1989, 10(A). Peace negotiations, while important in themselves, will have no lasting effect if the systematic murder of UP partisans is not stopped. Until it is, Colombia will continue in the absurd situation where it is more dangerous for those under arms to wage peace than it is to remain in the mountains.

39. *Amnesty Action* (May–June 1988), 4.

40. This is the basic conclusion reached in an article appearing in *Semana*, (May 1989), 34–7. Since the beginning of 1989, the government claims to have disbanded 23 gangs of hired assassins operating in Antioquia, Boyacá, Meta, Santander, and Caquetá departments. In April President Barco announced the creation of a Special Armed Corps (CEA) to combat organized crime. Although it will function under the command of the national police, the armed forces are expected to provide assistance.

41. Robert H. Dix, *The Politics of Colombia* (New York: Praeger Publishers, 1987), 136.

42. This was evident to the author, who witnessed civilian reaction to the military junta on the morning of Rojas' overthrow. Many of the thousands who swarmed into the streets of Bogotá demonstrated against the continuation of military government by shouting 'Civiles, sí; botas, no!' For a brief account of the coup attempts in support of Rojas' return, see Hartlyn, 'Military Governments and the Transition to Civilian Rule', 264–7.

43. Talkuder Maniruzzaman, *Military Withdrawal From Politics: A Comparative Study* (Cambridge, Massachusetts: Ballinger Publishing Company, 1987), 210–12.

44. Generally speaking, the military's corporate interests include ensuring adequate budgetary support, institutional autonomy, protection against encroachments from rival institutions, and, above all, its institutional survival.

45. Valencia Tovar ran for president in 1978 as a third party candidate, receiving less than 2 per cent of the popular vote. In February 1989 Landazábal Reyes formally requested legal status for the Colombian Integrationist Movement which he founded in 1987. He has spoken often of the need for basic reforms and his belief that 'What Colombia needs is a general to govern it'. He feels strongly that civilians have 'not let the military do its job' and urges the armed forces to 'reclaim their privileges'. For a Colombian journalist's reaction to Landazábal's politicking, see Fernando Cano, 'La balada de las balas', *El Espectador*, 4 March 1989, 2(A).

46. There is some reason to question current estimates on the size of Colombia's armed forces. In a letter to President Barco arguing for increased military expenditures, Defence Minister Samudio cited a dramatic increase in the size of the military over the past decade that is not reflected in the data. According to Samudio, in 1978 approximately 80,000 men in the armed forces and 40,000 police officers were covered by the budget; since then, the two forces have 'almost doubled in number, to 135.000 and 72,000 men, respectively' (*El Tiempo*, 13 June 1988, 1(A), 13(A)). An English translation of Samudio's letter appears in the FBIS *Daily Report: Latin America* (11 August 1988): 12–15. If correct, Samudio's figures indicate that the conventional wisdom about the size of Colombia's armed forces derived from the sources cited in the table is badly mistaken. Regrettably, the author was unable to obtain verification of Samudio's

figures from either US or Colombian officials prior to publication. However, given the source and the fact that the letter was directed to President Barco, I am not inclined to dismiss them as military hyperbole. In a speech on 6 August, 1988, celebrating Army Day, President Barco acknowledged that increasing the basic strength of the armed forces was an urgent priority of his government. He said that the standing army had increased by 20 per cent during the first two years of his administration, and that the country 'has more than 200,000 compatriots prepared to sacrifice their lives in the defense of sovereignty, liberty, and democracy' (*Revista de las Fuerzas Armadas*, vol. 43, no. 128 (July–September 1988), 271).

47. Nicaragua's renewed claim to Providencia and San Andrés, the international implications of drug trafficking, US policy in the region, and the on-going territorial disputes with Venezuela all contributed to the military's heightened concern with 'external security' after 1979. Along with the problem of insurgency, they stimulated a renewed interest in professional matters of size, budget, and readiness. For a review of Colombian foreign policy under Presidents Turbay and Betancur, see Bruce M. Bagley and Juán Gabriel Totkatlian, 'Colombian Foreign Policy in the 1980s: The Search for Leverage', *Journal of Interamerican Studies and World Affairs*, 27 (Fall 1985): 27–62.

48. *El Tiempo*, 13 June 1988, 13(A). Samudio's complaints confirm the impression that following Betancur's pacification initiative, the military found it difficult to convince the government that it needed modern arms to replace ageing equipment.

49. Dix, *The Politics of Colombia*, 218. The human and material costs to Colombia in its protracted guerrilla struggle are by no means negligible. General Samudio reported in 1987 that over the previous decade of fighting, 1287 soldiers, 3231 guerrillas, and 3502 civilians had been killed (*Latin America Regional Report: Andean Group*, 3 September 1987, 2). According to Colombian security sources, 563 soldiers, including officers, 158 policemen, 763 guerrillas, and 2157 peasants were killed as a result of political violence in 1988 (*El Siglo*, 3 January 1989, 1(A)). The number of soldiers killed in 1988 is almost double the number reported for any year since 1958, and almost half the number of casualties for the previous ten years.

50. Ruhl, 'The Military', 193.

51. *El Espectador*, 3 February 1989, 7(A).

52. In so far as Colombian public opinion can be determined, much less considered reliable, 59 per cent of a sample polled in April 1989 believed that the country is 'worse off' than it was during the National Front period. A majority supported some form of national union government that would include the leftist UP, but without the formal conditions of parity and alternation imposed under the National Front agreement. Over 70 per cent of the sample said they were prepared to vote for a president who is not from the party they support, suggesting that party identification has weakened. *El Tiempo*, 21 April 1989, 3(A).

53. *El Tiempo*, 15 May 1989, 6(B). Among new economic measures announced on 6 July 1989, the government called for a reduction in military spending, apparently on the grounds that military spending is 'out of control' (FBIS, *Latin America: Daily Report*, 6 July 1989, 58).

54. *Miami Herald*, 25 September 1988. The firm in question is Frost and Sullivan.

7 The military in a subsidized democracy: the case of Venezuela

Rita Giacalone and Rexene Hanes de Acevedo

During most of the twentieth century, Venezuela has presented a contradiction in the political behaviour of its armed forces, at least if we compare it with the actions of other national military institutions in South America. This state of affairs appeared more notorious when, in the second part of the century, civilian governments of countries considered to constitute models of political stability (such as Chile and Uruguay) fell, due to military coups leading to prolonged military interventions, while Venezuela, under military rule during most of its independent life, experienced after 1958 the establishment of a democratic political system which has proved to be lasting and capable of achieving a successful degree of integration of its armed forces.

It is a fact that after that date, the Venezuelan military withdrew from an active political role as power contenders, and a new political system developed in which increased oil rent, and agreement between major political and economic actors, and external support for the new institutions combined to give birth to what we have called a subsidized democracy. By this, we mean that the consensus around the political system hinges on the state's economic capacity to guarantee investment, employment, and services.[1] Political parties, however, provide the channels through which state resources have been distributed, although very unevenly, to every major sector of society, thus building a pyramid of support for democratic institutions. The success of this arrangement signified that, after 1958, the military had to find a new place for itself, more appropriate to the changes effected in the socio-political system, a process which forced a drastic reassessment of the traditional role of the military in Venezuela.

Our discussion of civil–military relations in Venezuela, both before and after 1958, is aimed primarily at providing an explanation of why the armed forces withdrew and what is the likelihood of their returning to a more active role in politics in the future. Our main contention is that, in the last analysis, in both cases, the withdrawal of 1958 as well as a possible return in the future, the principal responsibility lies in the ability of the political parties to build, maintain, and enlarge the necessary support for the institutions of the democratic political system among all major sectors of Venezuelan society. This chapter will be divided in four parts: in the first, we will give a brief historical overview of the development of Venezuelan military institutions prior to 1958; in the second, emphasis will be placed on the analysis of the political system we have characterized as a 'subsidized democracy;' in the third, discussion will be centred around the successful incorporation of the armed forces into that political system; while the fourth will deal with the present problems created by the deterioration of the fundamental pillars of that political system and how this may force a reassessment of civil–military relations in Venezuela. In the latter section, an effort will be made to place the Venezuelan armed forces into a larger perspective of what constitutes the norm of behaviour of South American military institutions. Thus, we will attempt to reinsert the particular Venezuelan experience into a broader interpretation of the role of the armed forces in South American politics.

A BRIEF HISTORY OF CIVIL–MILITARY RELATIONS

In spite of the fact that Venezuela has spent most of its independent life under one military ruler or another, the military as an institution is a relatively recent phenomenon. After the long struggle for independence from Spain, in which the Venezuelan army played a major role in the liberation of Andean South America, Venezuela became part of Gran Colombia, turning into reality one of the principal dreams of its liberator Simón Bolívar. Unfortunately, in 1830, internecine struggles for power led to Venezuela's withdrawal from this union of Colombia, Ecuador, and Venezuela. This set the stage for the weakening of the Venezuelan army, giving birth to two different factions: professional officers who were mostly loyal to the concept of the Gran Colombia, and the 'occasional soldiers' who had strong regional loyalties and a more parochial mentality.[2] When the latter seceded from Gran Colombia, the former disappeared from the political scene. Thus, the independence army was virtually disbanded, shrinking from over 12,000 men in the 1820's[3] to less than 2,000 in 1835.[4] The rest of the century witnessed a political situation of semi-anarchy, characterized by what could be called a '*caudillo* cycle', in which private militias formed the power base of each regional strongman in his struggle for political position.[5] For some 70 years, Venezuela was beset by almost constant military uprisings – 170 attempts to seize national power, of which only 13 were successful, but 32 of which involved relatively major upheavals.[6] The regular army was increasingly irrelevant, being supplanted by the personal army of whichever *caudillo* came to power, and would not regain relevance as an institution until well into the twentieth century.

It was only with the arrival of the Andean *caudillos* (Cipriano Castro and Juan Vicente Gómez) to national power in 1899 that a regular army again came into being. Both men considered an effective national army to be the necessary foundation for centralized power. To this end, each of them laboured to convert the armed forces into a more efficient tool at their personal service. In an effort to stave off regional challenges to his power, President Cipriano Castro initiated the centralization of regional militias and set up a general staff and chains of command under his control. Although he established a military academy in 1903, it did not begin functioning until 1910, two years after his overthrow by his Vice-President Juan Vicente Gómez.[7] In turn, Gómez built upon the gains made by Castro and, as soon as his centralized army was strong enough, prohibited the raising of state militias, [8] thereby removing the possibility of the emergence of new regional *caudillos* to challenge his rule. By this measure, he finally liquidated the age of the *caudillo* and ushered in the age of a military institution with national scope, a development which was to have telling repercussions in the future of Venezuela.

During Gómez' 27-year rule, professionalization of the armed forces was both furthered and constrained. In the first case, the military academy and the role of Chilean advisers helped create a new breed of officers. Meanwhile, Andeans, loyal to Gómez and formed in the battlefields, monopolized the higher ranks within the army. Professionalization for Gómez meant not only the academic formation of officers, but also the conversion of his ragtag followers into a well disciplined army, and perhaps even more important, its total loyalty to him. As an example of the duality of his approach, Gómez, at the same time that he hired foreign supervisors to train Venezuelan officers, also named his friend and confidant Félix Galavís as Chief Inspector of the Army, and, while presidents might come and go, he never gave up his own position as Supreme Commander of the Armed Forces.[9] Although the army continued to dominate his attention, Gómez also allowed considerable freedom for the navy to organize professionally, especially since it was not strong enough to present a threat to his hegemony. Later the air force would be granted the same treatment. Gómez' benign neglect, which favoured the professionalization of these branches but maintained them on the margins of power, was to sow the seeds of inter-service rivalries that would plague succeeding governments and play a significant role in future military coups.

As a general rule, the process of creating a professional army provokes tensions within the institution itself.[10] Venezuela was no exception to this rule and, after some years, a situation developed in which junior officers became increasingly embittered when they found their upward mobility blocked by the Andean officer corps. It is worth pointing out, as an indicator of the importance of this group, that during Gómez' regime, officers from the Andes (most of them from his home state of Táchira) represented between 75 and 90 per cent of all officers[11] and 100 per cent of the high command.[12] Still, Gómez preferred his loyal Andean cronies to quell the frequent insurrections and invasions of Venezuela over his newly professionalized regular army.[13] This situation occasioned a great deal of discontent, which found major expression in the unsuccessful revolts in 1919 and 1928 by junior officers graduated from the military academy. By the time of Gómez' death in 1935, the army was sufficiently strong to block any regional challenges to national power; henceforth, to be successful, any challenge would need to mobilize support within the military institution.

The death of Gómez provoked violent outbursts against his family and the secret police. When the violence subsided, the army emerged as the only viable alternative, due to Gómez' suppression of organized political parties. For the next ten years, two generals – Eleazar López Contreras (1936–41) and Isaías Medina Angarita (1941–5) – occupied the presidency. Basing their power on keeping intact the army which Gómez so carefully fashioned, they began a gradual and restrained process of democratization of Venezuelan society, after almost three decades of an iron-handed dictatorship. Part of their success in these precarious transition years can be related to the fact that they embodied the two principal strains among Venezuelan officialdom: they were both Andeans, the former forged in the battles of Gómez' rise to power and the latter a graduate and ex-director of the military academy.[14] While they did little or nothing to renovate the largely un-schooled Andean high command, they did continue and enhance the professionalization of the armed forces, which included the creation of a militarized police body (National Guard), primarily to safeguard the maintenance of internal order. This was particularly necessary as the process of opening up civilian society to the organization of political parties and trade unions created new possibilities of conflict. In the climate of intensifying politicization of the Venezuelan populace, it is interesting to note that the national guard, albeit primarily a police organization, was bestowed with the legal status of a fourth branch of the armed forces, largely to avoid interference with its activities by newly aggressive civilian politicians.[15] The military as an institution appeared to have achieved, in less than 50 years, sufficient power, upon which civil society dare not intrude.

The increasing professionalization of the armed forces deepened the internal clash of interests between the two main groups of officers, and by 1945, junior officers, trained outside the country secretly began to organize around a series of grievances, especially the questions of slow promotions and low pay for officers. Acknowledging the pro-democratic climate of the

1940s both within and outside Venezuela, they linked their discontent with the most organized political party of that time, Acción Democrática (AD). As Carlos Delgado Chalbaud, one of the leaders of the junior officers' conspiracy and soon to be Minister of Defence, openly admitted: 'A military coup without a social colouring is inconceivable in our time. It must have the support of the masses and Rómulo Betancourt [leader of AD] has that'.[16] When they joined forces to overthrow Medina Angarita in 1945, they demanded both a democratic system based on universal suffrage and the creation of a professional army, devoid of 'those elements that due to their senility and incompetence are responsible for its backwardness'.[17] In fact, the Venezuelan junior officers that put AD in power were demanding the right to control the armed forces. In order to keep them pacified, the government gave them lavish budgetary resources. By 1947, the defence budget had tripled, officers' salaries had been raised by 37 per cent and those of the troops by 57 per cent.[18] For a time, attempts against the government (mainly by displaced Andean officers) lacked any chance of success in this climate of plentiful resources and the army's willingness to look inward to its own organization, giving the AD government free political rein.

Free political rein did not, however, mean military withdrawal. The 1945 coup against Medina Angarita unleashed social forces too long restrained, but the inexperienced government possessed insufficient mechanisms to control them. Besides fulfilling the Junta's promise of providing universal suffrage for all citizens over the age of eighteen, this period witnessed an extraordinary degree of mobilization and incorporation of labour and peasants into the political system, who gave Rómulo Gallegos (AD) an overwhelming 74.4 per cent of the vote in the 1948 presidential elections. Nevertheless, such a drastic change in a very short time somehow managed to alarm almost every traditional political sector of society, and conflict escalated accordingly. Newly formed opposition political parties greatly resented AD's hegemonic pretensions over the newly incorporated sectors, arguing that AD was taking advantage of its position in the government to extend its hold on labour and the peasantry. For example, the Federation of Venezuelan Peasants (FCV), under AD's control, increased its membership from 6000 members in 1945 to some 43,000 in 1948, while the Confederation of Venezuelan Workers (CTV) organized more than 300,000 urban workers into thirteen AD-controlled federations.[19] In addition to the apprehensions aroused from seeing many of its members placed on trial for illicit enrichment with public monies, the reigning oligarchy feared the consequences of social and economic reforms on its privileged position, as well as the pernicious effects of escalating conflict on the possibilities of development. Appalled by a government decree attacking its educational prerogatives, the Church also began to mobilize its adherents.

The armed forces, which had helped to install the AD government, found itself shunted from key decision-making power once Rómulo Gallegos assumed the presidency. Having won by a large majority, Gallegos felt no great commitment to maintain the privileged role of the military, an increasingly uncontrollable social and political juncture notwithstanding. Less than eight months after he took office, efforts by opposing parties, the Church, and the upper class to mobilize the army against the government bore fruit. Even in these circumstances, however, the army moved only after it perceived itself to be threatened by two facts: 1 Registration in the Military Academies of several prominent members of AD, such as Valmore Rodríguez, Canache Mata, and Hernández Grisanti, led to heated accusations of attempted politicization of the officer corps, [20] a move strongly resented by the military institution. 2 Rumours, never substantiated but widely circulated, that AD was organizing paramilitary forces with the help of its trade union movement to provide a countervailing power to the army[21] served to make the officers coalesce around institutional interests and present a united front in the ensuing coup. The junior officers' initial objective in 1945 of professionalizing the armed forces had largely been achieved; at the same time, the military as an institution had developed the belief that it had a legitimate role to play in Venezuelan politics, at least in part to avoid dangers to its newly obtained institutionalization.

Another ten years of military rule followed, first, under the guise of a government of the armed forces, but which soon turned into a personalistic dictatorship under General Marcos Pérez Jiménez, one of the leaders of both the 1945 and 1948 revolts. The impressive unity of the armed forces and the almost unanimous support of opposition parties and traditional sectors for the coup which brought down the AD government in 1948 gradually began to wane, first with the assassination of General Carlos Delgado Chalbaud, President of the Military Junta, in 1950, and later with the arbitrary annulment of the elections of 1952 and the open seizure of power by Pérez Jiménez – a kind of coup within a coup. Public opinion, which accused Pérez Jiménez of being the intellectual author of the assassination of Delgado Chalbaud, was strong enough to prevent him from directly assuming the presidency in 1950. Even this was not enough to deter him in 1952, however, when the government was resoundingly defeated in national elections, which it had called in an effort to legitimize military rule. When the results began to be obvious, Pérez Jiménez ordered the counting of votes discontinued, accused Unión Republicana Democrática (URD), the winning party, of collaborating with the proscribed AD and PCV (Communist Party of Venezuela), 'invited' the winning candidate, Jóvito Villalba, to leave the country, and had himself proclaimed President of Venezuela.[22] Over time, support from the organized political parties had declined drastically, and at this point, only COPEI

(Christian Democratic Party) continued to operate legally. Although the military was not yet seriously divided, these events drove home the fact that a government of the armed forces no longer existed, only government by a clique of military officers, and some fissures began to appear in the military front.

While Pérez Jiménez continued to appeal to institutional unity to retain the support of the armed forces, he came to depend more and more on two civilian advisers – Laureano Vallenilla Lanz, Jr, the ideologue of the regime, and Pedro Estrada, the head of the feared political police organization Seguridad Nacional (SN). During this period, harsh repression under the direction of the SN was aimed not only at ending all the political and trade union activity encouraged during the three-year AD interregnum but any sign of dissent, whatever its source, including the military sector. Although the military was not directly involved in this disagreeable facet of government activity, it is not clear if this was part of a deliberate policy by Pérez Jiménez to deny the army more power[23] or just the result of his professional training as an officer, which inhibited him from involving the institution in this type of activity.[24] Whatever the reasons, the result was the same, and by the end of the decade discontent had grown much stronger inside the officer corps, fuelled not only by its marginalization from power but also because favouritism in promotions was once more the norm – in contrast to its ever-greater professionalization. The plebiscite of 1957 was the catalyst which mobilized both civilian and military opposition to the Pérez Jiménez dictatorship. For the first time, the armed forces were asked to participate actively in electoral fraud, requiring civilian employees to hand over the red electoral card after the election, as proof that they had voted with the blue card for the continuation of the regime.[25] Only fifteen days later, on 1 January 1958, an attempted coup led by Lt Col. Hugo Trejo marked the beginning of the end of the last military dictatorship in recent Venezuelan history.

The reasons given in 1958 by the military to justify intervention against the same government it had helped to create were that the SN was interfering in the army's affairs and persecuting officers of the armed forces, that the government had reached high levels of corruption and personalism and that this situation was creating strong resistance in civilian society, resistance that could affect the institution as a whole.[26] When the armed forces joined with the Junta Patriótica, a coalition of the four principal political parties (AD, COPEI, URD, and PCV), to overthrow Pérez Jiménez, genuine officers' discontent with the regime played a major role. However, given their prior involvement with the dictatorship, one could consider that they were following what has been a tendency among military regimes in South America:[27] that is, when a military government fails, it is not the institution but the individual officers involved who take the blame. In this way, the armed forces always protect their special status within the polity.

To assess civil–military relations in Venezuela prior to 1958 is no easy matter, since it encompasses a time span of more than one hundred years. Most of this period was dominated by two consecutive patterns of relationship: until 1899, a weak and almost nonexistent regular army coexisted with a very aggressive and armed civilian society that fought its own internal battles with private soldiers of occasion; and, from then until 1945, a professional armed body was formed and kept under control by a strong personalist government based on regional loyalties that even permeated the army. Relations changed after 1945 when that type of infiltration was abruptly ended by the action of the officers themselves. A truly professional army was born, one that for a while remained aloof from active participation in politics, until a new threat of political infiltration pushed the military back into the political arena in order to protect its achievements. When civilian pressure mounted against the military government they had put in power, the armed forces resorted to still another intervention in 1958. It should be noted that divisions within the armed forces permitted the successful transfer of power to civilian governments in both 1945 and 1958, while an impressive military compaction around institutional interests achieved a reverse transfer of power in 1948. Even in this case, however, the armed forces were responding not only to their institutional interests, but also to the socio-political context in which they were enmeshed. The new political system that developed after 1958 granted the armed forces the role of guardian of constitution and order, a role which they were only willing to honour after several years fraught with failed attempts to regain power and only after they were reassured that the well-being and the image of the institution would be adequately protected. It remained for civilian society to find a way to function without running the risk of feeding the officers' discontent and forcing them out of their barracks again. This was the task of the governments that sprang from the events of 1958.

A SUBSIDIZED DEMOCRACY: VENEZUELA SINCE 1958

An understanding of the Venezuelan political system which has developed since 1958 is crucial to any explanation of why the armed forces have withdrawn from overt positions of government. Nevertheless, the failure of the only other democratic experience of the twentieth century (1945–8) left an indelible mark on Venezuelan political leaders and severely constrained the possibilities of Venezuela's newly emerging regime. It is therefore with this first democratic experience that we must begin our analysis of the present political system.

One of the primary causes for the failure of that experience was the perception by political leaders of the lack of control over the process of incorporating new sectors into the political system. Rómulo Betancourt, the controversial but undisputed leader of that period, openly admitted the responsibility which fell on his own party (AD) for the military coup of 1948.[28] The military coup and ten years of exile and repression forced all of Venezuela's political elites to emphasize the paramount importance of control in a future return to democracy. As Daniel Levine succinctly pinpoints:

> Politics during the trienio [1945–1948] was characterized by widespread, bitter, and unceasing conflict, which culminated in a military dictatorship and a decade of brutal repression. The experience of these years profoundly affected Venezuelan political leaders. They became convinced that their incapacity to control and channel this widespread conflict was what had opened the door for a military coup. They also learned that political leadership involves more than simple adherence to ideology and program – conciliation and bargaining became key political values.[29]

But compromise, conciliation, and bargaining with other elites becomes impossible if political leaders cannot control the demands of their own organizations. Thus, an emphasis on discipline and the necessity for greater control arise as an integral part of the very conception of politics with the return to power in a democratic system in 1958. The same author notes the fragility of Venezuelan politics when he states that

> Political leaders seem to be constantly looking over their shoulders in Venezuela since 1958. They behave as if political institutions might fall apart at any moment, and therefore require constant care and attention to stay afloat. The memory of past conflicts and the fear of renewed military dictatorship arising in response to uncontrollable conflict drove many leaders to handle politics with extreme care.[30]

In an earlier analysis of Venezuelan elites, Frank Bonilla also sensed this fragility, pointing out that the most important constraint on Venezuelan politics is not objective, but rather subjective; this goes hand in hand with an 'acknowledged deference to power blocs with a marginally legitimate political role – the army, economic pressure groups, oil companies, the United States'.[31] Singly or in conjunction, these groups have enormous capacity to destabilize the new system, but, because their power does not rest on the mobilization of popular support, control over them lies largely outside the scope of political parties, the backbone of Venezuelan government since 1958. Thus, some sort of modus vivendi is mandated. Fear of uncontrollable conflict, renewed military intervention and the power of those important sectors with only a 'marginally legitimate political role' has been the cornerstone of Venezuelan politics since 1958, leading to the absence of overt political conflict, characterized by Moisés Naím and Ramón Piñango as the 'missing link in recent Venezuelan evolution' and the avoidance of conflict as 'the inviolable norm' of the democratic system.[32] In short, conflict must be controlled or avoided, at all costs, since open conflict alienates and frightens those power blocs over which Venezuelan parties, and, in consequence, Venezuelan governments, have only minimal control, undermining political stability and endangering the all-important goal of economic development. Betancourt understood this very clearly, proposing to a group of industrialists and union leaders in 1958 a 'pact of economic development and labour peace as the way to consolidate the regime of democratic institutions'.[33]

One of the first expressions of this attempt to avoid conflict can be found in the Pact of Punto Fijo (1958) among the three major democratic parties (AD, COPEI, URD), explicitly excluding the Communist Party, a pact that established a truce for inter-party conflicts and rivalries during the upcoming election, respect for its outcome, and a government of National Unity, regardless of which party won. Less explicitly, the Pact of Punto Fijo also determined which groups would have access to policy making in the new system. 'The principal actors would be the major political parties, the major employers' association, the major union, all to be protected by the armed forces and blessed by the Church.'[34] The cement which could hold together such diverse sectors of society during the ensuing coalition government would be the enactment of a 'Minimum Program' of social and economic reforms and an ambitious industrialization programmme, which together would assure political stability and economic development.[35] The importance of this 'Minimum Program' and the interrelationships among its components were made diaphanously clear in the AD party platform of 1962:

> We are aiming to put into practice a wide spectrum [sic] which will awaken and sustain private initiative through cheap credits and rational protective tariffs to fight the invasion of foreign products. This, and the increase in the buying power of the population through an honest and broad social policy, will increase the domestic market, a necessary step in the development of a national industry and agriculture. We do not make our fervent proclamation for a policy of bettering the conditions of workers and peasants only through loyalty to the principles of social justice ... We also recognize a scientific and practical reason: without this improvement, the internal market necessary for a Venezuelan agriculture and industry cannot be created.[36]

Without the availability of relatively abundant resources, however, Venezuelan leaders would have been hard put to ensure the survival and consolidation of the democratic system by means of social reforms and economic growth, while simultaneously controlling the levels of conflict. Those resources were based on Venezuela's oil rent, which had been strengthening the economic capacity of the state for more than fifty years and which, in the Constitution of 1961, had converted the state into the economic and social rector of Venezuelan life. Perhaps it should be noted that before the enactment of the Hydrocarbons Law of 1943, which envisioned a 50/50 split of the oil companies' profits, the Venezuelan state was essentially a weak state. By 1945, however, the state's economic capacity had been greatly enhanced, as oil income surpassed taxes as a source of revenue. Based on that income, the state was charged, in the Constitution of 1961, with guaranteeing social (Arts 72–94) and economic rights (Arts 95–109) to its citizens, as well as being the driving force in economic development. Over the years, the Venezuelan government has penetrated deeper and deeper into economic and social activities, leaving fewer areas outside its regulatory purview, with a consequent increase in its possibility for control over society.

In this way, Venezuelan governments after 1958 were able to act concurrently on several fronts and therefore to avoid the risks of zero-sum politics – both promoting the wealth of the private sector and providing social and economic policies favourable to workers, peasants, and the middle classes. In other words, it was only in conjunction with the fortuitous circumstance of relatively abundant resources from oil that successive governments were able to achieve their primary goal of consolidating the democratic system by offering something to every major sector of society, according to its potential disruptive power. It should be pointed out that President Betancourt made every effort to avoid a situation such as that in the 1945–8 period, when the AD government was accused of granting benefits to organized labour and peasants, to the detriment of other important groups. Now, resources were often channelled to the various sectors by means of infrastructural improvements (reproductive investments, education, health, and social services) rather than particular benefits such as salary increases. At one point, faced with severe economic difficulties, Betancourt even decreed a 10 per cent salary cut for all state employees, including members of the armed forces, but he simultaneously increased expenditures for education, health, and welfare programmes by 100 per cent.[37]

Even though it has been the state which has provided the prebends to guarantee adherence to the democratic political system, the big winners have been the political parties, through which the patronage resources of the state have been distributed. Little by little, the consolidation of the system made the political parties the most appropriate channels through which to grant access to credits, permits, exemptions, jobs, scholarships, etc. After all, this is quite logical in view of the fact that the parties that participated in the Pact of Punto Fijo have been the primary channels of control over the popular sectors. It is noteworthy that these sectors are not tied directly to the state, but only indirectly through the political parties, particularly the establishment parties: AD and COPEI.[38] These links have been based on the creation of clientelistic networks, which by their very nature involve the unequal exchange of goods and services as well as a large measure of control over the clientele's activities.

Until recently, the exchange aspect of this clientelistic relationship has been more prevalent, while the aspect of control has been more subtle, due perhaps to the lack of a deep-rooted legitimacy, in conjunction with the availability of resources at the state's disposal. Nevertheless, the fact that it has been more subtle is not to deny its importance. On the contrary, the degree of control that the parties can exercise has been strengthened by their ability to create a multiplicity of encapsulated clientelistic networks, thus diluting the possibility of generalized conflict by disaggregating demands. This manifests itself in the fact that political campaigns in Venezuela are not noted for their substantive content, and parties are not overly concerned with formulating coherent programmes of aggregated interests, which, in any case, are usually presented very late in the campaign.

In summary, the Venezuelan political system developed since 1958 has been based on the economic capacity of the state to subsidize democracy, providing the prebends necessary to maintain a certain consensus around the democratic system. In this process, the political parties have played a fundamental role. They have incorporated new popular sectors into the political system by means of enormous clientelistic networks, which are composed of a multiplicity of smaller networks. In this way, the political parties achieved an ample popular base for the political system at the same time that they diffused the conflict that could arise from electoral competition. This has given the system a certain representativeness while permitting other contenders, whose power base has nothing to do with the mobilization of popular support, to obtain access to the formulation of policy. As David Blank aptly states,

> The political parties since 1958 have been the crucial actors in establishing representative democracy; they have been relatively unimportant actors in the determination of economic development policy. ... No party government, in the sense that party program determined government policy, has existed in post-1958 Venezuela.[39]

Perhaps the most patent examples of just how true this statement is have occurred in the years since Blank published his book – in the first administration of Carlos Andrés Pérez (1974–9) and those of Luis Herrera Campíns (1979–84) and Jaime Lusinchi (1984–9) – when tensions between the government and the governing party reached levels such that the governing party appeared to be in the opposition. This would seem to offer undisputable proof that Venezuelan political parties function much more as channels to control conflict than as channels of access to policy making.

Once the system became more solid and institutionalized by the 1970s, the control aspect of the clientelist relationship took precedence over exchange, as support from traditional clienteles (peasants, organized labour, etc.) came to be taken for granted and less attention was paid to their demands. At this point, the 'captive' nature of popular-sector organizations as well as middle-class professional associations, etc., becomes quite evident. These organizations have been converted into appendages of the political parties, for all practical purposes, and the parties have found it to their advantage to maintain them with very little autonomy. On another level, the autonomous leadership that permits the conciliation and bargaining among elites, which is so characteristic of the Venezuelan political system, is found precisely on the level of control achieved over these organizations. That this pattern has been detrimental to popular and middle sectors becomes patently clear if we examine the distribution of national income, which, until 1970, had remained quite stable, but at that point began to become much more skewed, in favour of the wealthier sectors.[40] The docile acceptance by organized labour of economic measures implemented by President Jaime Lusinchi in 1984, designed to confront the debt crisis by reducing previous gains made by unions, provides a further example of the level of party control exercised over this sector.

Not only have traditional clienteles been neglected; neither have new clienteles been incorporated into the system, despite the impressive transformation of Venezuelan society since 1958 in the areas of urbanization, industrialization, education, and overall social complexity. Much as in other Latin American countries, those sectors, particularly the urban poor, unincorporated into the political system in the heat of its original development have remained so.[41] Political parties and successive governments, however, deeply involved in perpetuating their own power, have apparently failed to perceive this situation until recently. Conflicts, nevertheless, have not been resolved, only postponed. Thus, when a crisis, such as the present one of shrinking state resources, arises, old underlying conflicts are exacerbated, and often begin to surface at a time when the system is least capable of confronting them. Oil, which still provides almost all of Venezuela's foreign exchange and a large majority of total government revenues, in recent years has suffered a dramatic fall in prices – from over US $30.00 per barrel in 1979–80 to less than US $15.00 a barrel in 1988, thus halving government income. Parallel to this, Venezuela had accumulated, by 1983, a total external debt of US $38.421 billion[42] and the distinction of being the fourth-largest debtor of Latin America, in spite of its relatively small population.

As a consequence of the foregoing combination of circumstances, a sharp decline in the general standard of living has led to growing demands for distributive measures. Since, however, the economic capacity of the state to maintain adherence to the political system has been severely diminished, the state, and the political parties associated with it, must attempt to sustain and reinforce the mechanisms of political control by searching for other values to offer in exchange for disciplined political loyalty. One of these alternatives which has surfaced with ever-greater force in Venezuela in recent years is the possibility of political reforms, which could have the short-term effect of reinforcing political control and give the regime breathing space to implement its economic policy, but in the long run such political reforms would inevitably alter the very basis of control. Perhaps it is the consciousness of this contradiction that explains why political leaders in Venezuela have continually flirted with and then almost invariably reneged on political reforms.

In short, subsidized democracy made possible the integration of different sectors in the new political system after 1958, obtaining their support by means of the resources available to the state. The system has been characterized, at the top, by compromise, conciliation, and bargaining among elites, both political and non-political, including the armed forces. This has been facilitated by the role of the political parties as control networks reaching down to the grassroots. In spite of the existence of non-integrated sectors and a multiplicity of unfulfilled demands, the system has been able to survive for over thirty years.

THE VENEZUELAN ARMED FORCES: 1958–88

In 1958, the Venezuelan armed forces found themselves in an extremely delicate situation, due largely to the loss of prestige of its dominant body – the army – for its long-time association with the Pérez Jiménez dictatorship. That loss of prestige made dormant rivalries among the four branches much more acute, causing a great deal of internal conflict and leading navy and air force officers to participate actively in the overthrow of the Pérez Jiménez regime, as exemplified both by the uprising of the air force on 1 January 1958, and the navy's leading role in the formation of the new government. From his position as president of the interim junta that ruled Venezuela after Pérez Jiménez fled the country, Admiral Wolfgang Larrazábal decreed the creation of the Joint Chiefs of Staff to replace the centralized command system of the previous structure, in an effort to increase the influence of those branches heretofore marginalized. In the previous structure, centralized power was in the hands of the minister of defence and the commanders of the different branches primarily functioned as his secretaries. The new decree by the provisional government went far towards facilitating civilian control over the military in the new political system. Each of the branches of the armed forces acquired autonomy in matters of command, organization, training, administration, and budget. The objective of this decree was to create a 'structural equilibrium among the armed forces that ... grants equal representation to the ground, sea, and air forces'.[43] Even though this structure basically originated from inter-service rivalries, successive civilian governments found it to their own advantage to maintain it, since the autonomy of each branch required the existence of a superior coordinating figure to arbitrate inter-service conflicts, arising from competition over budgetary resources. The president came to fulfil this role and was thus able to exercise substantial leverage on the military institution.[44] For this reason, Rómulo Betancourt chose to uphold this decree and personally intervened to quell inter-service disputes, in spite of the army's resistance and various instances of conflict with the navy.[45] The creation of the Joint Chiefs of Staff, plus the elimination of a common training school for officers of the four branches (founded during the government of Pérez Jiménez), and the almost total autonomy of the various forces made possible the acceptance of civilian control by the military high-command.

Due in part to these internal divisions within the armed forces, the first democratically elected civilian government after 1958 was confronted by some 28 conspiracies from both the right and the left, in only five years.[46] In the first two years, major threats came principally from the right, from dissident elements within the army who reacted to the military's loss of power in the new regime. Gradually, these threats were overcome and supplanted by those from the left which, before the years of guerrilla warfare, involved navy officers (uprisings of Carúpano and Puerto Cabello in 1962), supported by leftist political parties excluded from the Pact of Punto Fijo. In these circumstances, military policy was crucial, especially in a situation where a feeling of mutual mistrust pervaded relationships between the military and civil society, for historical reasons.

Accordingly, the strategy which Betancourt assumed vis-à-vis the military was to be the pivot on which future democratic stability in Venezuela rested. In the ensuing paragraphs, we will analyse Betancourt's strategy on two levels: within the military sphere, and in civilian politics. On the first level, one of Betancourt's most important decisions was not to interfere with the military institution by changing the officers in command. He clearly sensed the risks involved in assuming such a position when he admitted:

> I was asked by some of the communists and some sectors of my own party to proceed with a massive and quick depuration of the high command of the National Armed Forces, in order to stabilize democracy. I did not follow that advice because it was bad advice. I could not proceed to effect those massive discharges, those changes in command, because then I would be the one discharged.[47]

He simultaneously took advantage of the policy implanted by the interim junta of reinstating officers who had been removed during the dictatorship, most of whom had been discharged for conspiratorial activity against the Pérez Jiménez regime. These officers would be favoured during his presidency with special courses to speed up their promotions and to permit their appointment to positions of command in key garrisons. Their reinstatement created claims of questionable constitutionality by the opposition, but the President simply paid no heed, because he needed a core group of officers loyal to the democratic system. Subsequent insurrectional attempts would provide the opportunity to purge from the armed forces officers compromised in those attempts, a measure that facilitated further depuration of disaffected elements from both the right and the left. At the same time, Betancourt continued and strengthened the policy initiated by the provisional junta of increasing the costs of military insurrection, as a measure to discourage their repetition.[48]

Betancourt also demonstrated his ability as a politician in his appointment as minister of defence for most of his administration of Brigadier General Antonio Briceño Linares of the air force, a branch which was not directly involved in the clash between the more reactionary army and the more radical navy,[49] and thus represented a more moderate balance. In addition, he took a personal approach to military problems in his constant visits to military bases, attendance at military parades and other events, lectures to officers and enlisted men, always stressing that he had been democratically elected and that the 'Armed Forces had contributed by their example to the recuperation of civilian republican institutions', that party politics would not enter the barracks during his term, and that his government would provide the reforms and resources necessary to make the armed forces 'a model of technical development and professional competence'.[50]

On the level of civilian politics, Rómulo Betancourt insisted, first and foremost, that relations with the military were his exclusive responsibility, and refused to allow any interference even by his own party. Although he was quite willing to form a coalition government and to permit opposition politicians to occupy sensitive ministries, he was adamant in his refusal to accept party oversight in any matter relating to the military. In his own words, 'I direct military policy, the constitution gives me that right and I am not willing to share it with the party. I'll be damned if I will be overthrown like Gallegos, that much I can tell you'.[51]

In spite of the political problems which this stance cost him in his own party, the existence of a united and coherent political leadership, based on the Pact of Punto Fijo, facilitated the maintenance of this policy. Perhaps this consensus achieved by political elites, with support from important economic sectors, the Church, and intellectuals, constituted the decisive factor in establishing a successful civilian pre-eminence over the military. The fact that no major sector of society was willing to participate in a new military regime did not make disaffected officers less prone to engage in conspiratorial actions, but did assure that, deprived of civilian support, a new military government would have little chance of success. For example, as early as 1958, when Defence Minister General Jesús María Castro León attempted to subvert the interim junta by offering the presidency to Eugenio Mendoza, a prominent industrialist, he was unable to persuade the conservative entrepreneur to accept.[52] Business elements had been won over to the new government not only by the promises implicit in its industrialization programme, but also by its decision to honour the enormous debt to the private sector which had been left by Pérez Jiménez.

A second aspect of Betancourt's strategy to provide a countervailing power to the military was the ubiquitous organization of Venezuelan society in political parties and trade unions, which he considered to be the two forces indispensable to secure and maintain the democratic order. This was useful in mobilizing mass support for the democratic government, when faced with the numerous uprisings of this period. Even during the transitional government, when the political parties were only beginning the process of rebuilding their own organizations, their power to mobilize supporters was already impressive: in both July and September, 1958, attempted coups were met with important manifestations of that power – the call for a general strike by major parties, employers, and workers' associations, threats that forced Wolfgang Larrazábal to be less tolerant of conspiracy among his fellow officers. In 1960, General Jesús María Castro León's second attempt to overthrow the government was frustrated not only by a general strike, but also by the peasants of the region where he invaded Venezuela, who effected his capture and turned him over to the military courts to be judged.[53]

As pressures escalated, the leftist menace replaced the right, especially after the 1960 expulsion of AD's youthful left wing, which joined with the Venezuelan Communist Party in calling for the removal of Betancourt from office. The government continued to use the same tactics of mass mobilization against the left, tactics which still proved successful. Thus, in the 1963 presidential elections, the leftist parties, now in open rebellion, called for a general strike (that was ignored) and for electoral abstention, threatening to employ violence against those who wanted to vote. Popular reaction to this threat was a massive electoral turn-out. In the words of Antonio José Urbina, then a communist militant, referring to the elections of 1963 in the city of Coro:

> every two hours we placed thunderous bombs in the proximity of voting centres in order to disperse the queues of voters. ... Upon hearing the explosion, the voters dispersed but ten minutes later even the old men ... and women returned to the queue to deposit their votes. There was no way to make them desist. We distributed flyers with the slogans 'do not vote', 'the government is antidemocratic', 'Betancourt's law of hunger',... well, all those slogans were useless: people accepted the flyers with a 'yes, my child', and flyers in hand, voted.[54]

Nevertheless, such loyalty to the democratic regime would not have been possible without the implementation of policies such as those represented in the 'Minimum Programme' of the Pact of Punto Fijo – agrarian reform, education, and other policies designed to improve the welfare of popular sectors, all feasible only due to Venezuela's increasing oil rent.

When the left resorted to guerrilla activity against the government, it inadvertently contributed to the strength of the democratic experience both by giving the armed forces a prominent role to play and by making Betancourt more acceptable to the military. Now the armed forces found themselves confronted by a state of affairs that required the application of their professionalized training, and for which they could count on support and resources from both the Venezuelan and the United States governments. The military was hailed by the government as a defender of the stability of democratic institutions, a mission which it was ready to accept after having failed to regain control of political power in previous years. The consolidation of this role of the military can be traced through its degree of participation in the war against the guerrillas. In the first stages of this war (urban terrorism), the main effort fell on the police and it was not until 1963 (rural-based guerrilla warfare) that the military assumed the central role in this struggle, after undergoing a process of preparation and training.[55] It is worthy of note that both the armed forces and the government were now more disposed to accept the new role of the military as guardian of the institutions of the democratic regime, instead of being a primary contender for power.

Betancourt also used this situation to promote himself as a moderate social reformer and an anti-Communist, thus making himself more acceptable to the armed forces. Perhaps it should be mentioned that, since 1940, Betancourt had often been accused of being a communist, an accusation that Pérez Jiménez repeatedly emphasized in his dealings with the military. The reputation thus acquired had been extremely difficult to refute: the left provided him with a golden opportunity. Moreover, the example of what had happened to the regular army in Cuba under Fidel Castro played upon the institutional fears of the Venezuelan armed forces, giving them more internal coherence and constituting a recurring theme in the President's speeches.

Betancourt's preoccupation not to alienate the armed forces led him to cede to their pressure to respond forcefully to subversive actions, and gave them free rein regarding repressive measures; however, he took great care to personally bear the brunt of responsibility.[56] In this way, he preserved the image of the armed forces as a positive institution, a fact that was reflected in the MIT–CENDES national survey of 1963, in which 64 per cent of respondents approved of the role of the military, while only 39 per cent approved of that of politicians.[57] These findings are quite interesting if we remember that only five years before, popular reaction had helped the political parties, organized in the Junta Patriótica, to overthrow a repressive military regime, and that resentment against the role of the military in that dictatorship had even affected the prestige of the armed forces as an institution.[58]

Another way of removing responsibility from the military, to which Betancourt often resorted, was to lay the blame for both military insurrection and leftist subversion on forces external to Venezuela. In spite of the fact that leaders of the various rightist attempts against the government were Venezuelan officers, Betancourt always managed to relate those attempts to external enemies, such as Leónidas Trujillo of the Dominican Republic and the exiled Pérez Jiménez, absolving the Venezuelan military of any blame.[59] On the other hand, as mentioned earlier Betancourt never missed an opportunity to ascribe to Castro the financing and supply of the Venezuelan guerrilla effort. This strategy meshed well with United States policy against hemispheric subversion and led to over US $60,000,000 in aid to Venezuela for military equipment and training, 'twice the amount of military aid supplied during the 1950s'.[60] Credits and grants for military assistance were continued throughout the decade, unlike economic assistance programmes which tapered off during successive administrations. In addition to the subversive threat from the left, the United States government recognized that the Venezuelan armed forces would be, in the final analysis, responsible for the demise or success of the democratic experience;[61] for this reason, they granted the resources needed to keep them within the system.

Civil–military relations during later administrations have basically followed the course laid down by Betancourt, suffering variations mostly in the direction of greater trust and normalization between these sectors. Proof of this is that from 1962 until 1972, military calls for action against the democratically elected governments declined dramatically. That year, former Minister of Defence General Martín García Villasmil hinted at a coup (a call which went unheeded) to prevent the return of Rómulo Betancourt as a presidential candidate in the elections the following year; however, García Villasmil was reacting not so much against the democratic institutions as against the person of Betancourt, whom he considered responsible for blocking his promotion.[62] This highlights a considerable change from previous calls to insurrection, where the decisive factor was related more to institutional mistrust than to personality clashes. It is, nevertheless, an interesting fact that Betancourt subsequently declined his party's candidacy.

One characteristic of both Betancourt's and following administrations has been the attention paid to the socio-economic welfare of military personnel, attention which encompasses a whole range of aspects from special housing programmes to professional training aimed at improving the qualifications and promotion of officers. Likewise, Venezuelan elected governments have been careful to maintain officers' salaries at a level similar to that of United States military officers. This has worked as an effective system of co-optation, giving birth to what has been called 'the golden marginality' of the armed forces.[63] The attractiveness of a military career can be seen in the greater number of candidates applying to the military academies after 1963, even though educational requirements had been raised substantially.[64] As John V. Lombardi has aptly summarized, the armed forces

> stayed with the government ... because the government gave them a mission and the resources to carry it out. Thanks to the guerrilla threat from the left, the armed forces had a job of internal security to accomplish, and the government lost no opportunity to equip the soldiers well and honoured their leaders extravagantly.[65]

The end of the guerrilla war marks the beginning of another period in civil–military relations – that of the decade of the 1970s. At this stage, the emphasis would change towards the military's assuming new roles in a pacified society, maintaining its preparation and responsibility for the stability of democratic institutions. One major accomplishment during this decade was the reduction of mutual mistrust between the armed forces and civilian society. It should be noted that the thrust for greater cooperation came largely from the military sector itself, [66] which now felt more at ease with Venezuelan society. As a reflection of this situation, the armed forces created the Institute of Higher Studies of National Defence (IAEDEN), with civilian participation both at the level of students and faculty. The importance of this institution can be seen in the fact that, even though Congress had approved unreservedly, in 1976, the Law of National Security and Defence (which was basically a copy of Argentine and Brazilian national security laws and, accordingly, highly authoritarian), only three years later the IAEDEN was involved in discussions directed towards the formulation of a new law adapted to Venezuelan democratic institutions.[67]

In light of diminishing problems of internal security and as an outgrowth of civic action programmes of the previous decade, the 1970s witnessed increased military participation in development programmes, such as the navy's role in the construction of an aqueduct for the island of Margarita and the army's building of highways in remote areas. In addition, the armed forces initiated and maintained welfare programmes for the population of marginal sectors (vaccination campaigns, programmes of dental health, etc.) and disaster or emergency relief (sheltering and feeding refugees from floods and mud slides, etc.). As well as providing much-needed services, these programmes also contributed to promoting the image of the military institution among the civilian population.[68]

Even though guerrilla activity was practically non-existent during these years, the quantity and quality of military purchases increased substantially, and the government made an effort to maintain a balance in the participation of the different branches of the armed forces. While these purchases were important from the institutional point of view, betterment of the economic situation of military personnel was never neglected. It has been calculated that in 1976, personnel expenditures alone represented over US $ 5000 per man in the armed forces, a figure 'almost two and one half times the national per capita income'.[69] Gradually, other subsidies have been incorporated to the system of privileges for the military (complete health and dental care for military personnel and their families, generous retirement plans, low-interest loans for education and housing, etc.). An example of the scope of the benefits from these programmes is found in the special military stores in five different Venezuelan cities, which each year sell approximately 400 million Bolívares of top-quality merchandise at discount prices. With the proceeds from these transactions, they are able to support most of the costs of the Military Hospital and to provide Christmas gifts and bonuses to military families.[70]

Increasing civil–military interactions began to produce a new phenomenon in the 1980s: open clashes between these sectors surfaced more often, but seemed to be more easily absorbed in the normal give and take of politics, without provoking more than a few ripples in the structures of the democratic system. This was evidenced by the debate over the purchase of F-16 fighter planes, a debate initiated in 1980, when the Air Force Commander publicly announced his force's intention to acquire a new fleet of these planes. He justified this decision on the need to strengthen national security, which was perceived as being menaced by the potential of Cuban aviation, which would be able to reach any corner of Venezuela after the completion of the Grenada airport. An unusual fact about this decision was that the Joint Chiefs of Staff, including the Minister of Defence, were unaware of the commitment until they read of it in the newspapers. Subsequently, they found out that the purchase had already been approved by President Luis Herrera Campíns (COPEI) and that the United States government considered the transaction to be definitive. The Minister of Defence and the Joint Chiefs of Staff produced a document stating that, even if the acquisition was justified in terms of national security, it was by no means acceptable to buy 48 planes of the same type from the same dealer, since this would create extreme dependence on one source of supply, and, perhaps even more important, it would reduce the possibility of acquisitions by the other branches. Meanwhile, the debate had reached Congress and the mass media. The Air Force Commander, in a speech towards the end of 1981, referred to 'supposed commercial interests and ideologies contrary to the national interest among those who oppose the purchase of the F-16s'.[71] When both AD and URD rejected this accusation, they created the first public confrontation between a high-ranking military commander and the political parties since the period of Betancourt's administration. At this point, the President intervened, declaring that the decision to buy or not to buy the fighter planes was not the prerogative of Congress. Thus, he brought to the fore the sensitive fact that military budgets were not under the purview of Congress, and in fact, were accountable to no one.[72] Finally, by May 1982, two agreements had been reached: one within the different branches of the armed forces to reduce to 24 the number of planes to be purchased and to distribute the remaining money among the other branches, and another agreement between AD and COPEI to support budgetary approval by Congress. This long-running debate was the first indication that civil–military relations had normalized to the point that politicians felt they could risk meddling in the military policy of the executive.

The new climate of normalization of relations was also to be seen in the call by the left-of-centre parties Movimiento al Socialismo (MAS) and Movimiento Electoral del Pueblo (MEP) for a constitutional amendment to give the vote to members of the armed forces, a move opposed by the establishment parties AD and COPEI. It should be noted that until the present decade, this policy proposal would have been unthinkable, especially coming from the left. During the 1980s, debates and criticisms in the mass media and in Congress over arms purchases and military participation in control of the drug trade has even reached the point of accusations of administrative corruption – a further consequence of normalization. While no high military officers have been found guilty of these accusations, the fact that ministers of defence have had to appear before congressional committees to provide information and/or to defend the institution is eloquent testimony that these matters are no longer taboo.

Party politics have also been instrumental in closing the gap between the civilian and military sectors of society, creating a mutual interdependence. Promotions below the rank of colonel are almost automatic and are the exclusive domain of the armed forces; above this rank, however, both the President and Congress have power over promotions. While this system has been criticized for politicizing promotions, [73] it has tended to further the identification of high-ranking officers with one of the two establishment parties, as a means of assuring their future careers. Tensions do surface annually when some officers consider that they have been unduly passed over, for partisan reasons, but the system survives, perhaps as a result of the fact that less than 5 per cent of nominations for military promotions have ever been questioned in Congress, much less rejected.[74] Moreover, those which have been questioned by one major party have almost invariably been supported by the other, such as that of García Villasmil, who had been passed over for promotion by Betancourt and AD, but was later promoted by COPEI, and that of General Carlos Carnevali, identified with AD, who complained of unfair treatment by President Rafael Caldera (COPEI, 1969–74). A different case is that presented by the retirement of Admiral Ricardo Sosa Ríos during the administration of President Raúl Leoni (AD, 1964–9), which was provoked by his reaction to Leoni's recommendation of certain promotions which had not previously been approved by the navy.[75] Such problems notwithstanding, we concur with Eugene Bigler that 'neither partisan nor personal favouritism over promotions and assignments has yet led to very grave abuses, such as the rise of raving incompetents'.[76]

In summary, civil–military relations have suffered a substantial transformation during the last three decades, due partly to changes in the military institution itself, but largely to changes in the political system and the consequences which this has had in the Venezuelan social and political context. If we compare the situation in 1958 with that of 1988, for example, it becomes easily observable that the armed forces have gained renewed prestige, which was at a very low level in 1958. Also, the character of military participation in politics has undergone a radical transformation: from active involvement in insurrectionary activities to a much more subtle identification with reigning party politics.

During these thirty years, Betancourt was the key figure in the transformation suffered in civil–military relations. His policies vis-à-vis the armed forces were based on two complementary levels of strategy: in civilian politics, the most important elements were the mobilization of organized popular support in conjunction with the conciliation and negotiation of conflict with opposing political elites, and the co-optation of other influential sectors devoid of popular support. In this way, he was able to make it more difficult for the armed forces to obtain backing for insurrectional activities outside their own institution. His strictly military policy involved the weakening of the vertical and unified command structure of previous years, the exclusion of officers implicated in conspiracies against the government and their replacement by officers committed to the idea of a democratic system, the development of a new role for the military in defence of democratic institutions, and the improvement of the status of the armed forces by granting them generous resources at both the institutional and individual levels. Once this pattern was established, civil–military relations have varied in the same general direction – towards greater normalization. We can distinguish the 1970s as a decade characterized by increased contact between civilian and military sectors and a reduction in the mutual mistrust of previous years. In the 1980s, normalization of relations even reached the point of public debate on military matters, a topic long considered taboo. Subsidized democracy appears to have demonstrated a relatively high capability to integrate civilian and military sectors into the mainstream of a common system.

CIVIL–MILITARY RELATIONS AND THE DEMISE OF SUBSIDIZED DEMOCRACY

The present socio-economic crisis in Venezuela may force a reassessment of civil–military relations. Since 1983, Venezuela has been hard hit by the simultaneous pressures created by a drastic fall in oil prices on the international market and the need to repay the huge public debt contracted during the years of the petroleum boom in the 1970s. It is hardly necessary to stress the importance of oil in Venezuela, which for years has been the fundamental pillar of the subsidized democratic system. In recent years, it has become increasingly evident that oil revenues can no longer sustain the co-optation of every major social sector, in this way exacerbating latent conflicts. At the same time, the debilitation of the state's capacity of co-optation has also weakened its capacity to control or avoid conflict within the society.

February 1989, witnessed the most dramatic manifestations of the new situation. Spontaneous popular protests, related to specific grievances against unauthorized hikes in bus fares, speculation in foodstuffs (causing undue scarcities), and the implementation of an economic shock programme (based on IMF guidelines) turned into massive destruction of private property, arson, looting, and loss of lives.[77] After two days of rioting in sixteen Venezuelan towns and cities, the government was forced to call out the armed forces, impose a 6:00 p.m. to 6:00 a.m. curfew, and suspend constitutional guarantees, in order to regain control of the situation. Even so, it took almost a week to re-establish order. Over 10,000 troops were mobilized to Caracas from all over the country, and were generally received with relief by the civilian population, which had been taken by surprise by the magnitude of the anarchy.[78] Although the armed forces had to resort to severe measures of repression before they were able to restore order, the military high command insisted that they were only acting on behalf of Venezuela's democratic system, which they were committed to safeguard. In spite of many rumours of a coup, the military returned to the barracks once normal conditions again prevailed. As an indication of popular reaction to military intervention in these events, a survey conducted by a major Venezuelan university shows an interesting result – Defence Minister General Italo del Valle Alliegro reached approximately an 80 per cent approval rate, over a month after the fact.[79] This was perhaps aided by the fact that political leadership was notoriously absent during the events of February, excepting the President's message announcing the imposition of martial law.

In light of severe economic deterioration, with its subsequent loss of resources for co-optation, plus the most aggressive popular reaction of the democratic period, is civilian rule in Venezuela likely to continue? An answer to this question rests mainly on the capability of party politics to regain control over the popular sectors – those hit hardest both by the crisis and government shock measures to resolve it. The options appear to be basically two: either political parties maintain and extend their control of civil society, in which case civilian rule will probably continue, or, if discontent becomes unmanageable, it is possible that the military will step in.

Regarding the first possibility – a continuation of the system by means of expanded party control, it should be noted that Venezuelan political parties possess a large reserve of organizational strength. Moreover, party politics permeate the entire society, on every imaginable level – from the appointment of an office-boy to the granting of government contracts. That the primary objective of such infiltration of civil society is greater political control is quite evident from the apprehension and mistrust with which independent movements are regarded by political parties, and the quick responses that these movements evoke. For example, when non-partisan neighbourhood associations began organizing in Venezuela, the political parties quickly sensed their potential and moved in.[80] As resources become scarcer, the need to identify with a political party is ever more important in order to obtain a share of diminished resources, thus providing an opportunity to extend the parties' leverage in society. Here a crucial factor may be the emergence of new leaders, able to aggregate not only material demands of the popular sectors but also their aspirations for greater participation in the political system. For this to function, however, the parties will have to develop new and more creative responses, breaking the bonds of bureaucracy and developing new forms of popular participation. One could begin to see an attempt in this direction in the various parties' efforts to organize debtors' clubs among owners who face the tripling of interest rates on mortgages, and in the new, more aggressive stance of the CTV, a stance assumed by labour leaders of the same establishment parties.

Now, when the government's ability to grant material demands in exchange for control seems too fragile even to satisfy existing clientele networks, the probability of extending control to those outside these networks is almost nil. The implementation of political reforms, which would permit greater majoritarian influence on the input side of the system, would appear to offer a logical alternative. Nevertheless, their implementation would involve a consequent relaxation of political controls and the increment of probable destabilizing effects, especially if done without the prior establishment of minimum rules of the game to channel conflict along a less dangerous course. However, the establishment of generally acceptable mechanisms of conflict management becomes ever more difficult. It is quite obvious, for example, at this point, that greater popular influence on policy would result in demands for changes in economic policy, such that the burden of economic problems weigh less heavily on the popular and middle sectors. Equally obvious is that demands for distributive measures run directly counter to external pressures, and also to pressures from a smaller but still powerful internal sector of society. Given the implications of political reforms for the future functioning of the system, it is quite understandable that Venezuelan governments have been more than a little hesitant to implement these reforms, despite the enlarging control gap.

Also, with the consolidation of the political system, party attention to popular demands diminished considerably while its internal bureaucratization and concentration on intra-and inter-party rivalries became the core of its activities. By ignoring the strength of popular demands and reacting to some of them only sporadically, the parties weakened their own ability to channel and control those demands and opened the door to other less institutionalized channels, such as violent demonstrations. In just such a way, the events of February 1989, caught political leaders wholly unaware of the degree of popular frustration. Given these circumstances, even if parties are able to accommodate to this new situation, it will take some time for them to be able to regain the level of control which they had previously enjoyed. Meanwhile, the escalation of violence would present a serious risk of military intervention, quite probably under the guise of protecting the democratic system.

If we look at the prospects of renewed military intervention in Venezuelan politics from the point of view of a broader analysis of how and why South American armed forces intervene actively in politics at the government level, some interesting features are apparent. In an effort to place our own study in the mainstream of theoretical observations on the military's political role, we will summarize some conclusions taken from George Philip's *The Military in South American Politics*, and then try to relate them to the present Venezuelan juncture. The main idea of his book centres around the concept that the 'South American military has an institution-maintaining role first, and a system-maintaining role as a necessary part of this'. (p. 362) Proceeding from this, the author states that 'military institutions in politics can be distinguished according to their level of unity and differentiation from civil society'. (p. 55) In the case of South America, he finds that the military is fairly united and highly differentiated from the rest of society – key propositions for understanding military behaviour in the region, because 'the ultimate loyalty of the military establishment is to its own institutional interest'. (p. 56) At the same time, the military is often perceived to intervene actively in politics when facing conditions of 'mass political upheaval, near civil war or complete political breakdown', (p. 363) Why is this so? For Philip, the paradox lies in the fact that the military as an institution committed to maintaining order can indirectly incite civilian opposition groups to promote disorder, whenever a critically unfavourable situation for the government develops. In his own words: 'the possibility of military restraint removes from civilian politicians much of the incentive for self-restraint'. (p. 366)

Applying Philip's framework to recent events in Venezuela it seems rather safe to state that if the government is unable to convince popular sectors that it can improve present conditions, in the short or medium term, if the parties lose their ability to channel demands into the system, and if violent demonstrations recur with some frequency, the probability of a military coup increases. Exacerbated popular demands would augment the need to employ the armed forces as an agent of repression, thus affecting their positive image in the eyes of popular sectors. It would also renew and deepen internal divisions between some groups opposed to engaging in repressive activities to protect politicians whom they consider responsible for the present situation, and others interested in imposing order through direct control of the government and the application of their own social and political recipes. Whatever the outcome of these divisions, the military institution itself would suffer severe changes, both in its level of acceptance by civilian society as well as in its internal cohesiveness. To avoid these risks to the military institution, the armed forces might become convinced that it would be in their institutional interests to overthrow the government. In addition, the opposing establishment party COPEI seems to be bent on continuing and escalating its opposition to the government, which had already reached a high degree of acrimony during the 1988 electoral campaign. The scene, then, appears to be set for the aggravation of social unrest and further involvement of the armed forces in repressive activities, which could lead to an eventual takeover of political power. Philip's analysis can be perceived as an accurate landscape of the present Venezuelan state of affairs.

It is worth remembering, however, that popular support for the government party can still be mobilized, making military intervention more costly and highly complicating the possibility of a smoothly functioning government of the armed forces, at least without investing considerable resources on repression. Moreover, there have been some hints of possible alternatives to a military coup in the attitude of former President Rafael Caldera, one of the signatories of the Pact of Punto Fijo, and some sectors of his party COPEI, who seem to be more receptive to the government's call to powerful political and social organizations to make a concerted effort to overcome the destructive consequences the socio-economic crisis can have on the future of the democratic political system. Concerted action at the highest level of the establishment parties may lead the way to reinforcing the channels of control over their own clienteles, but the other, more crucial, step lies in discovering means to incorporate into the system those expanding sectors who have been forming at the margins of those clientelistic networks.

In the very fluid atmosphere of Venezuelan politics at present, in which rumours of a coup are rife – to such an extent that President Carlos Andrés Pérez has had to acknowledge them publicly – it is extremely difficult to give a definitive answer to the question of whether or not civilian rule is likely to continue. As we have tried to demonstrate, however, the survival of the present democratic system in Venezuela will depend in large part on the capacity of the political parties to adapt to the end of subsidized democracy.

NOTES

1. Rexene Hanes de Acevedo, 'El clientelismo en el modelo político venezolano: un análisis preliminar', *Secuencia, Revista Americana de Ciencias Socciales*, (México) (Jan.–April, 1988), pp. 100–12.
2. Frank Bonilla, *The Failure of Elites* (Cambridge, Mass. : The MIT Press, 1970), p. 46.
3. Howards I. Blutstein, *et al. Area Handbook for Venezuela*, (Washington, DC: US Government Printing Office, 1977), p. 247.
4. Angel Ziems, *El Gomecismo y la formación del ejército nacional (Caracas: El Ateneo, 1979), p. 58.*
5. According to Gilmore, in the mid–1890's, 112 of 184 members of the Venezuelan legislature were generals. Robert Gilmore, *Caudillism and Militarism in Venezuela: 1818–1910* (Athens: Ohio University Press, 1964), p. 13.
6. David E. Blank, *Venezuela: Politics in a Petroleum Republic* (New York: Praeger, 1984), p. 18.
7. José Ramón Avendaño Lugo, *El militarismo en Venezuela: La dictadura de Pérez Jiménez* (Caracas: Ediciones Centauro, 1982), pp. 54–9; Gene Bigler, 'The

Armed Forces and Patterns of Civil–Military Relations', in J. D. Martz and D. J. Myers, eds, *Venezuela: The Democratic Experience* (New York: Praeger, 1977), p. 115.

8. Judith Ewell, *Venezuela: A Century of Change* (Stanford: Stanford University Press, 1984), p. 54; Blutstein, Area Handbook, p. 248.
9. Avendaño Lugo, *El militarismo*, pp. 59–63; Domingo Alberto Rangel, *Gómez, el amo del poder* (Valencia, Venezuela: Vadell Hermanos, 1975), pp. 196–7.
10. George Philip, *The Military in South American Politics* (London: Croom Helm, 1985), p. 90.
11. Blutstein, *Area Handbook*, p. 428.
12. Rangel, *Gómez*, p. 201.
13. Eduardo C. Schaposnik, *Democratización de las fuerzas armadas venezolanas* (Caracas: ILDIS, 1985), pp. 24–5.
14. Rangel, *Gómez*, p. 204; Ewell, *Venezuela*, p. 54.
15. Alberto Muller Rojas, 'Equipamiento militar, política de defensa y política exterior: El caso venezolano', *Política Internacional*, 2 (April–June, 1986), p. 22; Schaposnik, *Democratización*, pp. 26–7; Lugo, *El militarismo*, p. 102.
16. Cited by Schaposnik, *Democratización*, p. 49. Note: All translations from the Spanish are the responsibility of the authors of this paper.
17. Acta de Constitución de la Unión Patriótica Militar, cited by Andrés Stambouli, *Crisis Política: Venezuela, 1945–1958* (Caracas: El Ateneo, 1980), p. 49.
18. Rómulo Betancourt, *Venezuela: política y petróleo* (Caracas: Ediciones Senderos, 1969), pp. 551–2.
19. Blank, *Venezuela*, p. 26.
20. Schaposnik, *Democratización*, p. 55; Lugo, *El militarismo*, p. 143.
21. Lugo, *El militarismo*, p. 162; Blutstein, *Area Handbook*, p. 250; Stambouli, *Crisis*, pp. 255–62.
22. Avendaño Lugo, *El militarismo*, pp. 182–206.
23. Ibid., pp. 278–9.
24. Philip, *The Military*, p. 189
25. Schaposnik, *Democratización*, p. 174.
26. Stambouli, *Crisis*, p. 136.
27. Philip, *The Military*, p. 362.
28. Sanin (Alfredo Tarre Murzi), *Rómulo* (Valencia: Vadell Hermanos, 1984), pp. 270, 330; see also Ramón J. Velásquez, 'Proyección histórica de la obra de Rómulo Betancourt', in R. J. Velásquez, J. F. Sucre Figarella, and B. Bruni Celli, *Betancourt en la historia de Venezuela del siglo XX* (Caracas: Ediciones Centauro, 1980), p. 61.
29. Daniel Levine, 'Venezuelan Politics: Past and Future', in Robert D. Bond, ed., *Contemporary Venezuela and Its Role in International Affairs* (New York: New York University Press, 1977), p. 11.
30. Daniel Levine, *Conflict and Political Change in Venezuela* (Princeton, NJ: Princeton University Press, 1973), pp. 236–7.
31. Bonilla, *The Failure of Elites*, p. 318.
32. Moisés Naím and Ramón Piñango, *El caso Venezuela: Una ilusión de armonía* (Caracas: Ediciones IESA, 1984), pp. 553–4.
33. Velásquez, 'Proyección histórica', p. 59.
34. Diego Bautista Urbaneja, 'El sistema político o como funciona la máquina de procesar decisiones', in Naím and Piñango, eds, *El caso Venezuela*, p. 229.

35. Terry Lynn Karl, 'Petroleum and Political Pacts: The Transition to Democracy in Venezuela', in G. O'Donnell, P. C. Schmitter, and Laurence Whitehead, eds, *Transitions from Authoritarian Rule: Latin America* (Baltimore: Johns Hopkins University Press, 1986), p. 204.
36. Cited in ibid., p. 204.
37. Velásquez, 'Proyección histórica', p. 89.
38. Hanes de Acevedo, 'El clientelismo', pp. 106–7.
39. Blank, *Venezuela*, p. 129.
40. Asdrúbal Baptista, 'Más allá del optimismo y del pesimismo: las transformaciones fundamentales del país', in Naím and Piñango, *El caso Venezuela*, pp. 32–3.
41. Rexene Hanes de Acevedo, *El clientelismo político en América Latina: una crítica a la teoría de la dependencia* (Mérida, Venezuela: Librería Universitaria–Cruz del Sur, 1984), pp. 102–3.
42. *Brecha* (Montevideo), 10 March, 1989.
43. Schaposnik, *Democratización*, p. 239.
44. Alberto Muller Rojas, 'Rómulo Betancourt y la política militar' (unpublished manuscript, 1988), p. 15.
45. Schaposnik, *Democratización*, p. 243.
46. Sanin, *Rómulo*, p. 272.
47. Rómulo Betancourt, cited by Schaposnik, *Democratización*, p. 274.
48. Bigler, 'The Armed Forces', p. 121; Schaposnik, *Democratización*, pp. 272–4, 294; Sanin, *Rómulo*, pp. 357, 370.
49. Edwin Lieuwen, 'The Role of the Military', in R. R. Fagen and W. A. Cornelius, Jr, eds, *Political Power in Latin America: Seven Confrontations* (Englewood Cliffs, NJ: Prentice-Hall, 1970), p. 60.
50. Rómulo Betancourt, cited by Sanin, *Rómulo*, pp. 339–40; see also Velásquez, 'Proyección historica', p. 61.
51. Cited by Schaposnik, *Democratización*, p. 302.
52. Philip, *The Military*, p. 170.
53. Sanin, *Rómulo*, p. 353; Bigler, 'The Armed Forces', p. 119–21.
54. Cited by Imperio Rodríguez, 'El Plan República', *Revista Seguridad y Defensa*, no. 1, p. 35.
55. Bonilla, *The Failure*, pp. 284–5; Schaposnik, *Democratización*, p. 302.
56. Sanin, *Rómulo*, p. 385; Velasquez, 'Proyección historica', p. 82.
57. José Agustín Silva Michelena, *Crisis de la democracia* (Caracas: UCV–CENDES, 1970), p. 276.
58. Bigler shows that this loss of prestige was reflected in the low levels of recruitment by the Armed Forces Academies at the beginning of the 1960s. Gene E. Bigler, 'La restricción política y la profesionalización militar en Venezuela', *Politeia*, 10 (1981), pp. 94–5.
59. Velásquez, 'Proyección historica', p. 65.
60. Stephen G. Rabe, *The Road to OPEC: United States Relations with Venezuela, 1919–1976* (Austin: University of Texas Press, 1982), p. 146.
61. Ibid., pp. 146, 153.
62. Judith Ewell, *The Indictment of a Dictator* (College Station: Texas A & M University Press, 1981), pp. 157–8.
63. José A. Gil Yepez, 'El encaje político en el sector militar: el caso de Venezuela', *Nueva Sociedad*, 81 (Jan.–Feb., 1986), pp. 54–7.
64. Bigler, 'La restricción política', pp. 94–5.

65. John V. Lombardi, *Venezuela: The Search for Order, The Dream of Progress* (New York: Oxford University Press, 1982), p. 237.
66. Alberto Muller Rojas, 'La idea de la seguridad en los estados democráticos: Venezuela', *Política Internacional*, 8 (Oct.–Dec., 1987), p. 13.
67. Anfbal Romero, *La miseria del populismo* (Caracas: Ediciones Centauro, 1986), pp. 297–309; see also *Revista de Seguridad y Defensa*, 1, (Jan.–March, 1986), pp. 22–7.
68. It could be added that these measures, likewise, coincided with, and were at least partially inspired by, the influence of United States security programmes for the hemisphere. See Pablo A. Maríñez, 'Las Fuerzas Armadas en la República Dominicana: Profesionalización y politización', *El Caribe Contemporáneo*, 16, (Jan.–June, 1988), pp. 117–20.
69. Blutstein, *Area Handbook*, p. 260.
70. Jacobo Yepez Daza, 'Disertación sobre el Instituto de Previsipon Social de las Fuerzas Armadas (IPSFA) a la Confederación de Trabajadores de Venezuela (CTV)', *Politemas*, Año 1, 3 (Sept., 1987), p. 20.
71. Alberto Muller Rojas, 'Equipamiento militar, política de defensa y política exterior: el caso venezolano', *Política Internacional*, 2 (April–June, 1986), pp. 26–8.
72. Since 1983, a special military Controller General has been appointed to oversee military expenditures; however, he does not report to Congress, but directly to the President. Gil Yepes, 'El encaje', p. 53.
73. Angel Ziems, 'Una política militar en la Venezuela democrática del futuro', in 27 *Temas sobre Venezuela* (Caracas: Ediciones del Congreso de la República, 1988), pp. 701–23.
74. Schaposnik, *Democratización*, p. 376.
75. Ibid., p. 242, 376.
76. Bigler, 'Patterns of Civil–Military Relations', p. 125.
77. *El Nacional, El Universal, El Diario de Caracas*, 27 February – 8 March, 1989; 'El 27 de febrero', *Revista SIC*, Año LII, 513 (April, 1989), pp. 97–144.
78. *Arturo Sosa A.*, 'Qué fue lo que pasó?' in ibid., p. 104.
79. *El Universal*, 16 April, 1989.
80. Rexene Hanes de Acevedo, 'Conflict Management in Times of Crisis: Venezuela and México', paper presented to the XIV International Meeting of the Latin American Studies Association, New Orleans, LA., March, 1988, p. 9.

8 Civilian supremacy in Mexico: the case of post-revolutionary military

Roderic Ai Camp

Specialists on the military in Latin America have always been intrigued by the history of civil–military relations in Mexico. The reason for their continued interest is simple. Why, since 1946, has civilian leadership dominated Mexican politics, and what makes Mexico an exceptional case of long-standing civilian supremacy in Latin American and in the Third World in general? Although interest in Mexico has been high, it has not been translated into a body of scholarly literature on the country. Mexicanists are generally in agreement that the military is the least studied of such institutions in a major Latin American country, and the most difficult national institution to analyse in Mexico itself.[1] Moreover, when one examines the comparative literature for theoretical explanations helpful to understanding the evolution of Mexico's civil–military relations, and the reasons for the military's withdrawal from politics, the search typically is in vain. Basically, little has been published on Mexico of a systematic, comparative nature on the processes of military disengagement from politics.[2]

AN HISTORICAL REVIEW

Similar to most Latin American countries, Mexico achieved its independence from Spain in 1824. Also similar to many Latin American countries, its post-independence leaders could not agree on the type of political model best for the fledgling country. In Mexico, the removal of Spanish authorities left a political vacuum. The only institutions with some continuity with the past were the Catholic Church and the colonial militia. These two institutions shared one common feature. They had received special *fueros* or legal privileges in the colonial period, setting them apart from other, less influential members of society. In the years following independence, a democratic strain crept into the political values of some Mexican leaders. As part of that democratic culture, some politicians advocated removing special privileges. That idea, rather novel for Mexico, along with other important issues, contributed to a long period of civil conflict during the first half century of Mexican independence.

As the civil conflict grew in intensity, the legitimacy of all political institutions continued to decline. By mid-century, two competing groups of Mexicans emerged, Liberals and Conservatives. The Liberals offered a radical platform of decentralized government, and an elimination of Church privileges. The Conservatives, who favoured a more centralized form of government, corresponding more closely to the Spanish colonial heritage, allied themselves with the Church hierarchy. Since both sides needed military force to prevail, and since compromise was all but forgotten, the future role of the military was left undetermined. Indeed, as the fighting intensified in the 1850s and 1860s, culminating with a French invasion on the side of the Conservatives, military politicians became increasingly important. Most of these figures had joined the National Guard earlier in the century, later the source of Mexico's Federal Army.

In 1867, the Liberals, under the leadership of Benito Juárez, the most important civilian figure in their movement, defeated the Conservatives and their French allies. This defeat introduced a brief succession of Liberal governments, which changed hands through a representative political process, the first in Mexico's history. Yet, within four years, in 1871 dissident Liberal forces, led by one of the most prominent Liberal generals, Porfirio Díaz, attempted a revolt against the government. The rebellion of La Noria, as it was known, failed as most of the military remained loyal to the government. Five years later after Benito Juárez had died, Díaz tried again with his Plan of Tuxtepec. This time, without Juárez's prestige, and with the existence of dissension within his successor's government, Díaz and his military collaborators succeeded. They introduced a continuous government led or controlled by Díaz from 1877 to 1911.

Naturally Díaz, himself a military man, brought battlefield collaborators into his cabinet, and in control of important state governorships. Díaz legitimized military intervention in politics, not only because he himself had risen so high in the ranks, but because he obtained control through military force. Yet, a careful examination of his presidency reveals a gradual but persistent decline in career military backgrounds among his most influential collaborators. By the twentieth century, prominent military figures were only a small minority among influential politicians. This pattern suggests that even historically, in Mexico and elsewhere, the military does not have sufficient human resources to provide continuous political leadership over time, nor do military leaders themselves, even when firmly in control of political institutions, continue recruiting their comrades-in-arms to important political offices. The evidence suggests that, whereas President Díaz selected individuals personally loyal to him on the basis of shared career experiences, typically in numerous military encounters against the Conservatives, politics is essentially a civilian occupation, and civilians ultimately provide the lion's share of politicians.

It is ironic that at the point when military dominance over political offices was it its lowest ebb, the first major social revolution of the twentieth century should confront Mexico. This revolution, which had extraordinary consequences for the country's future social and political development, significantly flavoured Mexico's future civil–military relationships. Díaz contributed to the institutionalization of the Mexican military during his administration. His officer corps increasingly were trained at the National Military College. It would be fair to say that such training was an early form of professionalization. The army, however, did not defend Mexico from external enemies, rather it saw combat against various indigenous groups who were being suppressed and exploited by friends of the regime, and put down labour strikes. By the time of the 1910 revolution, the military, in part, became a paper force, rampant with corruption. In the eyes of the populace, it was feared, but it received little legitimacy or respect.

A POST-REVOLUTIONARY HERITAGE

The revolution accomplished what most popular movements have done in Latin America or in the Third World, it destroyed the influence and legitimacy of the organized military forces, replacing them with a grassroots substitute led by individuals who had earned their rank on the battlefield, instead of against poorly armed Indians and workers, or from officer candidate schools. General Alvaro Obregón, the first post-revolutionary president, had been a chick pea rancher, General Plutarco Elías Calles, his successor, a teacher, and General Lázaro Cárdenas, the famed agrarian reformer, a printer's apprentice. The Mexican Revolution, which endured on and off from 1910 till 1920, claimed the lives of nearly one out of ten Mexicans. Beginning in 1920, a succession of self-made generals, mostly from the north, dominated the presidency and political life in general. As in the time of Díaz, these veterans also controlled most gubernatorial posts.

Again, Mexican political history repeated itself. Although the generals dominated the presidency from 1920 through 1946, with a brief interregnum in 1929–30, they, like Díaz, quickly began recruiting bright, college graduates into cabinet posts. In the late 1920s, under orders from President Calles, the new army once again began institutionalizing itself, using a reconstituted Heroic Military College to train future officers. The revolution provided one other critical ingredient to this tried formula, similar to, but more intense and deeply felt than the nineteenth century civil wars, a desire for a lasting peace. Successive governments after 1920, just as their successive counterparts after

1871, had the advantage of governing a population willing to accept certain political deficiencies in return for peace and stability.

Mexico, therefore, embarked on a path in the twentieth century in which its untried political institutions have a certain advantage. Strangely, it might be suggested that the military did not withdraw from politics in the 1930s and 1940s, rather, the military had never, in the true sense of the word, intervened in political affairs in the first place. In other words, the military, as one of several quasi-state institutions with its own political interests had not intervened in 1910, rather, a civilian competitor defeated and replaced them. When violence became the only means through which civilian leaders could express their disagreements with established political authorities, then the means of force, and those most skilled at wielding them, became essential tools of political life. Those most politically skilled, however, were not the institutionalized military, that is the Federal Army, but rather the guerrilla forces. After 1920, forces loyal to the victorious revolutionaries put down rebellions by dissident peers fighting for political control.

The popular military leaders who led Mexico during the crucial transition period after the revolution encouraged the process of political withdrawal. They did so through a variety of techniques which have been carefully described by Edwin Lieuwen.[3] It is important to note, however, that many of these approaches were used successfully by Porfirio Díaz himself. But in the post-revolutionary period, the federal government, through its increasing budgetary power, and through the secretariat of defence, with its overwhelming control over the tools of violence, accomplished this task in a more centralized and formal fashion. Among these techniques were the persistent reduction in defence expenditures on a percentage basis, while increasing the absolute amounts each year. The government pensioned off hundreds of self-made colonels and generals, providing them with economic security, and an incentive to withdraw from the risky business of politics. Third, those interested in politics were permitted to hold various posts, but they gradually found themselves removed from influential cabinet positions, and instead were rewarded with lesser posts as governors, senators and deputies. Fourth, generals from popular or battlefield roots were replaced by those trained in the military academies, whose loyalty was to higher staff officials in the secretariat of defence, rather than to their gun-toting revolutionary peers.

COMPARATIVE THEORIES ON INTERVENTION IN MEXICO

The comparative literature on military intervention, while having little to offer that is relevant to Mexico, does provide a series of generalizations, some of which have some explanatory potential for the Mexican case. The most important suggestions for why the military does not intervene are: the institutionalization of civilian political values, the consistent but limited participation of the military in politics, and most important, the development of broad-based political institutions, especially a party, having legitimacy and support among the populace.[4]

A new political model

It is not entirely accidental that the last major rebellion within popular military forces against the government, led by General José Escobar in 1929, coincides with the establishment of Mexico's National Revolutionary Party (PNR), an antecedent to the Institutional Revolutionary Party (PRI). It is important to remember that this party was established by General Calles and other prominent revolutionaries to retain the reins of political power, and to institutionalize and legitimize their control. As Claude Welch suggests, long-term military disengagement is most successful in those countries in 'which political institutions have gained new bases of legitimacy as a result of revolution'.[5] While Calles and his collaborators enjoyed the natural legitimacy associated with their post-revolutionary governments, they understood the importance of trying to sustain that quality for future generations of political leaders.

The year 1946 marks this evolutionary process from military to civilian control in a symbolic and concrete fashion. General Manuel Ávila Camacho, a former revolutionary, aide to General Cárdenas, his predecessor, and secretary of defence, selected as his nominee for the party's presidential candidate, a young civilian politician, Miguel Alemán. Alemán's father, who was a revolutionary general, died fighting against the government in the Escobar rebellion, eleven years earlier. Alemán himself had supported, as a student, an opposition candidate for president in 1927.[6] The choice of Alemán represents several important characteristics of the Mexican system. First, Mexican politicians, including revolutionary generals, skilfully opened up their leadership ranks to dissident groups willing to join the system. This has included, remarkably, a number of defence secretaries. I do not know of any government in Latin American or the Third World that has recruited opposition figures to take over its defence ministry. Second, military leaders were instrumental in turning over political leadership to a much younger generation of civilians. In fact, Avila Camacho is the last defence secretary to be a serious official pre-candidate or PRI's nominee for the presidency. Third, Alemán's designation marks the beginning of a new Mexican professional politician, a college graduate, university teacher, career bureaucrat, and civilian. Fourth, under Avila Camacho, the military loses its separate representation as a major sector in the government party, and instead is incorporated into a popular sector. And fifth, under Alemán, the name is changed from the Mexican Revolutionary Party to the Institutional Revolutionary Party, symbolizing non-violent, evolutionary change, and the significance of institutions.[7]

The type of political model which emerges from 1946 forward, under the tutelage of Alemán's disciples, is one characterized by the following features:

1 The power of the civil state expands rapidly, not only in the size of the traditional bureaucracy, but in its control over economic sectors typically left in the hands of the private sector.

2 The military continues to decline in size and influence, measured both by funds allocated through the federal, budgetary process, and in its organizational size relative to the civilian bureaucracy specifically, and the civilian population generally.

3 The military controls the secretariat of National Defence, and the much smaller secretariat of the Navy, but generally has no other representative in the cabinet.

4 The Revolutionary heritage of the military is symbolized through the 1960s in the selection of a defence secretary with combat experience, first in the revolution itself, then against the successive revolts in 1923, 1927 and 1929, and the Cristero rebellion in West-Central Mexico, 1926–9.

5 The federal bureaucracy, and to a much lesser extent the party, institutionalized a political recruitment process in which the civilian power holders designate their disciples, consequently choosing Mexico's future political leaders. The preferred political recruitment channel is through the university and the federal government.

6 Civilian authorities have given the military symbolic respect, economic rewards, and intelligence and police tasks, without spending money lavishly on weaponry and military technology.

The Mexican military has not returned to a position of direct political influence, nor has it increased its political role substantially, for a variety of reasons. Although many factors have contributed to this pattern since 1946, the most important are: (1) the strength of Mexico's political institutions, (2) the attitude of Mexico's officer corps towards politics, (3) the socializing role of the military academies, (4) the attitude of the Mexican population towards the military, and (5) the autonomy of the military in internal matters, especially promotion, from civilian political interference.

Overall, the most important feature of the Mexican model is the increasing strength of its civilian political institutions, despite a significant decline in their legitimacy since 1968, and especially since 1976. As early as the 1940s and 1950s, military participation in politics had been transformed into military influence in politics, based on the increasing legitimacy of civilian and governmental institutions.[8] This is an important distinction. In effect, the military became one of several state-co-opted interest groups, sharing some similarities with labour, peasants, intellectuals and business people.[9] Some scholars have attributed this legitimacy to the influence of the PRI, but the essential ingredient actually has been the bureaucracy or state organizations. As Samuel Fitch suggests, as the military became professionalized, so did the civilian bureaucracy.[10] By any measure, quality of training, level of education, exposure to experiences abroad, and access to resources, the civilian bureaucracy advanced on a higher plane and at a faster pace than did the military. In fact, top civilian leaders in Mexico are generally better educated than their North American counterparts.

The rapid expansion and sophistication of the civilian public sector attracted the most ambitious future leaders. This has been true for some time. One reason is that Mexico's revolutionary heroes typically have been presented as civilians, despite their military exploits. Second, Mexico's military lacks prestige compared to other South American countries.[11] Third, anyone interested in the accumulation and management of public resources, and influencing public policy in Mexico, would not pursue a military career. This is reflected by the fact that frequently young men who are the children of successful career officers, follow public careers, such as Manuel Camacho, head of the Federal District Department in the Salinas cabinet. On the other hand, no child of a successful politician applies as a cadet to the military academies, hoping to become a career officer.[12] Typically, many future officers are the sons of career military men, as is the case of the present secretary of defence, or are from lower-middle-class families with no military connections.[13]

The strength of civilian institutions has been in question since 1968, when the president, in response to increasingly belligerent student demands, over-reacted and brought in the army to curb a student demonstration in Tlalteloco Plaza in downtown Mexico City, resulting in the deaths of hundreds of students and bystanders. The political ramifications of this incident were enormous, not only on government relations with students, but with all other societal groups. Moreover, the legitimacy of the political, economic and social model the government represented, came under severe criticism. The military, having played the unpopular, police role, itself lost prestige, and therefore its legitimacy also declined.

The military, realizing the extent of the damage to its institutional image, demanded a high price from the government. For the first time since Miguel Alemán's administration, a new military zone was established. Furthermore, three new battalions were created, an infantry, parachute and military police battalion, a company of combat engineers in the presidential guards, and other additional positions.[14] Not long after these changes, a large group of senior officers, representing the old-style field commander, were retired, replaced by younger, academy-trained staff officers.

OFFICER CORPS VALUES

The attitude of the officer corps towards its own role in society, and its own self-definition has also contributed significantly to why the Mexican military lacks an active interest in politics. In the first place, the officer corps has felt positively about how they are perceived by the government, particularly the president. According to Franklin Margiotta, who interviewed officers during three administrations through the 1970s,

> all officers seemed satisfied that the political system would continue to reward them. Mexican officers often discuss their pay and benefits as though they had received them personally from the President. Deep personal respect, at times approaching reverence, for the individual presidents was expressed. Presidential concern for military status seems to have had a salutary effect upon civil–military relations in Mexico and may have helped ensure political stability'.[15]

This positive image of civilian interest has been a remarkable achievement given actual military expenditures. As documented by Merilee Grindle, from 1967 to 1980, the military budget increased on average 2.6 per cent, compared to an average increase in federal government expenditures of 12 per cent, and a Gross National Product of 5.51 per cent.[16]

The Mexican military's attitude towards civilian leadership is affected by the direction of their loyalties. According to George Philip, a significant distinction between South American military officers and Mexican officers is that the former owe their loyalties to their own institutions, whereas Mexicans willingly have committed themselves to civilian politicians and leaders.[17] The most influential element in retaining military loyalty is the officers' belief in the civilian leadership's ability to maintain order. As long as the government demonstrates its capacity to sustain order, and retain limited respect from the population, the military will support civil authority. As one Mexican officer told an interviewer, '"Authority is first, since order cannot exist if there is no authority which sustains and imposes it". The military mind, therefore, may be able to tolerate many things, but it can never accept nor understand disorder'.[18] As we shall see, military academies have played a crucial role in instilling the military's attitude of subordination to civilian authority in Mexico.

Some scholars have also suggested that the Mexican military, similar to officers elsewhere in Latin America, have a strong strain of anti-Communism built into their values. Opposition to Communism has been a typical reason cadets joined the officer corps.[19] Edward Williams believes the military leadership's ideology on Communism counters Mexico's favourable leftist rhetoric in its foreign policy statements, notably towards Cuba and Central America.[20] Regardless of its policy effects, the military is not likely to abandon present government civilian elites for another alternative if they consider its replacement to be more receptive to the left. Although the new Cardenista party front in Mexico operates symbolically in the name of General Cárdenas, through his son and party leader Cuauhtémoc, the military shows no special concern for the poor. Their social philosophy, according to Lieuwen, has been moderate, middle class, basically in line with civilian attitudes.[21]

Any military officer expressing an interest in politics is allowed to participate. But, it is important to note that an officer wishing to run for elective office, or be appointed to a political post, is given leave of absence, and is prohibited from using his military rank while on leave.[22] Time taken off for political office-holding may not be counted towards time-in-grade in calculating future promotions. Consequently, the enforcement of these rules leads to downplaying the military's importance, and to a strong separation between military and civilian political careers. As can be seen from the discussion of promotions, political careers are not helpful to military advancement. Even as early as the 1950s, when military officers commonly straddled political–military careers, military officers who followed orthodox army careers claimed that these officers 'in general enjoyed little prestige among the military professionals and that any "understanding" about their appointment was a symbolic recognition of the army's role in the revolution rather than a significant political linkage'.[23]

The socializing role of the military academies has been instrumental in embedding an attitude favourable to subordination to civilian control among the officer corps. The Mexican military, according to many observers, has one of the 'highest levels of discipline in Latin America or the Third World. Its discipline is omnipresent and overwhelming, stifling individual behavioural norms and reinforcing the effect of common experiences upon cohesion'.[24] The average officers, according to North Americans who actually attended Mexican service academies, spend much of their time waiting for guidance from their superiors.[25] The Mexican academy system is built on a stringent superior–subordinate relationship. Obedience to one's superior, and respect for civilian control, is repeatedly taught and presented in the official Army/Air Force magazine. It has been suggested that the setting at the Higher War College, which produces most of Mexico's future officers of general rank, establishes behaviour patterns which are re-enacted in the civil–military arena. Michael Dziedzic concludes that the typical Mexican officer will obey the president in the same way that he obeys his superior officer.[26] In those few cases where an officer publicly criticized the government or the president, they were summarily removed from their position or command.[27]

Military socialization processes share certain similarities from one culture to the next. Studies of North American officers who enter West Point reveal very clearly that among those professing 'liberal' views, twice as many resign as remain in the service. The majority of 'conservatives', on the other hand, remain on active duty.[28] This means, of course, that most officers are from a select group from society, that they do not represent society as a whole, not necessarily from a social class perspective, but from an attitudinal view. Mexican officers are not likely to be any different. As Mora suggests, the Mexican 'officer who is willing to totally subordinate himself to the system, and is willing to make the ultimate sacrifice, is an individual who knows what rewards the system has to offer. He will likely complete the school'.[29] Even at the Higher War College, which takes the cream of the officer corps from junior officers who are graduates of the Heroic Military College, only 55 to 60 per cent complete the rigorous three-year programme.[30]

The content of the military education programmes are influential on the officer corps because of the percentage of officers who are graduates, and the length of time officers have studied in military academies. As Ackroyd suggests, the typical cadet joins the Heroic Military College around 15 years old. Between the ages of 15 and 26, the typical officer will have spent 6–8 years in military training programmes, culminating in the Higher War College.[31] Before the 1970s, most high-ranking officers did not attend the Higher War College. In the mid–1970s, the number of officers with staff and command diplomas at the secretariat of defence, and among zone commanders in the field doubled and tripled from 25 and 33 per cent respectively, to 50 and 55 per cent.[32] Today, approximately 90 per cent of all officers are graduates of the Heroic Military College. All officers holding a departmental directorship in the secretariat of defence in 1987 were graduates. A small percentage still obtain direct commissions. According to Steve Wager, 'it is generally recognized within military circles that without a diploma from the Superior War College, the highest rank an officer can hope to attain is Lt Colonel'.[33] Consequently, all future leaders of the officer corps pass through a disciplined environment requiring subordination to superiors, and to civilian authority.

SOCIETAL ATTITUDES

A major reason why the military does not intervene in any society, frequently ignored in the literature on Latin America, is the attitude among civilian politicians and citizens in general towards military political participation in politics. A significant pattern in Mexico is that opposition groups do not have special ties to, nor do they attempt to elicit support from the military.[34] This in part is a by-product of a modified one-party state, and the continuous relationship between an established civilian leadership and the officer corps. The major opposition party of the right, the National Action Party (PAN), which has operated since 1939, is identified with business interests and the Catholic Church, and indeed has some ties to each. Yet, there has never existed any alleged or real connections between the military and any political opposition party, including PAN. This situation is the result of the separation taught at the military training schools, and the harsh punishments meted out for overt political activities, especially in the electoral arena, within the military. But it is also the consequence of an informal agreement among civilian politicians, who regardless of their disagreements on other issues, are 'both singularly united in their commitment to limiting the political role of the military and successful in gaining military acquiescence to this role definition'.[35]

Civilian leadership alone cannot impose civilian supremacy on the military. The separation of military-civilian spheres of responsibility are much sharper, and durable, if the citizens themselves strongly support such norms. The fact that the Mexican military accepts a fairly narrow level of responsibility, and that society supports their limited role, can be measured statistically by its size and the financial support the Mexican military receives vis à vis other militaries. For example, in the mid-1970s, only 0.13 per cent of the total Mexican population, compared to 1.32 per cent in the United States, and approximately 6 per cent in most other Latin American countries, were in the military. In terms of expenditures, Mexico's military received 0.86 per cent of GNP, while most Latin American militaries were at a level of 2–3 per cent, and the United States was at nearly 7 per cent.[36]

The prestige of the service can be measured by the reasons people give for making it a career. Most young people, who are not connected to the military through their parents or relatives, join the services for economic reasons. For example, among army recruits, Mora found that the majority enrolled as officer cadets because it offered 'an alternative to the poverty they had grown up with'.[37] Similarly, the typical enlisted personnel also joins for economic reasons. In 1980, the basic pay for a recruit was generally twice as high as for a farm worker or unskilled labourer.[38]

The Mexican military does not attract individuals because of a prestigious reputation. According to most citizens, those Mexicans who deserve the most respect are parents, teachers, and priests. Those who deserve the least respect are political bosses and politicians, followed by military men and bankers.[39] But when institutions are examined, as distinct from occupations or individuals, the military scores better than all political organizations. Again, schools and Church are easily at the top of the list. Strongly in the middle, with the legal system, is the military, in which 48 per cent of the population expressed confidence. Legislators and bureaucrats, however, received a positive vote from only about a quarter of all Mexicans.[40]

The critical issue is not the military's prestige, but the attitude of the population towards military participation in the government. In a national poll taken by PRI in 1983, 50 per cent of the population said that the military should never participate in the government. Twenty-three per cent said the military sometimes might be justified in participating, and 26 per cent said they should be involved in governing.[41] Mexicans were much more definitive about the Church not participating: nearly two-thirds thought the Church should stay out of politics. This is not surprising considering the fact that civil wars were fought over this very issue, and that numerous provisions, specifying such a politically restricted role, to the extent of not even recognizing the legal status of the Church, appear in the 1917 constitution. The constitution makes no mention of any restrictions concerning the military. The difference between the two institutions can be conveyed in one other way. Constitutionally, a congressperson cannot be a minister of any religious cult, but he can be a member of the armed forces. (Article 55, Section VI) The average Mexican's attitude towards the military is conveyed less formally, on the basis of experience, filtering gradually into the Mexican value system over time.

CIVILIAN INTERFERENCE

Finally, Margiotta speculated that the absence of civilian interference in the internal matters of the military, such as promotion, discipline and assignments, might help explain their non-interventionist attitude.[42] I discovered considerable evidence to support this belief, and that the absence of civilian interference distinguishes Mexico's military from other services in Latin America. The insularity of the Mexican military from political affairs can be measured on several levels. For example, it is worth noting that the secretariat of national defence is the only cabinet agency since 1946 which has not had a change in secretary mid-way through an administration.[43] The top leadership of the military is characterized by extraordinary stability, and the secretary of defence always comes from a senior officer. In fact, by comparison with politicians themselves, senior officers, and defence secretaries, are older than their civilian counterparts, and more recently, presidents.

A more in-depth appraisal of promotions, perhaps the single most important internal military process, reveals an extraordinary consistency. Promotions can be predicted with considerably accuracy on the basis of years of service and time in grade. My examination of hundreds of officers reaching general rank indicates that individual officers have not followed a fast track within the service.[44] Whereas it is indeed true that personal ties within the service, just as in politics, are critical to career success, ties with civilian politicians, even kinship, does not guarantee a successful military career. To be promoted through the ranks to Lt Colonel, one has to receive favourable ratings from a superior officer, score among the top candidates on a competitive examination, and complete a minimum time requirement in service, which is 8 years for 1st Captain, 11 years for Major and 14 years for Lt Colonel. Colonels are recommended by a board of senior officers, their names are submitted to the secretary of defence, and they must be approved by the Senate.[45] The Senate, which has normally functioned as a rubber stamp of the executive branch, has, since the 1940s, resisted any efforts on the part of the president to selectively promote an officer from colonel to general, or from one general rank to another, before minimum time in grade. The Senate, on more than one occasion, has refused to approve such presidential recommendations.[45]

CONCLUSIONS

These have been some of the reasons why the Mexican military has not indicated a desire to intervene in the last forty years. Mexico has been unique in that a military elite, more accurately a political–military elite, transferred the basis of power from the army to a civil state. A few other examples exist, as in Iraq and Ethiopia, but they too followed a revolution.[46] Given the historical distance of Mexico's revolution, the extent of Mexico's economic crisis since 1979, and the rise of a powerful populist political opposition, some observers believe that the potential for a changing attitude towards political–military relations may exist.

For the military to pursue an activist role in the governing process, 'the armed forces must prove that the PRI is no longer the legitimate inheritor of the Revolution. They must, in effect, go against political behaviour that has embedded itself over a period of more than half a century in Mexican life and thinking'.[47] A splinter group from PRI, headed by Cuauhtémoc Cárdenas, allied with established, tiny, leftist parties, demonstrated the level of decline in PRI's legitimacy, obtaining in 1988 the largest percentage of votes ever received by an opposition party, and according to some observers, actually defeating the PRI. It is clear that many Mexicans associate their declining standard of living with the government, and that more importantly, the moral character of its leadership, that is their legitimacy to lead, is very much in question.

These changing views of the Mexican government, however, do not mean that the military will substitute for civilian leadership. If the government were to collapse, without an available alternative in the wings, then the military is likely to consider reasserting its political role.[48] Instead, if the capabilities of the government to lead, in face of deteriorating social and economic conditions continues to decline, a more likely scenario is greater use of para military groups, and in the extreme, military control over such groups.[49] The most probable change that may occur, in fact, already has begun, is the alteration of civil–military relations in terms of the military's role within the state, rather than in politics per se. In other words, the military in the foreseeable future is not likely to intervene directly in politics, usurping civilian authority, but rather it will play a larger and somewhat differently defined role in the decision-making process.[50]

To some extent, an expanded military role has already been introduced. In recent years, the number of military zones has increased, so that three states, Guerrero, Oaxaca and Chiapas now have two each.[51] The military has expanded its patrols on the local level in rural areas. And most visibly, the military has taken over the lion's share of the battle in the war against drugs. This activity not only expands its social responsibilities, it could impact favourably on its image, since the average Mexican is very much concerned about ridding drugs from Mexico's culture.[52] It appears, however, that so far, because of allegations in the United States media that several high-ranking officers allegedly have been connected with drug trafficking, that the military has stained rather than enhanced its reputation in the drug eradication programme.[53] A more likely activity forcing the military to make some hard choices is its role in elections and maintaining civil order, if dissident voters take to the streets to decry fraud. The military was called on to perform such internal police functions in 1985, and to a lesser extent in 1988. In recent newspaper accounts, an enlisted man seeking political asylum in Canada claims that he and other troops were ordered to execute civilian political prisoners, and these executions took place at Military Camp No. 1 in Mexico City.[54] In other confrontations between government authorities and groups over such highly charged issues as abortion, civilian groups have directed petitions to the secretariat of national defence, rather than to the appropriate civil ministry.[55]

A change with longer-term consequences is taking place within the military educational structure. The military recently established, as a capstone facility, a new National Defence College. This facility was set up to educate officers having the greatest potential as future leaders.[56] Initially, the college proposed to use civilian instructors and guest lecturers, as well as military officers. It also decided to make greater use of civilian materials, including books by foreign authors.[57] The Mexican decision followed a pattern instituted in Peru, at the Centre for Higher Military Studies (CAEM), and in Brazil, at the Superior War College. Scholars believe that civilian sources and instructors play a significant role on the ideology of military graduates, and on their self-definition and perceived political role.[58] In 1989, the first civilian students, five individuals holding public positions, will join their military colleagues at the National Defence College. This introduces a new era in military education. Another source also exists for the introduction of alternative ideologies in the services. The navy, unlike the army and air force, accepts lateral entry for officer ranks from civilians, giving them a rank on the basis of their education and skill, similar to the United States services' direct-commission programme. The other two Mexican services accept such candidates only under very special conditions.[59] The navy does not require any indoctrination courses for civilian professionals who enter laterally.

This influence is tempered by the fact that the Mexican navy accounts for only a small percentage of military forces, and that among naval officers, civilian entrants are probably a small percentage, and may not, like earlier political-military officers, have the same level of respect among orthodox career officers. However, in recent years, disputes between the army and the navy have surfaced publicly, including such sensitive political issues as to whether or not the military should run a presidential candidate.[60] Also, during the 1985 earthquake in Mexico City, the navy earned a favourable public image by pitching in to help uncover victims, whereas the army appeared to be more interested in maintaining control and keeping order.[61]

Finally, the government continues to stay out of internal military affairs. However, there is some evidence that in times of political crisis, the president has used his promotion powers to retire some officers and promote larger numbers of younger officers, as if trying to reward the military's loyalty.[62] This is an old technique used by Porfirio Díaz, by Victoriano Huerta when he revolted against the constitutional government in 1913, and by the revolutionaries themselves, after each successive revolt against the government. Implemented too frequently, officers may begin to expect something special in return for traditional loyalty to civilian authorities.

In summary, in many respects, Mexico's civilian supremacy corresponds strongly to some universal characteristics Claude Welch suggested. Those were: that some constitutional constraints on the political impact of the military exist, which in Mexico, have emerged more through custom than legal statute; that some type of social relationship exists between both sets of leaders (this was true after the revolution, but is not true today, since both groups tend to come socially from somewhat different origins), that civil and military institutions each have their own hierarchies, with civilians in control; that historic reasons permit the maintenance of a relatively small armed force with narrow responsibilities; and that there is widespread acceptance within the armed forces of an ethic of subordination.[63]

Only a major political upheaval is likely to alter these patterns in Mexico's immediate future.

NOTES

1. David Ronfeldt, 'The Mexican Army and Political Order Since 1940', in Abraham F. Lowenthal ed., *Armies and Politics in Latin America* (New York: Holmes and Meier, 1976), p. 7.
2. Claude E. Welch, Jr, *No Farewell to Arms? Military Disengagement from Politics in Africa and Latin America* (Boulder: Westview Press, 1987), p. 10.
3. Edwin Lieuwen, *Mexican Militarism* (Albuquerque: University of New Mexico Press, 1968).
4. Claude E. Welch, Jr, *No Farewell to Arms,?* p. 17.
5. Ibid., p. 17.
6. Roderic Ai Camp, 'Camarillas in Mexican Politics, the Case of the Salinas Cabinet', *Mexican Studies* (1990).
7. The three names of the party, National, Mexican and Institutional are the only words which have changed since 1929. The party colours are the same as the national flag. Both attempt to capture and monopolize the revolution as the singular heritage of the government party, implying by inference that others are mere impostors. See Robert Scott, *Mexican Politics in Transition* (Urbana: University of Illinois Press, 1964), for an analysis of the party's evolution.
8. Claude E. Welch, Jr, 'Civilian Control of the Military: Myth and Reality', in Claude E. Welch, Jr, ed., *Civilian Control of the Military, Theory and Cases from Developing Countries* (Albany: State University of New York Press, 1976), p. 22.
9. For some comparisons, see my *Entrepreneurs and Politics in Twentieth Century Mexico* (New York: Oxford University Press, 1989).
10. Samuel J. Fitch, 'Armies and Politics in Latin America: 1975–1985', in Abraham Lowenthal and Samuel Fitch, eds, *Armies and Politics in Latin America* (New York: Holmes and Meier, 1986), p. 37.
11. George Philip, *The Military in South American Politics* (London: Croom Helm, 1985), p. 17.
12. Based on an analysis of the family backgrounds of more than 3000 politicians in my *Mexican Political Biographies Project*, covering prominent political figures from 1884 to the present.
13. Steven J. Wager, 'Civic Action and the Mexican Military', Unpublished paper, Department of History, United States Military Academy, 1982.
14. Guillermo Boils, 'Los militares en México (1965–1985)', *Revista Mexicana de Sociología*, 47: 1 (January–February, 1985), p. 175.
15. Franklin D. Margiotta, 'Civilian Control and the Mexican Military: Changing Patterns of Political Influence', in Claude E. Welch, ed., *Civilian Control of the Military*, p. 221.
16. Merilee S. Grindle, 'Civil–Military Relations and Budgetary Politics in Latin America', in *Armed Forces and Society*, 13: 2 (Winter, 1987), p. 258.
17. Philip, *The Military in South American Politics*, p. 78.

18. William S. Ackroyd, 'The Military in Mexican Politics: The Impact of Professionalism, Civilian Behavior, and the Revolution', *PCCLAS Proceedings*, 12 (1985–6), p. 101.
19. Daniel Mora, 'Profile of the Mexican Company Grade Officer', paper presented at the Rocky Mountain States Latin American Conference, Tucson, Arizona, February, 1984, p. 3.
20. Edward J. Williams, 'The Mexican Military and Foreign Policy: The Evolution of Influence', paper presented at the Role of the Military in Mexican Politics and Society, Center for U.S.–Mexican Studies, UCSD, La Jolla, California, March, 1984.
21. Lieuwen, *Mexican Militarism*, p. 149.
22. Steven J. Wager, 'Modernization of the Mexican Military: Political and Strategic Implications', unpublished paper, Department of History, United States Military Academy, 1983, p. 40.
23. Lyle N. MacAlister, *et al.*, *The Military in Latin American Socio-political Evolution: Four Case Studies* (Washington, DC : Center for Research in Social Systems, 1970), p. 241, for their prestige; and for evidence of career success, see Roderic A. Camp, 'Mexican Military Leadership in Statistical Perspective Since the 1930s', in James W. Wilkie and Peter Reich, eds, *Statistical Abstract of Latin America Supplement Series*, vol. 20 (Los Angeles: UCLA Latin American Center, 1980), pp. 595–606.
24. William S. Ackroyd, 'The Military in Mexican Politics: The Impact of Professionalization, Civilian Behavior, and the Revolution', paper presented at the Pacific Coast Council of Latin Americanists, San Diego, October 1982, p. 13.
25. Michael J. Dziedzic, 'Civil–Military Relations in Mexico: The Politics of Cooptation', unpublished paper, University of Texas, Austin, 1983, p. 27.
26. Ibid., p. 38
27. Ackroyd, 'The Military in Mexican Politics', p. 14.
28. Gary Spencer, 'Methodological Issues in the Study of Bureaucratic Elites', *Social Problems* vol. 21 (Summer, 1973), p. 92.
29. Mora, 'Profile of the Mexican Company Grade Officer', p. 11.
30. Ibid., p. 9.
31. Ackroyd, 'The Military in Mexican Politics', 1985–6, p. 98.
32. Boils, 'Los militares en México', p. 174.
33. Steven J. Wager, 'Basic Characteristics of the Modern Mexican Military', in David Ronfeldt, ed., *The Modern Mexican Military: A Reassessment* (La Jolla: Center for U.S.–Mexican Studies, University of California, San Diego, 1984), p. 95.
34. Roderic Ai Camp, 'Opposition in Mexico: A Comparison of Leadership', in Judith Gentleman, ed., *Mexican Politics in Transition* (Boulder: Westview Press, 1987), pp. 245–6.
35. Grindle, 'Civil–Military Relations and Budgetary Politics in Latin America', p. 263.
36. Lind L. Reif, 'Seizing Control: Latin American Military Motives, Capabilities, and Risks', *Armed Forces and Society*, 10: 4 (Summer, 1984), p. 571.
37. Mora, 'Profile of the Mexican Company Grade Officer', p. 5.
38. Vicente Ernesto Pérez Mendoza, 'The Role of the Armed Forces in the Mexican Economy in the 1980s', unpublished MA thesis, Naval Postgraduate School, Monterey, California, June, 1981, p. 24.

39. Enrique Aldúncin Abitia, *Los Valores de los Mexicanos, Mexico: Entre la Tradición y la Modernidad* (Mexico City: Fondo Cultural Banamex, 1986), p. 176.
40. Alberto Hernández Medina, *et al., Como somos los Mexicanos* (Mexico City: Centro de Estudios Educativos, 1987), p. 110.
41. Partido Revolucionario Institucional, Instituto de Estudios Políticos, Económicos y Sociales, 'Encuesta Nacional de Partidos Políticos', April 1983.
42. Margiotta, 'Civilian Control and the Mexican Military', p. 253.
43. Roderic Ai Camp, *Mexican Political Biographies, 1935–1981* (Tucson: University of Arizona Press, 1982), p. 419.
44. Roderic Ai Camp, 'Generals and Politicians in Mexico: A Preliminary Comparison', in Ronfeldt, ed., *The Modern Mexican Military*, p. 136ff.
45. Wager, 'The Mexican Military', unpublished paper, 1983, p. 21.
46. Philip, *The Military in South American Politics*, p. 77.
47. Ackroyd, 'The Military in Mexican Politics', 1985–6, pp. 102–3.
48. Alden M. Cunningham, 'Mexico's National Security in the 1980s–1990s', unpublished paper, no date, p. 17.
49. Francisco J. Suárez Farías, 'Notas para una historia de la relaciones políticas entre gobierno y ejercito Mexicanos', unpublished paper, Universidad Metropolitana, Mexico City, 1978, p. 31.
50. David Ronfeldt, 'The Modern Mexican Military', in Abraham Lowenthal and J. Samuel Fitch, eds, *Armies and Politics in Latin America* (New York: Holmes and Meier, 1986), p. 234.
51. Williams, 'The Mexican Military and Foreign Policy', p. 20.
52. *The New York Times*, 26 October, 1986.
53. *Washington Post*, 6 February, 1989.
54. *The New York Times*, 19 February, 1989.
55. Roderic Ai Camp, 'Mexico', in James Malloy and Eduardo Gamarra, eds. *Latin American and the Caribbean Contemporary Record*, Vol. 7 (New York: Holmes and Meier, 1989).
56. Cunningham, 'Mexico's National Security in the 1980s–1990s', p. 17.
57. Ronfeldt, 'The Modern Mexican Military', p. 232; a case in point was my book *Mexico's Political Leaders*, published in Mexico by the Fondo de Cultura Económica, which received a request from the secretariat of national defence to do a non-profit edition for the army, 1986.
58. Christopher Brogan, 'Military Higher Education and the Emergence of "New Professionalism": Some Consequences for Civil–Military Relations in Latin America', *Army Quarterly and Defence Journal*, 112 (January 1982), pp. 23, 26.
59. Vicente Ernesto Pérez Mendoza, 'The Role of the Armed Forces', p. 21.
60. *Acción*, 18 January, 1982.
61. Roderic Ai Camp, 'The Military', in George Grayson, ed., *Prospects for Mexico*, (Washington, DC : Center for the Study of Foreign Affairs, Foreign Service Institute, 1988), p. 87.
62. For some allegations of this under Luis Echeverria, see Judith Hellman, *Mexico in Crisis*, (New York: Holmes and Meier, 1978), p. 166; Martin C. Needler, 'A Critical Time for Mexico', *Current History* (February 1972), p. 83.
63. Welch, 'Civilian Control of the Military', pp. 5–6.

9 The Dominican military's conditional retreat

Jan Knippers Black

In 1978, the Dominican armed forces interrupted the ballot count with the apparent intent of nullifying the election of Antonio Guzmán, of the centre-left Dominican Revolutionary Party (PRD), to the presidency. That intervention was thwarted, in part by the timely intercession of United States diplomats and military officers expressing the displeasure of the Carter administration with such anti-democratic initiatives.

For Latin America as a whole, the retreat of the Dominican military marked the beginning of a process of military withdrawal that was to continue for more than a decade. The wave of militarism that had swept the hemisphere in the 1960s and 1970s had left all but about three Latin American states under dictatorial rule, directly or indirectly controlled by the military. By 1989, the situation was reversed. Only the armed forces of Haiti, Panama, and Chile ruled without benefit of a civilian facade.

For the United States, the deterrence of military intervention in the Dominican Republic proved to be the finest hour of the Carter administration and the vindication of Carter's human rights policy. That initiative also illustrated once again the special place of the Dominican Republic in US history. The republic's small size and population, its proximity to the United States, its poverty and the insecurity of its elites have made it more readily manipulable than most countries and thus a choice proving ground for new initiatives in US policy. Largely frustrated in their efforts to leave their marks on the unwieldy United States, US presidents nevertheless have readily left their marks on the Dominican Republic.

For the Dominican Republic, the turning point of 1978 has been followed by more than a decade of relatively free expression and association, of greatly broadened political participation, of greatly diminished government-supported violence, and, for most of that period, of something approximating social peace. It has also been a period in which the armed forces, traditional monitors of public affairs, have maintained an exceptionally low profile. Does that mean that for the Dominican Republic the long era of militarocracy or military tutelage has passed and that freely elected civilian officials may now respond to their popular constituencies without fear of military reprisal? Not necessarily.

The more things change in the Dominican Republic, the more some things stay the same. Politics at the highest level, for example, remains a *pas de deux*. Defying the odds of time and fortune, the two grand old men of letters, Joaquín Balaguer and Juan Bosch, the primary contenders for power when Trujillo was abruptly removed from the scene in 1961, continue to dominate the political arena at the end of the 1980s. Balaguer is now serving his sixth term, and Bosch, leading a well-disciplined centre-left party, enjoys such personal popularity that he is still clearly a force to be reckoned with. Among the military officers who must be conspiring even now to ensure that Bosch is not returned to the presidency are many of the same officers who toppled his government in 1963 and engaged in combat with his supporters in 1965. Along with the two remarkably durable octogenarians, even the supporting cast of characters remains much the same as it was in the 1960s.

Another characteristic of Dominican life that has changed little over the years is the hardship of it for most Dominicans. The benefits of the Caribbean Basin Initiative of the 1980s, like those of the economic miracle of the 1970s and the Alliance for Progress of the 1960s have mostly been siphoned off long before reaching the deprived majority of peasants and blue-collar workers or would-be workers. On an island blessed like few others with varied mineral resources, fertile soils, lush forests, and plentiful fish and fowl, an ingenious and industrious people continues to struggle with little relief or progress against the ravages of hunger and disease.

Finally, even as the anticipated 'American century' draws to a premature close, as the South American states diversify their commercial and diplomatic relations and Central American ones are kept in the backyard only through massive show or use of force, the Dominican Republic resignedly remains a virtual appendage of the United States. The all-important decisions as to what will be produced, at what cost, for what price, with what technology, and for what markets continue to be made beyond its borders and without reference to the needs of its people.

The very important and very positive changes that have taken place in Dominican public life over the last decade are not to be discounted. However, the crucial elements that remain unchanged – in particular, the steeply pyramidal social structure and the high level of dependency – should temper overly optimistic expectations.

This chapter will address in broad outline the history of Dominican civil–military relations; the reasons for and the process of transition to more nearly democratic rule; the contemporary restraints against renewed political activism by the military; and the prospects for civilian supremacy in the foreseeable future.

CIVIL–MILITARY RELATIONS IN HISTORICAL PERSPECTIVE

Dominican independence in the nineteenth century was never very secure. As in the case of many other Latin American countries, the military campaigns that secured independence left the armed forces (or at least a variety of armed bands) in a power position that was wholly out of keeping with constitutional and legal clauses stressing civilian supremacy. In the Dominican case, however, that general pattern was reinforced by the fact that Dominicans had to fight repeatedly for their independence.

Struggles in the nineteenth century against the would-be colonizers of Spain, France, and Haiti gave way at the turn of the century to a new kind of struggle against a new kind of threat. In this struggle the military, at least the largest or most successful elements of it, was to become a tool of the colonizer, and later, with the passing of direct occupation, of the hegemonic power in a neocolonial relationship.

The origins and subsequent development of the modern Dominican armed forces and the nature of their relationship with civilian sectors and institutions cannot be disaggregated from the ambitions and fears of the United States with respect to its client state and, in particular, from the role assigned by the United States armed forces to the Dominican constabulary. The constabulary approach to the problem of 'instability' in Latin America was extended to the furthermost states of South America after the United States emerged from World War II as the unchallenged hegemonic power of the hemisphere. That approach had been tested much earlier, however, in Central America and the Caribbean, and had been found to be reasonably effective.

The strategy for containing and controlling political change was firmly established in the 1930s when US marines, retreating from Central American and Caribbean countries they had occupied, left behind well-trained and well-funded local constabularies to protect the claims of US corporations and the governments and political leaders favoured by US policy-makers against challenges from less favoured local contenders, particularly those who presumed to speak for the lower classes. These constabularies understood very well that their firstline base of support was the US government rather than any element of their national societies.

US occupation and the Dominican constabulary

Before the United States occupation (1916–24), the Dominican military consisted of hastily armed and mobilized bands who fought on behalf of competing regional *caudillos*. Since that occupation, the military has served more consistently as an instrument of US policy than as the instrument of any class or regional interest in the Dominican Republic. First and foremost, however, among the interests served by military power have been those of the institution itself and of its highest-ranking officers. The same might be said of the national police, which was united with other armed bodies in the Dominican Constabulary, established during the US occupation.[1]

The new force, created by executive order of the US military government in April 1917, was called the Guardia Nacional Dominicana, or Dominican National Guard. By 1918 the full complement of 1200 men had been recruited. The nucleus of the new Guard came from the now defunct Guardia Republicana, an unruly group, notorious for preying on civilians.

All ranks above lieutenant were reserved for North Americans. In fact, few Dominicans having the required education and status wanted the stigma of serving the occupation forces, so temporary commissions were given to enlisted men among the US Marines. Dominicans recruited to serve under them generally came from the lower middle class. One such recruit was Rafael Leonidas Trujillo, who joined the Guard in 1919.

One of the most important responsibilities of the Guard was to supplement the efforts of US Marines in putting down a guerrilla uprising in the east. The seeds of insurgency, particularly in the provinces of Seybo and San Pedro de Macorís, antedated the occupation; in those areas the expansion of modern sugar-producing plantations was already displacing peasants who had engaged in subsistence farming, leaving them landless and desperate. But the occupation itself contributed to the spread of insurgency, as the land registration act and other measures adopted by the military government accelerated the displacement of subsistence farmers. Furthermore, tactics employed by the marines and their Dominican understudies and informants, including the brutalization of entire communities in areas that had been 'cordoned off', alienated the population and intensified nationalistic fervour.[2]

Insurgency in the Dominican Republic was by no means an isolated phenomenon. Guerrillas – who, in those days, the United States called bandits – had materialized in virtually all the countries under US occupation. Though no leaders emerged in the Dominican Republic of the stature of Nicaragua's Sandino, the Dominican insurgents held out against the superior arms of the US occupation forces for 5 years. The insurgency ended, with hundreds imprisoned and hundreds more accepting amnesty, only after the United States had drawn up plans for withdrawal.

A factor leading more directly to the US withdrawal was the mounting resistance of articulate, urban Dominicans. Owing perhaps to the indifference of urban upper and middle classes to the plight of peasants, and perhaps also to censorship, there was little notable urban support for the guerrilla campaign in the east. Nevertheless, by 1920 specific abuses associated with martial law, together with the humiliation of foreign occupation, had spurred urban Dominicans to the organization of a more effective nationalist movement. Under the banner of the Unión Nacional Dominicana, nationalists increased their agitation and acts of defiance at home, while mounting an international campaign of diplomacy and propaganda against the occupation.

The international campaign caused embarrassment to the Wilson administration, which began in late 1920 to draw up plans for withdrawal. The US government soon found, however, that it is far easier to launch an intervention than to withdraw from one. The US occupation forces were determined, for example, to ensure that those who most actively resisted their presence should not profit from their departure. In that they were successful; when the United States finally withdrew in 1924, it was not the Dominican nationalists but the US-sponsored constabulary, under the leadership of Rafael Trujillo, that moved in to fill the power vacuum.

Trujillismo and its aftermath

The National Guard became Trujillo's vehicle for attaining control of the government, and once in power, he used it to crush opposition and maintain himself in power; but he stripped it of independent political influence. After Trujillo's assassination, the military emerged as the strongest institution in the country. The 31-year dictatorship of General Trujillo left no aspect of national life unscathed. No political institution had any domestic base independent of Trujillo and his thugs. Politicians such as Joaquín Balaguer, who had associated themselves with the regime, were widely discredited, especially among the educated in urban areas. Those like Juan Bosch, who had fled into exile, remained untainted but also unschooled in the grisly reality of Dominican politics. Thus, both Bosch and Balaguer, the towering *caudillos* of the post-Trujillo era, were rendered less effective as national leaders by the legacy of that awful tyranny.

The confrontations that followed were not of a clear-cut military versus civilian nature; rather, they were struggles among changing alliances of civilian and military cliques. Nevertheless, civilian leaders remained less than comfortable in dealing with military men whose acclimation to their roles had taken place under the brutalizing leadership of Trujillo. As head of government under the Triumvirate, Donald Reid Cabral once confided to a friend that he was very careful about what he said around military men. They were accustomed to taking drastic action on very subtle commands, or even comments, from Trujillo. A comment like 'So-and-so annoys me', for example, might have been taken as a command for execution.[3]

After Trujillo's death in 1961, Balaguer, who was serving as puppet president, yielded to pressures from the Kennedy administration and from the Dominican population and stepped down. Power was transferred to a Council of State, which scheduled elections in 1962. The elections resulted in a solid victory for Juan Bosch and his centre-left Dominican Revolutionary Party (PRD); but after only six months in office, Bosch was overthrown. The country's traditional reactionary forces – in particular, the oligarchy, the military, and the Church – had united to bring down the PRD government and to dominate the so-called Triumvirate government that succeeded it.

In April 1965, the Triumvirate was itself toppled by an uprising dominated by pro-Bosch, or constitutionalist, forces. A civil war ensued, as reactionary elements of the military, encouraged by US military advisers, launched an attack against the constitutionalists and their PRD civilian supporters in Santo Domingo's poorest neighbourhoods. Facing the prospect of a victory by the pro-Bosch forces, President Lyndon B. Johnson sent in the marines.

During the civil war of 1965 the armed forces nearly disintegrated as an institution. Colonel Francisco Caamaño led many younger officers and several whole contingents in support of the constitutionalist movement. After order was restored, loyalist leader General Elías Wessín y Wessín and constitutionalist leader Colonel Caamaño, along with several officers who fought with them, were sent abroad (exiled) to diplomatic posts. Nevertheless, the move nearly toppled the provisional government, and rumours of impending military intervention were heard throughout the 1966 election campaign.

In elections in 1966, supervised by the US Marines and their military cohorts from a few other Latin American countries, Balaguer and his Reformist Party (PR) soundly defeated Bosch and the PRD. Balaguer was re-elected in 1970 and 1974 in elections boycotted by the PRD and most other parties.

One of the provisions of the so-called Institutional Act imposed after order was restored was that the constitutionalist forces should be reincorporated into the regular army, but that did not take place. Those of the rebels who were not imprisoned or exiled were isolated in a single base where they remained well into the 1970s. Some constitutionalist officers have been reintegrated, however, since the PRD returned to power.

Containment through factionalism and perquisites

In the 1970s, the highest-ranking officers were generally engaged in power struggles among themselves, and a semblance of civilian control was maintained through the adroitness of President Balaguer in playing off one faction against another. He frequently reshuffled the top military positions.

This was done to ensure that no officer gained clear ascendancy over the others or retained his command long enough to establish a personal following among his subordinates. At the same time, however, Balaguer was exceedingly generous with his supporters in uniform. During his first term, the armed forces held only one cabinet seat, but they held two in his second and three in his third. Promotions were accelerated, resulting in a top-heavy command structure. Whereas there had been only six general rank officers on active duty when Balaguer assumed the presidency in 1966, there were 48 by the time he relinquished power in 1978.

The military share of the budget also rose steadily under Balaguer, amounting in his final years, to almost twice the appropriated figures; funds were transferred, without legislative approval, from education and health and welfare programmes into military coffers. It was estimated that actual military spending in 1977 was about $75 million, although only $42.7 million was appropriated for that purpose. Furthermore, military officers were assigned to administer state lands and industries and even welfare programmes, and their use of such sinecures for personal enrichment was carefully overlooked.[4]

TRANSITION AND THE NEW DEMOCRATIC REGIME

Latin America's post-war generation of military leaders, convinced by their US mentors that politics, as an extension of the Cold War, was too important to be left to the politicians, settled into the presidential palaces for the long haul. But the strengths of military rule proved to have been overrated. By the late 1970s, several factors that tended to make government by sheer force of arms untenable had converged with factors, like economic crisis, that would weaken any government. Internal cleavage, or factionalism, plagues any ruling elite, military or civilian. Patronage has its limits; for every loyalist who can be rewarded with high office or some other licence to steal, there are many others who will feel slighted. And factionalism is a more serious matter for military rulers than for civilian ones because an actual or simulated *coup d'état* is their only means of rotating leaders in and out of the highest office.

Finally, some regimes found that there are limits even to the obvious utility of brutality and terror. In the 1970s, human rights abuses became so flagrant as to punish not only the inarticulate poor but also legislators, clergymen, academicians, journalists, and others having ties to politically articulate groups in the United States. Growing awareness in the United States of abuses by Latin American client regimes gave rise to a new human rights policy, expressed first by Congress – primarily in the denial of military assistance to systematic abusers – and adopted by the incoming Carter administration in 1977. Thus while other factors came into play, it was no coincidence that the retreat of the generals began with Carter's assumption of power.

Military disunity and the crumbling support base

In the Dominican Republic, the deepening of the economic crisis occurred after the transition and thus may have contributed to the subsequent restraint of the military, but apparently had less to do with the transition itself than was the case in other Latin American countries. Internal cleavage, or factionalism, was an important contributing factor, however, as was external pressure.

During the long reign of Balaguer, virtually all political activists, including some now aligned with him, suffered death threats, narrow escapes, detainment and deportation. They learned both to accept risk and to exercise caution. Thus it was a moderated and subdued PRD that contested and won the elections of 1978. Even so, military officers seeking to block its accession to power backed down only after the Carter administration interceded in support of the democratic process. As Bosch had defected to form another, more leftist, party, the Dominican Liberation Party (PLD), the PRD's standard-bearer this time was Antonio Guzmán, a wealthy rancher.

Little wonder that as the 1978 elections approached the armed forces and the National Police were unhappy at the prospect of the replacement of Balaguer and his personalistic Reformista Party (PR). They were especially unhappy at the prospect of the return to power of the PRD, which they considered a socially disruptive, if not communistic, element. Nevertheless, facing that outcome the uniformed services were unable to present a united front. One reason was that there was intense rivalry among the officers most loyal to Balaguer, especially between General Nivar Seijas, chief of the National Police, and General Enrique Pérez y Pérez, commander of the army's First Brigade. Balaguer himself had cultivated such rivalry as a means of preventing successful conspiracy against him; in 1978, however, it worked against his interest, as Pérez and others refused to follow the lead of General Nivar Seijas.

Another obstacle to military unity was widespread resentment among colonels and other field-grade officers of the monopolization of corruption in the upper ranks and what they saw as the stagnated promotion system. They saw little reason to put themselves at risk only to ensure the sinecures of their superiors. Officers of this persuasion, who came to be known as the 19th of May Group, had begun meeting about a year before the election. By the time of Guzmán's inauguration, they constituted a majority of the younger colonels and lieutenant colonels.

Finally, the politicians in uniform were stunned by the levels of domestic and external opposition to the interruption of the vote count. They had always assumed that they could count on the backing of the US military; finding, in this instance, that their ultimate base of support was not supportive was a frustrating and sobering experience. In the end, the conspirators remained a minority faction, and, as pressure mounted and Balaguer vacillated, they withdrew, claiming that there had never been a coup plot and that nothing out of the ordinary had happened.

As a fall-back position, with the obliging assistance of the PRD-dominated Congress, the armed forces sought to insulate themselves from civilian control through legislation before the PRD government assumed power. Legislation passed in the lame duck session raised military pay; directed the Department of National Investigation (DNI) (a secret police and intelligence unit often used by Balaguer to repress the PRD) to report to the secretary of the armed forces rather than to the president; stipulated that the armed forces secretary must have been a major general for at least five years; and provided that officers could not be transferred by civilian authorities before they had served two years in a given post. Balaguer then reshuffled and further promoted his loyalists so that each of them would have a full two years to serve before Guzmán could move them.

As the ultimate insult to the incoming civilian government, the *comedores económicos*, or 'soup kitchens', for the urban poor were transferred to the jurisdiction of the armed forces. This was done so that Major General Melido Marte Pichardo, Balaguer's presidential security chief, who had been administering the programme, could continue to use it for his personal enrichment.

Guzmán takes charge

Even those senior officers who had been hesitant to participate in the abortive election day coup were prepared to give Guzmán no more than a six-month probationary period, and it appeared that the PR's eleventh hour legislation had indeed placed Guzmán on a short leash. But Guzmán managed to turn the tables. Strengthened by an intensely anti-military popular mood at home and by continued support from Washington, Guzmán disregarded the tainted legislation and moved quickly to rid his government of those officers who most clearly threatened it. Nivar Seijas and Pérez y Pérez, who had been linked, in the early 1970s, to death squad activities, were among the 23 senior officers retired in short order. More than 240 potentially disloyal commissioned and noncommissioned officers were also replaced by more reliable ones.

The armed forces did not necessarily accept Guzmán's initiatives with good grace. In fact, a coup was plotted in 1979, but Guzmán was able to crush it before it unfolded. In the meantime, his promotions of junior and middle-ranking officers who had been dead-ended or derailed by Balaguer boosted morale among that long-disgruntled set and attenuated their hostility to the PRD.

Guzmán opened up the system, eliminating restraints on civil liberties and urging respect for human rights. He also pledged to rein in runaway corruption, to promote economic growth and modernization, and to provide long-neglected social services. His political position was weak, however, as he encountered fierce opposition from within his own party as well as from Balaguer's PR. And his assumption of power coincided with a steep economic decline. The sugar market had gone limp. Most other exports were in low demand as well, and petroleum, all of which had to be imported, was scarce and expensive.

A bad situation was made worse by a devastating hurricane in 1979. Thus, social services continued to be neglected, and economic development programmes were sustained only at the expense of a sharply mounting foreign debt. Corruption scarcely abated. In fact, it is generally believed that it was embarrassment over his own daughter's involvement in shady deals that drove Guzmán to suicide shortly before the end of his term.[5] Meanwhile, Senator Salvador Jorge Blanco, one of Guzmán's arch-enemies within the PRD, had been elected to the presidency for the term beginning in 1982.

Jorge Blanco had no considerable popular following of his own, but he brought to the presidency the reputation of a serious and honest lawyer-politician with a constructive programme. He pledged to maintain and strengthen the social and political liberalism introduced by his predecessor; to stem the tide of corruption, to which the PRD itself had fallen prey; to trim the size of the bureaucracy, which had mushroomed under Guzmán; and to expand services and protection to the disadvantaged majority. Sadly, it has been in the nature of things – the urgency of majority needs, the scarcity of national resources, the extent of private greed, the omnipresence of military intimidation and US guardianship, and the crushing pressures from foreign creditors – that Dominican presidents rarely leave office with their political stock intact. Economic and political circumstances largely beyond his control combined with the weaknesses of his own administration to make Jorge Blanco's presidency a troubled and disappointing one.

Jorge Blanco, portrayed by Guzmán himself as a leftist, was even less acceptable to politically-oriented officers than Guzmán had been. Having so much to overcome, Jorge Blanco was exceptionally generous with the military. Salaries were raised, and housing facilities and commissary offerings expanded. A new Social Security Institute, including a hospital, was established exclusively for the armed forces and the police. Jet planes and

modern patrol boats were purchased, and extra-legal enterprises were overlooked.

Nevertheless, Jorge Blanco never achieved the levels of control over and
respect from the officer corps that Guzmán enjoyed. In fact, they simply
refused to accept his first choice for commander of the army; he was forced
to back down and withdraw his nominee and to accept General Jose Ernesto
Cruz Brea, reputedly a right-wing hardliner, in that position.[6]

Facing the spectre of default on a number of important foreign debts, Jorge
Blanco caved in also to the demands of the International Monetary Fund
(IMF) for the imposition of austerity measures that severely penalized his
own constituency and deepened the factionalism within the PRD. In particular, the peso devaluation of April 1984 resulted in sharp price increases for
a number of essential commodities and ignited riots in Santo Domingo that
went on for three days and left more than 100 dead. His government never
recovered from that episode, and it sunk ever deeper into unpopularity as
charges of corruption mounted during its final months.

The PRD thus faced the elections of 1986 with a severely divided party,
a reputation besmirched by corruption, and an economy in shambles. Little
wonder that many voters looked back through rose-coloured glasses upon
the 'good old days' of Balaguer's rule. Running at the head of a newly
constituted Social Christian Reformist Party, he took a plurality of some 41
per cent of the vote, leaving the PRD's Jácobo Majluta with 39 per cent and
Bosch, heading the Dominican Liberation Party, with 18 per cent.[7]

The PRD legacy

PRD governments, during their 8-year tenure, attempted to depoliticize the
armed forces. Officers charged with attempting to influence votes during the
previous elections were reprimanded. Nevertheless, Jorge Blanco's
Secretary of State for the Armed Forces, General Manuel Antonio Cuervo
Gómez, who was later indicted for corruption, issued a strong warning to the
left in an interview published in November 1984.

The fierce military factionalism of the 1970s has not reappeared. Nor has
there appeared a new centre for political intrigue comparable to the Armed
Forces Education Center (CEFA) of the 1960s. Some critics contend that
military officers are too busy getting rich to want to bother with politics. Even
in the 1980s there were unsolved murders that many attributed to the armed
forces and the police, but such murders were not necessarily political; some
appeared to be related to drug-trafficking and to illegal currency exchange
operations. Following the kidnap-murder of a prominent banker, Héctor
Méndes, in January 1985, General Ramiro Matos González, minister of
interior and police, dismissed the National Police Chief and assumed that

position himself. Witnesses had alleged that Méndes was kidnapped by the police.

PRD leaders maintained that civilian control over the armed forces had been institutionalized, but they clearly preferred not to test that hypothesis. They remained particularly concerned about the extent of US training of Dominican officers.[8] All of the country's military cadets train at US schools in Panama and some two dozen high-ranking Dominican officers are graduates of the US Army Command and General Staff School. The Dominican armed forces opened their own command and general staff school in 1984, modelled on its US counterpart. The republic also has an elite unit known as the Cazadores de la Montaña (Highland Rangers), trained by US specialists in counter-insurgency, which trains other services.

CONSTRAINTS AGAINST RENEWED MILITARISM

More than a decade has passed since the Dominican military overtly threatened to intervene in an election and determine its outcome. To what do we owe such an unprecedented period of apparent civilian hegemony and relatively unfettered electoral competition?

Can the role of the military have changed dramatically while the cast of characters in leadership positions – both military and civilian, the economic hardships suffered by the majority, and the status of dependence and subordination to the United States have changed so little? The simple answer, I believe, is no – or, at least, not yet. The withdrawal of the military has thus far been only partial and conditional. The generals have by no means retreated far enough to give democracy a free rein.

Four factors, which might be seen as temporal or conditional rather than as structural or long-term, have contributed to the restraint of the military over the last decade. They are: the role of the International Monetary Fund (IMF) in protecting elite interests; the nature of executive–legislative relations in the United States and the usefulness of a civilian facade; the pacifying role of corruption; and since 1986, the political adroitness of Balaguer. There is a fifth factor that may not yet have come fully into play, but that should prove the most important one for the long run. That factor, the politics of the tourist industry, will be addressed in the final section.

The usefulness of the IMF and the civilian facade

Even in countries having a firmly established tradition of military intervention, military establishments rarely move against civilian governments entirely on their own. The necessary unity within the military itself generally comes about only when important elements of the civilian economic elite and/or of the hegemonic power, seeing their interests threatened, weigh in in favour of intervention. The interests of foreign and domestic elites in the Dominican Republic, as elsewhere in Latin America in the 1980s, have been protected to some extent by the fact that military withdrawal has been incomplete. Meanwhile, the more immediate task of protecting those interests – that is, of ensuring that debt servicing is maintained without threat to the existing economic structure – has fallen to the IMF.

When foreign creditors demand sacrifice as the price of extending further loans, the rich make the usual choice about whether or not to accept that sacrifice, and the sacrifice is borne by those who have no choice. Civilian elites who can no longer blame the military for such grossly inequitable policies can now pass the buck to the mysterious and seemingly omnipotent IMF.

A party such as the PRD, popular and reformist in its origins, would ordinarily be a source of anxiety for economic elites and a target for military repression – as indeed it was throughout most of its history and as recently as 1978. Because of that history, in fact, it was a much subdued PRD that assumed the presidency in 1978. Even so, the most modest of its promised welfare measures were thwarted by the austerity measures imposed by the IMF, while the military lurked in the background. Seeing themselves under constant threat – feeling the pull of the short leash – PRD executives, Jorge Blanco in particular, made concessions to creditors and to other foreign and domestic elite interests, that even the notoriously conservative Balaguer might have resisted!

Such an outcome, allowing a reformist party to take 'power' only to discredit itself, while their own reputations are protected along with their interests, has obvious appeal for economic elites, as for hegemonic powers. In the United States in the 1980s, a government representing the ideological right finally discovered what more seasoned conservatives had long recognized, that in a client state a civilian government that is uninterested in acting upon or unable to act upon a popular mandate and unwilling or unable to control military and paramilitary forces is a better hedge against social change than a repressive military government. That learning process was expedited by a Congress that under popular pressure to end support for human rights violation insisted on taking a firm position on both sides of the fence; particularly with respect to Central America it made the maintenance of a 'democratic' civilian facade a condition for the on-going provision of military aid. The lesson learned so well in Central America should be equally applicable to the Dominican Republic.

Corruption as a pacifier

The durability of Dominican presidents has always hinged to some extent on their approach to corruption. In fact, the fortunes of Dominican presidents since the fall of Trujillo reveal a great deal about the role of corruption in Dominican politics and about Dominican attitudes towards corruption.

Bosch was overthrown in part because he tried to pull the plug on military corruption. The *coup d'état* of 1963 that so abbreviated his presidency had many authors, not the least of which, according to Bosch himself and to his friends and enemies alike, were agents and agencies of the US government.[9] But the Dominican armed forces had their own motives, which went well beyond the publicly paraded ones of maintaining order and fighting Communism. According to a retired army officer who had been among those selected by their peers to deliver to the president a briefing on military grievances, Bosch's insistence on curtailing US arms purchases threatened to put an end to some of the armed forces' most lucrative rackets.

Jorge Blanco fell into disrepute – and later under indictment – because he allegedly tried to take over and orchestrate military and other rackets. He took refuge in April 1987 in the Venezuelan Embassy and later fled to the United States for an indefinite period of 'medical observation', but he returned to the Dominican Republic in the spring of 1989 to stand trial. Widely accredited charges against him range from the massive allocation to friends and political cronies of tax exemptions for the importation of cars and industrial products to conspiracy in currency exchange and narcotraffic deals. Moreover, it is widely rumoured that several million dollars allotted annually to 'national security' simply disappeared. His highest-ranking military and police appointees are also on trial, largely as a consequence of denunciations originating from within the military. It appears, then, that career military officers feel strongly about the right of the institution to run its own rackets without interference or competition from civilian authorities.

As before, Balaguer is being careful not to impede institutional (as opposed to PRD-based) military rackets. He found during previous presidential terms that most officers were willing to surrender considerable political power and to address total loyalty to him in exchange for the opportunity to enrich themselves at the public's expense.

A particularly well-connected political insider maintains that in the 1980s the three services have become highly specialized in their profit-making endeavours. The air force, he says, has the narcotraffic protection franchise. The navy has the concession for protecting illegal exit to Puerto Rico. Army enterprises are rather more diversified, but on the Haitian frontier the army monopolizes the taking of bribes from Haitians entering illegally and the confiscation of their purchases as they leave. The police are left with the generally less lucrative *mordidas* (petty bribes) they can extract from traffic offenders and street operators.

Balaguer, meanwhile, maintains an ascetic lifestyle and is universally acclaimed for his 'personal' integrity. Even Bosch and other political opponents give full credence to Balaguer's assertion that the corruption stops at the door to his office.

THE ADROITNESS OF BALAGUER

Balaguer's political skills are legendary. Friends and enemies alike credit his intelligence and political acumen, and even those who know him best describe him as enigmatic. Under the tutelage of Trujillo, he learned to listen and not to speak unnecessarily; he also learned how to reward and discipline supporters, co-opt the uncommitted, and punish his enemies. He was adept at combining authoritarianism with paternalism, but, always the pragmatist, he has adapted with ease to operating in a more open and democratic system, building on his strengths in bargaining and conciliation.

Now in his sixth term, Balaguer has profited, ironically, from his failure to establish a real party or any other civilian institution of consequence. No one seems to begrudge his solitary style of decision-making; and even his would-be enemies wish him good health, largely because of the uncertainties that would accompany his demise.

No new generation of leaders is apparent in Balaguer's Social Christian Reformist Party (PRSC) or in any other party. Balaguer's early cabinet appointments were a veritable Who's Who of the centre to right, including many of his one-time enemies. The aristocracy, which has not always been on good terms with Balaguer, was represented by Donald Reid Cabral, who headed the very conservative Triumvirate government of 1963–5; Reid Cabral served as minister of foreign affairs until he was replaced by Balaguer's nephew, Joaquín Ricardo. Foreign investors might have been reassured by the placement of Carlos A. Morales Troncoso in the vice-presidency. Morales Troncoso, previously a local manager of Gulf and Western properties had become a major stockholder in the properties of the Fanjul brothers, who bought out Gulf and Western in early 1985.

The Christian Democrats, whose recent merger with Balaguer's Reformist Party provided Balaguer with valuable international ties and legitimacy, have not reaped much yet from the bargain. Their leaders still believe that they stand one day to inherit Balaguer's base in the peasantry. In the mean time, however, Balaguer has mainly used them to fill subcabinet positions where it is important to have competent people who can be counted on not to steal.

Balaguer's initial choice for secretary of the armed forces was sure to displease some of the military's career officers, but might have been reassuring to the Pentagon and the CIA. General Antonio Imbert Barrera is one of two survivors from among those who, in 1961, at the behest of the CIA, assassinated Trujillo. The interior secretary, in charge of the police and of 'public order', was the omnipresent General Elías Wessín y Wessín. Wessín masterminded the coup against the government of Juan Bosch in 1963 and, with the help of the US Marines, put down the uprising of Bosch's constitutionalist forces in 1965. He also conspired a time or two in the early 1970s against the government of Balaguer.

At any rate, the military leaders in the cabinet are essentially *gastado*, or burned out, having little following of their own. This leaves Balaguer free to mediate among services and factions whose loyalty is above all to him. Some speculated that Balaguer had drawn Imbert and Wessín into his cabinet in order, figuratively (he is almost blind), to keep an eye on them. It was clear that confidence between the president and each of these officers was less than complete. Balaguer in late 1987 vetoed and pushed into early retirement Imbert's nominees for chiefs of the three services. In June 1988, following rumours of a coup attempt, Balaguer dismissed Imbert, replacing him with Wessín as secretary of the armed forces.

Given the country's dire economic straits, and particularly a steady decline over several years in the standard of living of the poor majority, the ambience that prevailed until early 1988 was remarkably calm and stable. There had been few manifestations of civil unrest. A general strike in July 1987 generated no disorder (due in part to the curiously passive role played by PLD-dominated student and labour groups), and police did not fire a single shot – a restraint duly noticed and publicly praised by human rights monitors.

The record of the new born-again-democratic Balaguer in this regard stood in stark contrast to that of previous Balaguer governments as well as to the government of Jorge Blanco, [10] though the rights of the poor are poorly protected even in the best of times, and Haitians in the Dominican Republic remain particularly vulnerable to scapegoating or worse. Until 1988, even Balaguer's political enemies conceded that relatively speaking this government had shown sensitivity to human rights concerns and restraint in maintaining order. In fact, the Balaguer government had shown such skill in conciliation that instead of the polarization that might have been expected amidst economic desperation, the political scene as 1988 began was more aptly being characterized as a *sancocho*, or stew, and most of the country's ills were being blamed on Balaguer's runaway predecessor.

That climate changed suddenly and dramatically during the third week of February. The protests that began at that time, over low wages, the soaring costs of basic goods and services, and the scarcity of such amenities as electricity and potable water, were remarkably widespread. At least eleven of the country's twenty-seven provinces were crippled by general strikes, and incidents of violence were reported throughout the country, particularly in the capital, Santo Domingo, and in a half dozen northern cities. By 2 March, casualties included 10 dead and at least 20 wounded, and several thousand protesters had been arrested.

Along with the use of military force to crush the unrest, Balaguer's offer of a substantial wage hike to public employees on March first may have contributed to a lull later in the month. But violence erupted once again on 6 April, as thousands took part in street demonstrations throughout the country. Bombs exploded in Santo Domingo and in Santiago, the country's second-largest city. Twenty persons were injured in the bombing in Santiago, and many more were injured in Santo Domingo in confrontations with riot squad police. A National Strike Committee, comprised of labour confederations and civic and neighbourhood organizations, called for a 48-hour nationwide general strike to begin on 7 April.

Negotiations between labour and business leaders mediated by the Catholic hierarchy served to quell the unrest for the short term. But strikes have been common in 1989 and riots have erupted from time to time. Balaguer is now on notice that the bargaining and conciliation that have served in the past to mitigate conflict among elites are no substitute for addressing the urgent needs of the masses.

PROSPECTS FOR CIVILIAN SUPREMACY

The Dominican Republic has weathered remarkably well the political and economic crises of the 1980s, but the calm that prevails as the decade draws to a close should not be mistaken for stability. A very great deal of economic readjustment and diversification has taken place, but it is not clear that those changes will solve even the long-term problems of balance of payments and debt servicing; and they are not even addressed to the shorter-term problem of the economic insecurity of the majority.

The collapse of the world sugar market in the early 1980s, followed in short order by a massive cut in the Dominican quota of the US sugar market, left the country economically destitute and terminally indebted. The tourist industry, growing exponentially, has since become the country's major foreign exchange earner. Nontraditional export crops grown on land formerly devoted to sugar cane and light industry in the proliferating duty-free zones have also contributed to a measure of economic recovery. Nevertheless, the country remains utterly dependent upon dollar remissions from the nearly one million emigrants now living in Puerto Rico or the United States and on hard currency loans contracted at great cost to national sovereignty and social peace.

Balaguer's approach to the country's very severe economic problems – printing pesos to cover a new public works programme, and more recently to stimulate agricultural production – has generated new jobs but has also resulted in devaluation and accelerated inflation (the cost of rice, beans, and other staples doubled, and in some cases even tripled, in 1988).[11] Meanwhile the foreign reserves accumulated first of all from remittances from Dominican emigrants, second from tourism, and to an unknown degree from drug deals cannot be expected to adequately service a foreign debt of some 4 billion. A new class of financiers, however, has learned how to profit from the country's economic prostration – through currency exchange deals and speculation in scarce commodities. This group competes for influence with another new rich sector, the *narcotrafficantes*, some of whom are plying their trade in the Dominican Republic, while others are merely laundering there money earned elsewhere. Whether the sense of threat to more nearly traditional economic elites and their well pampered military allies comes from the perennially poor or the newly rich, the fluidity of the situation cautions against complacency.

Nor is the political prospect reassuring with respect to military restraint. The tug-of-war over inheritance of Balaguer's PRSC remains unresolved, and no definite new leadership has emerged. The PRD remains profoundly discredited by the economic failures and the much heralded corruption of the Jorge Blanco government. It is also irreparably split between the factions of Jacobo Majluta and José Francisco Peña Gómez. Majluta, generally viewed as an able but corrupt politician, is believed to have a firmer grip on party 'machinery', particularly in the provinces; but Peña Gómez's popular base among the poor of Santo Domingo probably gives him better long-term prospects of reviving the party.

The Dominican Liberation Party (PLD), which Bosch established in 1973 as his new political vehicle, has gained followers at the expense of the sinking PRD and may have benefited as well from Balaguer's relatively benign attitude towards it. Bosch charged in the spring of 1988 that in some military barracks bombs were being prepared as part of a plot to create havoc and blame it on the PLD – this in order to discredit Bosch and his party in anticipation of the 1990 elections. Within 72 hours of Bosch's denunciation of the plot, Balaguer had dismissed the commanders of the National Police and of the air force.[12]

Both Bosch and Balaguer have reserved their harshest criticisms for the PRD. Meanwhile, the PLD is generally acknowledged to be the best organized party in the country now. It claimed 18 per cent of the vote in the last election and has been growing very fast since then. The question then would be whether or not the US and Dominican armed forces would allow him to take office; the answer to that one may have more to do with developments in the United States than in the Dominican Republic.

Meanwhile, though, the country's new leading industry provides new grounds for optimism; more than most profit-making enterprises, tourism offers a modicum of insurance for the constitutional system. Since tourists tend to shy away from countries experiencing civil turmoil or military rule, an emphasis on tourism may give party leaders greater incentives to resolve their differences without resort to agitation in the streets. Tourism should also give leaders of the business community, domestic and foreign, an unaccustomed dread of military intervention and a predilection to support constitutional government and civilian rule.

NOTES

1. The National Police has since become a separate body in form, but in practice, particularly with respect to political issues and conflicts, it operates as a branch of the armed forces; its senior officers are drawn from and circulated back to the other services.
2. For elaborated coverage of the US occupation and Dominican resistance, see Bruce J. Calder, *The Impact of Intervention: The Dominican Republic during the US Occupation of 1916-1924*. (Austin: University of Texas Press, 1984).
3. As told to Social Christian Party leader Alfonso Moreno Martínez, Interview with Moreno Martínez, Santo Domingo, 2 January 1985.
4. G. Pope Atkins, *Arms and Politics in the Dominican Republic* (Boulder, CO: Westview Press, 1981), pp. 107–22.
5. Guido D'Alessandro, who as minister of mining and commerce in 1975–6 had tightened national controls over the partially US-owned gold mining company, Rosário Dominicano SA, believes that the Guzmán government paid private shareholders far more than the mine was worth because Guzmán's daughter, Sonia, had invested in the company.
6. Sources include Richard Hines, political counsellor, US Embassy, Santo Domingo, interview 3 January 1985; and Colonel Wayne Wheeler, US military attaché, US Embassy, 8 January 1985.
7. Michael J. Kryzanek and Howard J. Wiarda, *The Politics of External Influence in the Dominican Republic* (NY: Praeger, 1988), p. 58.
8. J. Winston Arnaud, Acting Secretary-General, Partido Revolucionario Dominicano (PRD), interview with the author, 10 January 1985.
9. Former President Juan Bosch, interview with the author, Santo Domingo, 12 January 1988.
10. The slow-moving machinery of the UN Human Rights Commission ruled in late 1987 in favour of reparations for those brutalized by the Jorge Blanco government's tactics in the course of the 1984 riots.
11. Vito Echevarria, 'Balaguer's Bid to Stop the Dollar Deluge', *South* (UK), February 1989, pp. 36–7.
12. Roberto Brito, 'Destituyen a los jefes de la policía y de la Fuerza Aérea', *El Diário-La Prensa* (Santo Domingo) 25 May 1988.

10 Coup, withdrawal and economic development in Gabon

Elena V. Dorabji

Of the countries represented in the United Nations, about a third are on the continent of Africa. Many are a mystery to the English-speaking reader, whether layman or professional. Some might be known because they were dominated by the British, and these speak our language, send us their students and ask us for aid, while others, having lived under the yoke of French colonialism, seem too distant and exotic to grapple with. Nor do we really see the point of trying to understand them, since France has continued to monopolize the trade in aid and cultural interchange with these former colonies since independence. This is not to infer that we are blaming France for our ignorance. We in the English-speaking world have done the same with the former colonial possessions of Great Britain (of which there have been a great number). We have monopolized relations and ideas with them in just the same fashion, but living inside the circle of this reality we have chosen not to focus on the parallel universes existing beyond our line of sight.

This brings us to Gabon, a fascinating and neglected country. Gabon is not a household world in the English-speaking West, despite a book of enlightenment attempted by America's first ambassador to the newly independent country in the 1960s.[1] Few people will know that this former French colony is situated below the Cameroons and Congo (Brazzaville), on the western coast of Africa; that it straddles the equator; and that this country, the size of Italy, began independence with less than half a million people. Today's population, thirty years later, stands at about a million and a half, with 350,000 living in the capital city of Libreville. And if asked, even fewer people will be able to identify correctly that it is Gabon which can boast of the highest per capita income in sub-Saharan Africa.[2] This income in 1987 averaged $5500 per person.[3]

Gabon also boasts of a functioning civilian government, and an essentially uninterrupted history of constitutional rule, and a thriving economy based on timber production, the extraction of uranium, manganese, iron ore and petroleum. Its exports of $2.2 billion in 1984 exceeded imports by $1.5

billion.⁴ Gabon has also enjoyed a highly favoured status with France, a relationship extending back beyond independence.

Given all of the above-mentioned information why has Gabon been included in an anthology on military-civilian rule? The reason, simply enough, is that Gabon also, for a brief 48-hour period, in the month of February 1964, fell into the hands of a group of junior army officers. These officers, outraged at being excluded from the bounty harvested after independence by the civilian government in power, managed, in a matter of hours to storm the presidential palace, seizing the then head of state, Leon Mba, and carrying him off to the bush. But, unlike similar coups conducted in French-speaking Africa in the preceding year of 1963, the Gabonese coup was to end in a different manner. Within two days of the bloodless coup, which succeeded with barely any military resistance or popular civilian outcry, Mba was back in his post as president, thanks to the immediate intervention of the French government. Unprecedented in the history of French Africa, foreign troops had been sent to intervene in the internal problems of a former possession, where they had not been so used under similar circumstances, either before or after. The outcome of this intervention was the immediate reestablishment of civilian rule. However, more important, it resulted in the successful functioning of civilian rule ever since.

It is this story, of unique French intervention in Gabonese internal affairs, which deserves to be spotlighted in this chapter. And ironically, perhaps, it is the story of this unique event which highlights all the common problems befalling the newly independent countries of Africa: economic neocolonialism; states existing without national purpose, character, and impulse; and leaders out of step with their people and with each other. In short, Gabon is a microcosm of the struggle of post-independent Africans searching for a place to call their own in a world grown at the same time more interdependent and more egocentric. And how Gabon is handling her problems, how she is dealing with the three biggest problems of the twentieth century – economic development, national sovereignty, and stable democratic rule – may well provide us with a mirror to our own.

PRELUDE TO THE COUP

Gabon was a colony of the French prior to independence. Although trade along the coast line had been active for hundreds of years, the hostile climate and topography of the equatorial rainforest had pre-empted any serious European penetration. Struggle within the overwhelming invasiveness of the rainforest had also greatly burdened the local populations of the region, and disease, and scarcity of tillable land had been contributing factors to its very low population density. In addition the impenetrability of the forests had resulted in population clusters of isolated subsistence economies, self-sufficient and xenophobic. Clannishness, always a characteristic of isolated subsistence economies, was extreme in this part of equatorial Africa, where one's only salvation was one's closest kith and kin, everyone else being part of the hostile exterior environment.

Colonialism only served to strengthen feelings of negativity towards strangers, for colonialism by its very nature was exploitive and demeaning, justifying its harsh rule with ideologies of superiority of civilization and race. In comparison to other African countries Gabon's colonial experience was relatively limited. Although some knowledge of its enormous mineral wealth existed before independence, the hostile interior environment prevented easy access, so serious exploration and exploitation were delayed. Also, unlike gold and diamonds, the natural resources which Gabon was known to have (uranium, manganese, iron ore and petroleum) enjoyed a greater demand later on in the twentieth century, as the world's economy became more industrialized and as more easily accessible sources of these minerals became exhausted. Thus, because pressure to exploit Gabon's store of mineral treasures was delayed, her economy remained fairly untouched. Except for the capital city, whose economic ties reached out to France and other French-owned African coastal locations, the bulk of Gabon's interior stayed as it had always been: small kinship groups eking out a self sufficient if precarious existence in the hostile environment of the rainforest. There was no traditional economy of interdependence through trade and conquest as many of West Africa's city-states had experienced. The Gabonese also were spared the effects of a settler influx which pushed Africans off their own holdings and into a wage-economy as landless labourers. Likewise, the Gabonese were not subjected to poll taxes and hut taxes to force them wholesale into the mines or onto plantations, as colonial subjects elsewhere in Africa had been.

Conversely, few roads, railroads, or bridges were built to transport minerals, give settlers access to upcountry sites, or to protect strategic holdings. Thus, Libreville at independence had not yet been confronted with the consequences of urbanization due to the economic pressures of more penetrated colonial societies. Few people in Gabon considered moving into town, steeped as they were in a traditional economy that still met their needs, not yet educated enough to question the truth of continuing in its path, not close enough to roads or rail to bring them to the capital, even if they had so desired. Gabon, in a nutshell, was not at independence a nation waiting to be born but a state just conceived.

The impulse for nationhood had not, primarily, been an internal one. Few Gabonese thought about nationhood. Few had been to school, fewer still to university. Those who had been educated, invariably in France or another

French colony, were the ones who wanted a new political order. They also were expected by everyone to be the new rulers of an independent Gabon, once independence was granted. There had been no protracted popular struggle, nor had the boundaries of the Gabonese state been drawn according to any patriotic imperative or sense of historical inevitability. Gabon just 'happened', thrown together because of some long-ago reason having, of course, nothing to do with common Gabonese needs, hopes, or goals. At the same time Gabon was preparing itself for the 'possibility' of nationhood in the 1950s, it was being tantalized with other political alternatives: union with France as an integral part of its polity, and alternatively, membership in a regional structure of government, consisting of contiguous African sister-states from the same colonial background. All in all, the political imperative towards independence as a Gabonese nation was weak, artificial, and arbitrary. Gabon became Gabon in 1960, not out of a popular sense of destiny but out of an elitist impulse to be part of the modern community, to shed its perceived yoke of inferiority and backwardness, so that it could hold its head high among the civilized communities of modern men.

Yet, as the present Gabonese President, Omar Bongo, himself has pointed out, in 1960, the 'heavy heritage of independence' was not yet evident to the world community. It was colonialism that was perceived as an evil so oppressive, that its simple removal would be enough to right the wrong of generations and sometimes centuries of abuse and exploitation. No one had expected the scar of colonialism to leave such a deep and lasting mark: 'We all felt that independence was the end of the road, not its beginning, and that the terrible effects of colonialism had been wiped out with its achievements. Instead we faced a new and painful struggle to overcome, a heavy heritage to take on.'[5]

Bongo himself has added some valuable insights to the political problems faced by the Gabonese at independence. First, there were very few Western educated and trained Africans who understood the dynamics of running a modern state. Gabon itself had no university of its own and very few matriculated graduates. Second, France had excluded the Gabonese from positions of political and economic power until after World War II, when the first Gabonese were elected to the regional Second Constituent Assembly for Gabon – Middle Congo. The Gabonese who involved themselves in national politics for the most part espoused views which were a 'parasitic reflection' of political ideas and conflicts in France. In other words, according to Bongo, they parroted ideas and processes from the homeland and did not approach politics from the fresh perspective of Gabon and her unique needs and viewpoints. Their artificial approach to political action alienated the masses and made them indifferent to modern political struggle. Not only could the people not relate to the way the Gabonese elite contested political power, but the elite themselves could not rise above the petty and egocentric use of parties as a cover for fighting personal battles as well as regional and ethnic ones. As a consequence, politics after independence was reduced to the worst form of parochial and personal infighting imaginable.[6]

Not only was political conflict threatening the integrity and well-being of the state from the outset, but economic interests also inhibited the true formation of an independent Gabon. Economic exploitation after all, was the impulse that had driven colonialism. And the French had developed an elaborate network of economic interdependency which the Gabonese, especially those directing the new state, could not dissolve without serious consequences. Since the leaders of Gabon had committed themselves unhesitatingly to the ideal of economic development, their options for divorcing themselves from economic interaction with the French were quite small. If they threw out the French contractors, bakers, and bankers, who would build their roads, bake their bread, and give them development aid? The Gabonese leaders at independence and in the years thereafter were caught up in the heavy web of neocolonial exploitation and this, as much as the weakness of their political infrastructure, made independent, effective national decision making so difficult.

In Gabon the economic dependence on France was classic. After independence most teachers were still French, as were most doctors and other professionals. Among the advisors to the government the French were liberally represented. From electricians to plumbers to aeroplane pilots, the French owned and ran the bulk of the economic infrastructure of the country, which in essence was the infrastructure of the capital city. The hinterland was essentially without roads, hospitals and secondary schools. This situation grew worse in the first years after independence as national leaders living in Libreville appropriated the lion's share of funds to modernize the capital city and its infrastructural needs (with such things as an international airport, four-lane highways into town, parliamentary buildings). What jobs the French did not control were taken by the more westernized Congolese and Dahomenians from neighbouring French colonies. These people, having lived under French rule in more accessible locations, had been exposed to modern opportunities and expectations longer than the bulk of the Gabonese.

In spite of these factors, the Gabonese did not seem to resent the French continuing domination of their economy after independence. In fact a common myth at independence was that the French and Gabonese had not had a hostile, exploitive relationship during colonial rule. They were like older and younger brother; Gabon's association with France had been voluntarily entered into by Gabon's tribal leaders during the nineteenth century and freely maintained. No other country stood in such close relationship to

Gabon.[7] The Gabonese expressed pride at the civilizing influence of French culture, at the schools, hospitals, and roads that they had built.[8]

After independence the French continued to funnel in huge amounts of aid as well as more lucrative types of assistance. According to Charles Darlington, who was Gabon's US Ambassador at independence in 1960, the French were much better aid providers than others, especially the Americans. They paid the salaries of a host of Frenchmen, from doctors and teachers to financial experts and engineers. They financed all manner of capital projects and economic and engineering studies and provided equipment from bulldozers to hypodermic needles. From Darlington's point of view French assistance was not only large but well selected and efficiently executed. The French were able to conceive, finance and implement programmes in a fraction of the time it took Darlington and the cumbersome checks and balances system under the American Congress. Not only was the French Foreign Office freed from the burden of having everything approved and directed by the French Assembly, but Paris' foreign policy was not up for review every year by the congressional chairman of a foreign affairs subcommittee. All in all the French outclassed all potential rivals and maintained a firm economic grip on the country after independence.

Incredibly the biggest economic web was not between the French government, protected French business interests, and the Gabonese Libreville elite. It was between the large mining companies and the western countries who owned shares in their operations and required the materials they produced. These companies operated outside the confines of the urban economy of Libreville. The minerals had to be mined where they were found and typically their location was in some inaccessible and forsaken spot. At the time of independence there were several of these large mining companies operating in Gabon. One was a mine at Moanda, which was said to have the largest reserves of high-grade manganese in the free world. Since the United States was the sole customer of this manganese, the French not being manganese users, American interests were major stockholders. US Steel owned 49 per cent of COMILOG, which mined the ore, and had an investment of over $60 million.[9] The other shareholder was France with 51 per cent. This mine was located in the southeastern corner of Gabon, as far away from Libreville, on the north-western coast, as any location in Gabon. Its self-contained mining community was serviced and administered by French personnel. The US Steel company acting as technical advisors made the operation a capital-intensive one requiring few Gabonese labourers. The availability of the ore a few feet below the surface enabled the use of immense bulldozers. The ore was crushed and washed and then loaded into buckets swinging on an aerial cableway called *téléferique*. It moved the ore a short 45 miles into Congo–Brazzaville, where the Congolese railroad carried it to the Congolese port of

Pointe Noire for shipping to America. The COMILOG concession was serviced by no Gabonese rail line or road to its own coastal port but did have an airstrip which brought it whatever could not be supplied by road from the two neighbouring Congos. Near it was the uranium mine of Franceville, which supplied half of France's uranium needs, France being a nuclear power. This, too, was trucked to Porte Noire in precious barrels worth $5000 each for shipping to France.

In this pattern of economic interaction one sees the typical costs and benefits of neo-imperialism, that is, the continued post-independence economic exploitation by a former imperial power of a former colony. Except for the taxes or royalties paid to the Gabonese government, the profit from the sales and from the remaining economic 'by-products' of these mining enterprises are divided up by non-Gabonese. The only exceptions would be the wages paid to the relatively few common labourers who work in the mines. As for the trained engineering, advisory and managerial personnel, they are all foreign, usually French. Their sizeable economic needs – from food to clothing to building supplies for houses – are all provided by foreign merchants, again usually French. Transportation lines are owned by the foreign country of Congo (Brazzaville), or in the case of the *téléférique*, are of no use to the indigenous Gabonese population. The manganese and uranium are themselves metals of no use to the Gabonese, and so cannot be transformed into finished products in Gabon to be sold as exports. The local economy in essence benefits hardly at all. And when one recalls that Gabonese development plans hinged on these schemes to make Gabon self-sufficient and advanced[10] one can only marvel at the optimism of the leadership.

In the 1960s Gabon was known to Western business interests as one of the richest African states in natural resources. Americans were moving in fast on traditional French markets and jockeying for position to 'help' in the country's economic development. Besides the 49 per cent share in COMILOG, Bethlehem Steel of America owned 50 per cent of SOMIFER, which mined iron ore at Belinga one of the richest reserves in the free world. The remaining shareholders were a Common Market consortium. With independence came the expectation that Gabonese leaders could now make their own decisions, based on what was best for Gabon. Foreign countries were sending Gabon their very own ambassador and lobbying Gabon for economic consideration in return for lavish promises of development aid.

There was considerable pressure on the French government to ensure that French business interests were protected as the process of independence unfolded for Gabon. The first hurdle to overcome was ensuring the election of a Gabonese government in time with French interests. This in itself was not a difficult task, since the Gabonese contending for power in the new government were all products of French schools and most had lived a part of their lives in Paris. The top contenders to lead the Gabonese government in the days before independence were Hilaire Aubame and Léon Mba. Aubame had been the darling of the French intellectuals and liberals for years but the powerful forestry concerns of Gabon put their weight behind the more pragmatic Mba, whose business interests he seemed more eager to protect than the leftist leaning Aubame.[11]

In the territorial elections held in 1957 before independence, Aubame campaigned at the head of Gabon's first political party, which he himself founded in 1947. As its founder and present leader Aubame enjoyed an edge in popularity and support over newcomers to the political arena. His party, the Union Democratique Socialiste Gabonaise, UDSG as in the past, did well, winning 19 out of the 37 seats being contested. Mba's party, called the Bloc Democratique Gabonais, BDG, came in second with 8. Various regional and independent candidates accounted for the remaining 10 seats. Not an overwhelming consensus, but, legally, the UDSG had seats enough to form a parliamentary majority and government with Aubame at its head. However, internal parliamentary manoeuvering by the BDG convinced all 10 independents to join in coalition with the BDG, giving it 18 seats to Aubame's 19. Still short of a majority, the BDG enticed 3 French UDSG members of the Assembly to switch political allegiance. Thus fortified with a newly-won majority, the BDG approached the French Governor to form a government under the *Loi Cadre*, existing French law. As a reward for their flexibility and insight these three French turncoats were made ministers in the new Gabonese government.[12]

From then on the BDG enjoyed a position of dominance in Gabonese politics. Although initially Mba was not as well known as Paul Godjout, who was the leader of the BDG, Léon Mba steadily increased his own power within the government. Mba accused Aubame of catering to the regional interests of the Fang ethnic clan, of whom he was a member. Although Aubame loudly denied the charge, politics in Gabon aligned themselves quickly according to the common denominator that everyone, especially the ordinary electorate, could understand. This common denominator was kin affiliations and personal connections. Added to this was the lubrication provided by the money of the business cartels and French government assistance. Politics in Gabon was to be played as a power struggle for absolute control of all available resources, not as the give-and-take of compromise which allowed everyone to have a share in the spoils of independence.

While the French were in power, they saw to it that political and economic power (what was left after they took their lion's share) was spread out among the various factions. This was done as much to keep power dispersed as from any altruistic sense of fair sharing. However, after independence the allotments of economic and political power increased, and the leadership felt the winners were entitled to carve up the spoils in any way they saw fit. As Bongo later asked himself, was this autocratic stance a reflection of traditional tribal authority patterns, where the chief's word was law, or was it based on the belief that the national leader was the symbolic patriarch father of the nation and that his word could not be challenged? [13] Or we may ask ourselves, was it emulation of more modern role models; perhaps, an imitation of the pattern of autocratic colonial rule, where the civilized had an obligation to guide the savage and ignorant? Or, perhaps as Ambassador Darlington has suggested, the Gabonese leaders looked to the contemporary example of President de Gaulle, who made no secret of his belief in the virtue of presidential rule, of the sacred right of the few to rule and guide the many.[14] Whatever the inspiration, the pattern became established early. Power was to be concentrated in the presidency; opposition was to be viewed as a disloyalty to the popularly mandated authority, who was Mba, duly elected leader of the Gabonese people.

At independence Mba, who had been Deputy President of the Council of Ministers of the territorial government, became President of the Republic, while Gondjout became president or head of the Assembly. The newly elected heads of government now gave themselves the task of rewriting the Constitution bequeathed to them by the French. The question was whether to go with a document which shared power between the presidency and the Assembly or whether to concentrate more power in the hands of the executive. The political struggles which France was grappling with at this time under de Gaulle were also being played out in her former colonies. The role model of de Gaulle was a very real and vivid one, with his image having been elevated to that of a demigod by many of his admirers, especially in the colonies.

Mba manoeuvred and played constitutional games for several years, managing to effectively squeeze out his opponents from positions of real power over the course of this time. What happened to Aubame during this period is a case in point. Aubame was first forced to become a junior partner in a one-party system created soon after independence under a Government of National Unity. Naturally, as head of the one party, Mba could now call the shots in the Assembly as well as the presidency. However, as Minister of Foreign Affairs, Aubame and two other UDSG colleagues also holding ministerial positions were still kept within the power loop. For two years this system was maintained. During this time period the French also consolidated their economic hold on the country. Much to the American ambassador's dismay, the Gabonese tariff structure favoured imported French goods over anyone else's including American.[15] The French in 1965 supplied 58.8 per cent of Gabon's imports while they bought 46.2 per cent of her exports. The

USA, on the other hand, bought 21.8 per cent of Gabon's exports while selling her only 11.7 per cent of her imports.[16] In addition, the French controlled the powerful Gabonese Chamber of Commerce, which regulated the number of businesses which could operate in the country. Since the chamber favoured the established French-owned businesses, newcomers of any ethnicity, even Gabonese, were discouraged from competing. As a consequence, near monopoly conditions existed in Gabon and companies pretty much set their prices and conditions. Certainly, the high prices they charged did not reflect the low wages they paid their Gabonese labourers.[17] Manipulation of the government extended to getting them to set a low wage structure for Gabonese workers, uncovering privileged information that would give them the competitive edge in new business ventures (such as the right of way to where the new railroad was being built) and putting their economic force behind candidates they favoured. Corruption and graft abounded in the French business community, [18] and was especially serious because of the amount of economic resources in Gabon that they owned or controlled.

The lack of a national Gabonese vision – either by the leadership, the mass of people or the French – made divisive sectional politics a problem from the very start. In 1962, the Congo–Gabon riots in Libreville brought these problems starkly into focus. During colonial times French rulers had some-times encouraged movement of their subjects from their communities to other areas of the empire, as the need arose. In Libreville, a sizeable number of Congolese had settled, along with some Dahomenians, to take up the economic niches of petty clerics, tradesmen and merchants. Many of these Congolese people had been living in Libreville over a decade and had married into local families. Still, according to their customs they were distinct from the kinship grouping of Gabon and could never become part of their country.

In September, 1962, news of a scuffle below the opposing sides (Gabon vs Congo, Brazzaville) of a football match in Brazzaville turned into ugly communal riots in Libreville. Mobs of Gabonese freely roamed the streets beating, maiming, and killing any Congolese that could be found. They apparently were avenging insults which had befallen their Gabonese football team while in Brazzaville. Hardly an international incident, one would think. However, when seen as the fruits of colonialism, the anger generating such riots becomes more understandable. The disappointments over independence were beginning to express themselves; not everyone was prospering under independent rule, and foreigners were still exploiting the ordinary Gabonese. National sovereignty was a hollow promise. Not even at a foreign football match could one get respect! And the rage, so long suppressed, even now below the level of consciousness, could not realistically be directed against the white demigods still controlling the streets of Libreville. The common man probably did not have a clear picture of French post-colonial exploitation. But he did know that he was not in the promised land and that those traitorous Congolese foreigners were robbing him blind when he shopped and that they sat in all the air-conditioned offices monopolizing all the nicest clerical jobs. *Divide et impera* was coming home to roost.

For two days the police, still officered by French commanders, did nothing to stop the riots.[19] Perhaps they were grateful, the people's rage had not turned in their direction, and hoped that they would exhaust themselves in this orgy of rioting. In any event once the police gave a show of force the rioting stopped. The government insisted on the expulsion of all Congolese without exception. Even the mayor of Libreville, his wife and seven children were included.[20] The French ambassador, when asked why the French had stood back and allowed such carnage, replied that giving African states their independence meant also that they would have to make their own mistakes, without interference.[21]

THE COUP

Mba was finding it increasingly difficult to govern Gabon, under the conditions of less than total loyalty and obedience that he felt he deserved. Mba was not comfortable with the idea of dissent and in the few years between independence and the coup became increasingly autocratic. After working within the framework of a coalition-type government called the Government of National Union until February 1963, Mba grew increasingly suspicious of Aubame and the other ministers who were not from his party. He forced Aubame and the others out of the government, but as an offering of conciliation appointed Aubame president of the Supreme Court, a position of prestige but very little power. Likewise he moved Gondjout to the presidency of the Economic and Social Council, where he could keep a tight reign if he so wished. As Mba grew more suspicious he relieved more and more officials of their positions. Even country prefects and subprefects were arbitrarily moved about, especially if it was known they had gained a following with the local population.[22] According to the American ambassador's perception of the situation, Mba was trying to rule Gabon (1965 population of only 600,000) like a village chief.[23] He did not trust the idea of delegating authority, nor did he believe that opposition could be loyal, nor could he prioritize matters of individual importance. By the end of 1963 Mba was overcome with the suspicion that Aubame was plotting his overthrow. Part of his paranoia was no doubt due to the knowledge that in next-door Congo–Brazzaville his contemporary, Fulbert Youlou, had been overthrown in August while pushing too hard for a single-party state.[24] Aubame had not helped the situation when he openly criticized the president's political behaviour from his ivory tower of the Supreme Court. An unsigned tract circulating in Libreville was attributed to Aubame and gave Mba the excuse he needed: Aubame had to resign from the Supreme Court or the Assembly, it now being illegal to belong to both. Aubame angered Mba by choosing the assembly seat over that of the Supreme Court. Mba retaliated by dissolving the Assembly and calling for new elections.

After the tensions and infighting of the preceding two years, opposition to Mba's government had grown stronger. Even in the countryside active dissatisfaction with his rule was widespread. Fearing the potential success of this opposition Mba moved to arrange the way the election was to be contested so as to exclude as many of his opponents as possible even from running. Mba prohibited anyone having held appointive office from running; this eliminated Aubame. Mba required high deposits from candidates and stipulated that parties run only with complete lists of candidates for all 47 seats. With $160 deposit per candidate each group running had to come up with $7500 even to file. American ambassador Darlington writes that an opposition leader approached him for financial help to put up a list of candidates, in the interests of democracy, to oppose Mba's government party. Darlington refused.[25] That was 23 January 1964. There would be no group of opposition candidates filed in those three weeks before the coup of 18 February 1964. For the opponents to Léon Mba, the pathways to legal opposition had closed down. The future looked grim.

The coup itself took place without great fanfare or turmoil and succeeded with embarrassing ease. A few junior officers, under the leadership of Lt Valere Essone who led the first company of the Gabonese army, seized the presidential palace. No shots were fired; no one was injured. The troops simply told the few police on duty that this was just a military exercise and were allowed to proceed.[26] In the early hours of the morning the soldiers entered the palace and forced President Mba at gunpoint to sign his abdication and announce it in a statement which was repeated over the radio the next morning. At dawn the rebels rounded up the ministers of the government, detaining them all in the barracks. Mba himself was taken by car to an undisclosed location in the bush.

Meanwhile the French learned from the minister of foreign affairs, who alerted the French ambassador, that the coup had occurred. General Kerga- ravet, Commander of the French Forces of the Second African Zone headquartered in Brazzaville, was ordered by President de Gaulle to overturn the coup and restore Léon Mba to the presidency. He began moving troops under cover of night a scant 20 hours after the coup. The first French troops met no resistance at all, and aroused no suspicion, because they said they had been sent in only to protect French lives and property. The Gabonese rebels were caught completely off-guard by the influx of French soldiers. Having seen the policy of non-intervention practised by the French in the 1963 Dahomenian and Congo–Brazzaville coups, it never occurred to the rebel soldiers that the French would alter this policy when confronted by a coup in Gabon.

For the French, Gabon was an investment which could not be so easily sacrificed. Several reasons have been proffered by analysts to explain France's intervention. On the legal level, France's justification had centred on a secret agreement between de Gaulle and a few favoured leaders at independence which promised French assistance in cases of internal turmoil or danger.[27] A formal, written request had been made to France by Vice President Yembit, on behalf of the fallen government, but it was dated more than 24 hours after French troops had attacked and defeated the rebel soldiers in their barracks at Barake.[28] The government, of course, was very grateful that it had been restored to power with such speed and efficiency, so it did not question France's motives or their technical legality.

On the economic level the French would have hated to risk losing the huge economic investment in Gabon: all that trade, all those businesses, all that money invested in mines and personnel – all that France would be loathe to let slip out of her grasp. However, France had not interfered in the domestic violence of three of her other former African colonies, where one could argue similar economic seeds had been sown and had taken root. In Gabon's case, it seems there was an additional emotional component; losing Gabon appeared to mean to France the loss of face and the loss of a dream of glory. For Gabon had become tangled up in de Gaulle's dream of a powerful France, one whom everyone would respect and fear. France was developing its own nuclear capability and Gabon's uranium was supplying half of France's needs. Perhaps, losing this lifeline to glory, de Gaulle's *force de frappe*, [29] was more than France's leaders could bear. And no doubt, adding to the insult was the fact that Mba and de Gaulle had shared a close personal friendship and that Gabon had been held up as one of France's colonial triumphs. All in all, France unhesitatingly took the plunge. By day's end of the 21st of February, the officer's barracks had been surrounded, 18 Gabonese and 1 French soldier had died, the captive government ministers had been released, and a bedraggled Mba had been found and returned to the Palace. Barely a hiccup even in Gabon's short four-year history of independence.

MEANING OF THE COUP

According to the soldiers who engineered the coup, it was severe economic disappointments which drove them to overthrow their own government. While they and their families languished and were cut off from the benefits of independence, the politicians in Libreville were accumulating the spoils of self-rule. Even the generals, who lived in pleasant houses in town away from the common soldiers, had been co-opted by the system. But the common people had continued to be excluded and the soldiers had wanted to alter the balance.[30] Whether Aubame or any other members of the disgruntled opposition had added encouragement before the event has never been determined, but it seems fairly certain that it was a military uprising, above all else, succeeding because army power had not yet been suppressed by Mba's drive to take over total power in Gabon.

After the coup, the economic frustrations of the mass of the people were brought clearly into the open and the connection to the source of the inequities – the French – was made. Whereas before the coup the tendency had been to focus blame on other Africans who had succeeded economically, whether Congolese, Dahomenian, or political elites, after the coup the French got the brunt of the heat. Disbelief, anger and a sense of violation were the reactions from the Gabonese as well as much of the international community, including voices from within the French government itself. But curiously the focus from abroad was more on the political betrayal of sovereignty, not on its underlying impulse: continued neocolonial economic exploitation.

Even Gabonese people who were clearer on the issue did not react towards the French with violent acts of mayhem as they had done with the Congolese. They felt violated but even the opposition leadership not directly beholden to the French expressed their disappointment in more philosophical terms. And after all, what could they do? The French were still their role models, the former masters, the *evolués*, whom they had been educated to emulate. And if the Gabonese wanted to be a modern, civilized, economically developed nation (which they did), they needed French assistance (or if not French, some other equally invasive capitalist country's help). They needed help and the trade-off was making it financially worthwhile for France. That was the bottom line, for it was becoming very very clear by 1964, that nobody except maybe Albert Schweitzer in Lambaréné, was going to do it simply for the satisfaction of helping.

And now the coup had proved that in order to keep the existing economic order intact one also needed the help of French troops to keep one's own population from upsetting the apple cart. The only alternative was to bring the population into the economy and that would take time, effort and sacrifice. The coup in Gabon brought the dilemma of economic neocolonialism into clear focus. France after independence was proving to be as domineering as France before independence and it would take the elites' continued subordination to France's needs and desires for them to stay in power, and share in the wealth.

BONGO TAKES CONTROL

After Mba regained his position, his rule became even more autocratic. He dismantled the entire army and dismissed every single soldier. The new army was only slowly built up to replace it, containing only tribal groupings loyal to him. For effective protection he relied on the good will and military might of the French, who kept him safely in power until his death in 1967. Militarily, Gabon has remained weak. Probably the absence of disputes over borders or the lack of any secessionist groups has made it less vital for Gabon to maintain a strong armed presence.[31] And with experience as a putsch victim, the government's need to keep the army under control would logically have the greater precedence. Neither Mba nor Bongo have used the army to strengthen their own power base. Although a failed coup attempt in 1985 was not met with added reprisals, President Bongo remains cool towards the army. Even today the army stands at only 1900.

However, Gabon's political integrity was under great stress by 1967 when El Hadj Bongo assumed power at Mba's death as the heir-apparent. Although the number and type of players who were permitted to act in the political arena had been severely restricted under Mba, he had always stopped short of completely defying or abandoning constitutional necessities. Much of the competition had been muzzled but there was still the framework of the rule of law.

In fact after giving vent to a few political tantrums, the dismantling of the army being a typical example, Mba's deteriorating health forced him to take long leaves in Paris. Mba's friendly policies towards foreign investors, especially the French, continued and an economic boom set in during the mid-1960s. Libreville expanded, prices stabilized and salaries increased.[32] Although the economic expansion centred around Libreville and the mining centres, and the hinterland lagged behind, the economic expansion helped bring more Gabonese into the modern economy and put pressure on the economic monopoly held by the French. With time, increasing numbers of Gabonese were educated and trained under Bongo's expanding educational system. They slowly moved into positions of economic power alongside the French and steadily diluted their power. The key to Gabon's success has been its steady, continuing economic expansion and the small population which had to share this wealth.

Bongo assumed the mantle of the presidency with both the blessing of Léon Mba and with the legitimacy of a 99.9 per cent electoral victory behind him. As Mba's choice he had the tacit approval of the French, who had kept the peace for Mba for three years. Bongo was apparently a compromise candidate, coming from an insignificant southern kinship grouping with no great national support.[33] He also was an able administrator, and at 31, had a more modern view of the nature of authority in a nation-state than Léon Mba.

Bongo is also more of an intellectual than Mba, and has written several books, which have tracked the evolution of his thinking. When he took office in 1967, he knew that he would need to practise a policy of reconciliation to rectify the overbearing authoritarianism of Mba.[34] However, he was also convinced that opposition was a negative, destructive force in Gabon, and he was not prepared to revert to a Western-style multiparty system of decision making in the national assembly. He felt that a sense of nationhood was missing in Gabon and that the 'old demons' (*vieux démons*)[35] were tearing the polity apart, for they prevented the creation of a national outlook.[36]

Bongo also expressed resentment that he even had to apologize to Western critics and justify to them why a multiparty system of representative government would not work. Who were they to assume that it was the only democratic choice? Why was he even put in the position of being defensive about seeking alternatives? Upon taking office he felt he had two choices: (1) rule with an iron fist like other African rulers, or (2) open dialogue and 'extend a hand' to all sides.[37] He opted for the second solution, which led to the creation of a single party of national unity, the Partie Democratique Gabonaise in March of 1968. This single party would shape the 'modern' man of Gabon. It would become the 'crucible of national unity', permitting a safe environment for debate and discussion while educating and steering people towards the correct path.[38] It would be a more benevolent and persuasive form of control; however, control would remain with the leadership, specifically with Bongo.

CONCLUSION

Bongo has been in power now for 20 years and enjoys great personal authority. A 1984 government sanctioned publication entitled, *One Man, One Country*, led us to conclude that he alone has shaped Gabon into the nation-state it is today. Bongo firmly believes that conflict is divisive and has suppressed all expression outside the confines of his single party, which he feels most constructively channels and resolves differences of opinion. In the 1984 publication just mentioned Bongo went to great pains to explain the eclectic character of his single party. Its orientation was neither to the left nor to the right, rejecting both the injustices and inhumanity of capitalism and the inefficiency and dictatorial nature of socialism.[39]

Nevertheless there have been reports of human rights violations in Gabon and political prisoners were set free in 1985[40] A very recent coup attempt in September and October of 1989 points to the fragile nature of Bongo's control. Both the inability to tolerate dissidence and relative ease of overthrowing a whole political system through coups are hallmarks of politics in former colonies like Gabon. As such they point to an immature polity still lacking in consensus as to how conflict should be resolved. Bongo understands the fragile nature of his authority and has not been willing to entrust the protection of his person to Gabonese nationals. Because Gabonese society lacks agreement as to who should hold power and how resources should be divided, recurring coup attempts have happened. There appears to be a struggle among the elites for personal monetary gain. Outside business interests are invariably involved to lend support to one faction or another who seeks to tap into the country's riches. Bongo has kept control by not entrusting his personal safety to Gabonese citizens but rather assigning a French National responsibility for security within the palace and making Moroccan bodyguards an elite unit of 'personal security guards' to the president. Most likely, this multinational system of protection is not going to change in the future. Recent information confirms that it was a Gabonese citizen, Lt Col. Georges Moubandjo, the upcoming appointee as a new head of a president's 'personal security guard', who engineered the most recent coup.

Whatever the injustices of the system he picked, Gabon has been politically stable and economically developing since Bongo took power. In fact economically, Gabon has been steadily becoming wealthier since independence, an anomaly for Africa. The discovery of oil was the biggest boon, especially in the OPEC cartel days of the 1970s. Bongo still proclaims the greatest affection for France and in the Twentieth Anniversary Book celebrating two decades of independence, he gives France credit for its generous assistance of aid and cooperation, its technical and teaching help after independence. He also points out that harmonious relations have been maintained, that new accords were signed in 1974 and that France was the first to participate in the construction of the Transgabonese Railroad. France remains, according to the Anniversary Book, one of the best clients and principal suppliers to Gabon.

However, Gabon is now far from being a French puppet and has expanded her economic and political horizons to embrace countries formerly considered 'frightening' because of their ideologies. Who these are he does not say. But Bongo also included countries of the East and the Arab States. In fact he has welcomed public cooperation with all governments and private investors capable of helping Gabon develop. He has been travelling the globe and in the course of his travels has succeeded in forging technical commercial agreements and has uncovered foreign investment opportunities.[41] In short, the $5500 per capita income for Gabon has been no accident, Bongo has actively pursued it. Income, nevertheless, despite the small population, is still unevenly distributed and the hinterland lags way behind. However, the

Gabonese are being made economic partners in the system to a very real extent.

On the plus side, rural education is a high priority and Gabon has boasted its own university since 1970. On the negative side, Gabon has aroused the hostility of some African neighbours with its 'neutral' policy towards hated South Africa and its willingness to subordinate ideology to economic considerations. Whether Bongo's political rigidity could be a problem for the future is beyond the scope of this discussion. As for the coup, the fact that it happened when it did, is completely understandable, given the situation at the time. That the French intervened, was an aberration which, though an un-pleasant affirmation of the weakness of Gabonese sovereignty, permitted the growth of a politically stable government which in turn could allow economic development. And though exploitive of the Gabonese, in that the lion's share of profits has continued to go to foreigners, over the thirty years since independence the stable political environment meant funds were not diverted to fighting civil wars, destruction of infrastructure and maintaining large armies, as they have been elsewhere in Africa. Gabon today follows a completely different path from Ghana, Zaïre, Angola, and most of her other African sister-states. Whether the failed coup is what made the difference is something we might ponder. Whether Gabon has succeeded in her goals is another question we might ask. Of her three quests: economic development, national sovereignty, and stable democratic rule – she has certainly subordinated the latter two to achieve the former. In studying Gabon we have to ask ourselves what politically drives nations like her today? Is it independent living within one's own national borders? Is it equal access to and participation in one's national affairs? Or are these just metaphors for what she really wants? An acceptable way to corner as many resources for herself as she can?

NOTES

1. The book is by Ambassador Darlington and his wife: Charles and Alice Darlington, *African Betrayal* (New York: David McKay Company, 1968).
2. *Africa* (Global Studies), 2nd edition, An Annual Editions TM Publication. 1987, pp. 74–5.
3. Ibid.
4. Ibid.
5. El Hadj Bongo, *Un homme, un pays* (Les Nouvelles éditions Africaines, Dakar, 1984), p. 53.
6. Ibid. p. 54.
7. Darlington, *African Betrayal*.
8. Ibid.
9. Ibid. p. 62.
10. Ibid.
11. Ibid. p. 45.

12. Ibid.
13. Bongo, *Un homme, un pays*, p. 64.
14. Darlington, *African Betrayal*, p. 118.
15. Ibid. p. 66.
16. Ibid. p. 67.
17. Ibid. p. 114–17.
18. Ibid.
19. Ibid. pp. 329–31.
20. Ibid. p. 330.
21. Ibid.
22. Ibid. p. 121.
23. Ibid.
24. Ibid. p. 122.
25. Ibid. p. 124.
26. Ibid. p. 130.
27. Ibid. p. 138.
28. Ibid.
29. Ibid. p. 146.
30. Ibid. p. 139.
31. There is a group, the 'Gabonese Movement for National Renewal', living in exile in Paris. Called MORENA, it formed a government in exile in 1985.
32. Ibid. p. 174.
33. Ibid. p. 175.
34. Bongo, p. 64.
35. The old demons of tribalism: nepotism, favouritism, and division.
36. Ibid.
37. Ibid. pp. 65–7.
38. Ibid.
39. Bongo, p. 71.
40. *Africa (Global Studies)*, p. 75.
41. *Independence Book*, no pagination.

11 Sierra Leone: civilian–military republic[1]

Benjamin Kline

In 1961 a Sierra Leone newspaper, *Shekpendeh,* warned that the country's newly achieved independence could be endangered by the actions of the armed forces. It cautioned the military and police to 'understand that whatever might be their political complexion or outlook their duty lies with the legitimate government. ... Nothing could be more dangerous than tribalism and politics entering the ranks of the army and police force'.[2] In a country as fragmented as Sierra Leone, with its many tribal loyalties, client–patron relationships, and penchant for corruption, it seems almost foolhardy to believe that these warnings would have been heeded. In fact, they were not. Still, the result was not quite what people in 1961 might have imagined. Sierra Leone has managed over the years, despite military coups, to maintain the semblance of civilian rule. From the civilian-run multiparty system of the 1960s–1970s, to the establishment of a single-party state under Siaka Stevens in 1978, to the unification of both political and military authority under Brigadier-General Joseph Momoh in 1985, the intrusion of the army into government affairs has been an evolutionary process resulting in a hybrid; a single-party civilian–military republic. When Sierra Leone's only legal party, the All People's Congress (APC), chose Brigadier-General Momoh, the army commander, as the successor to Siaka Stevens in 1985 it made the military–political marriage a fact and the two became one.

Ironically, while tribalism and politics have certainly entered the ranks of the military it cannot be said, under the existing system, that it has forgotten that its 'duty lies with the legitimate government'.

HISTORICAL BACKGROUND TO 1967[3]

Sierra Leone was established in 1787 when the British abolition movement created a settlement at Freetown for the purpose of settling freed slaves. In 1807 the territory around Freetown, which had been administered since 1791 by the Sierra Leone Company, was transferred to the British government and became a Crown Colony. Eventually British authority was extended into the interior by the establishment of a Protectorate in 1896. By the end of World War II Sierra Leone continued to be governed as two largely separate units, the Colony and the Protectorate, under British colonial rule. The attempt to organise countrywide political parties dates only from the controversies over the 1951 constitution, which provided a majority of seats in the legislature for Africans, and more importantly, gave the hinterland enough seats to outvote the Freetown peninsula. The resulting election helped crystallize the division between Creoles and hinterlanders which prompted the formation of the first political parties: the National Council of the Colony of Sierra Leone for the Creoles, and the Sierra Leone People's Party (SLPP) for the hinterland. The National Council was doomed by its small base of support and the SLPP emerged as the dominant political party.

The first leader of the SLPP was Milton Margai, the son of a Mende trader. In 1957 Sierra Leone received a new constitution and the SLPP won the forthcoming election. As the party's leader, Margai consequently became the head of the civilian government. In 1960 Sierra Leone's parties formed a coalition to go to London for the Lancaster House Independence Conference to work out arrangements for independence. Siaka Stevens, primarily known as an opponent of the SLPP and a Union leader, was a member of this delegation. Protesting the conference's report because it did not call for new elections, he returned home and joined the Election Before Independence Party, later known as the All People's Congress (APC), which combined many of the others who had been left out of the Mende-dominated government: i.e., the Creoles, the Temne, and the Limba. Siaka immediately rose to the top of this party relying on the prestige of a dead Limba father, a Temne tongue, and Creole manners and friends. When independence was declared in 1961 Milton continued as prime minister, his brother, Albert, became the finance minister, while Stevens returned as leader of the official opposition.

The most important conflicts by the time of independence were derived from the largely Mende and southern leadership of the SLPP (the Margais were Mende) and its elitist attitude. The APC was much more northern and Freetown based. In the 1962 elections it won 16 seats, all in the Northern Province and the former Colony, now called the Western Area; its ally the Sierra Leone Progressive Independence Movement (SLPIM) in Kono won 4 more, against 28 for the SLPP and 14 independents. The fact that the independents and also the Paramount Chiefs, who held a further 12 seats, supported the SLPP denied the APC any chance of forming a government.[4]

Since independence in 1961 the civilian government in Sierra Leone had been successful in controlling the military. During the government of Milton Marqai this task was made easier by the fact that the British officers held most of the staff and line commands. Margai was in favour of this arrangement because of his concern about the long-term repercussions of rapid Africanization upon colonial or quasi-colonial systems of civilian control.

When Milton died in 1964, Albert took over as prime minister. Albert was more radical in foreign policy, but his domestic policy, which clearly favoured Sierra Leone's southern, largely Mende, population alienated many citizens. Once Albert had assumed office, he instituted policies designed to create an indigenous officer corps that could be controlled by the civilian authorities. Subsequently, instead of there emerging a polarity of interests between civilian and military, the two groups joined together in the defence of mutual interests. A common ethnic and regional identity particularly after the Mendes came to predominate in the upper echelons of both sectors aided the formation of this alliance. This relationship, facilitated by the close proximity of the army barracks and government offices in Freetown, led to a close client–patron arrangement. The army officers needed identification with prominent civilians to raise the formers' status in the wider community and, indirectly, to further their military careers. The politicians were in turn reassured by the presence of soldiers who could step in with support should the population lose faith in its civilian leaders.

The potential for civil disorder arose when the poor state of the country's economy and accusations of government corruption under Albert's rule began to undermine his position. Between 1961 and the end of 1966 Sierra Leone's net foreign exchange reserves declined from Le29 million to a level of Le11.4 million, a figure that was slightly less than two months' worth of imports. Brian Quinn, the IMF's resident representative in Sierra Leone from 1966 to 1968, believed that this decline in external reserves could be attributed directly to the diversion of funds belonging to the Sierra Leone Produce Marketing Board (SLPMB) into a number of oil palm and coffee plantations with few controls over how the money was actually spent.[5] The Forster Commission of Inquiry established during the rule of the National Reformation Council, revealed that by 23 March 1967 Sir Albert possessed assets worth Le250,000, based on an annual salary amounting to Le4000.

Added to the economic woes of the country was the growing disunity within the army. Senior military officers had quarrelled with each other on an almost round-the-clock basis during 1966 so that by early January 1967 the officer corps was in disarray. Most of the participants in these altercations sought to dramatize accumulated frustrations over alleged nepotism and the glaring incompetence of the military command. The army commander, Brigadier David Lansana, personally bore the brunt of this discontent and, by the end of 1966, there existed a considerable number of officers who wished to remove him.

Apparently, faced with the prospect of imminent electoral defeat at the 1967 elections but unwilling to hold a fraudulent general election, Albert had turned more and more to the army as his only remaining alternative. Almost immediately command and staff billets were organized along sectional lines. Southerners and easterners whose loyalty to the government seemed reasonably assured monopolized all the company commands and presumably most of the platoon commands; only Mende rank and file received arms. Subsequently, praetorian tendencies increased as the army experienced a significant role expansion in the weeks prior to the election. For the first time in post-independence history, soldiers were engaged in widespread internal security duties throughout the country. The use of soldiers to back up the police both in Freetown and the provinces became commonplace when rioting in Kono on nomination day between APC and SLPP partisans led to a declaration of a state of emergency in that district.[6]

By election day, 17 March 1967, civilian cliques, came to be identified with army cliques and vice versa. Added to the economic and social problems was the fear that Albert was moving to impose a one-party state upon the country. Northern citizens rallied around labour leader Siaka Stevens, and his All People's Congress party (APC). Virtually none of these cliques, whether of the civilian or military variety, was motivated by clear political philosophies, but rather by elementary patron-client relationships. Groups of people lined up behind certain 'big men' who were expected to act as providers of protection. As the flow of election results continued to arrive it slowly became clear that the APC had won a major victory and that the electorate had chosen to end the rule of Albert Margai. Siaka Stevens was to be Sierra Leone's new leader.

By the morning of 21 March a crowd of APC supporters had gathered near State House to cheer the expected appointment of Siaka Probyn Stevens as prime minister of Sierra Leone. When the governor-general invited Stevens to form a government, Brigadier David Lansana, who supported Margai, siezed power. Faced with the impending appointment of a man who would no doubt call a halt to his military career, Lansana embarked upon a course of action that would sabotage Sierra Leone's popular civilian-government tradition. Subsequently, it was the ruling civilian elite, including many politicians, which joined with the military to impede the transfer of power to the victorious APC. By the end of 1966 that loose coalition of traditional rulers, educated elites from the provinces, and Freetown professionals, known as the Sierra Leone Peoples Party, had found its future political prospects seriously jeopardized and consequently turned to the military for support.

NATIONAL REFORMATION COUNCIL (NRC)

A show of military force became inevitable as Lansana found himself obligated, by his relationship to Albert Margai and the SLPP, to defend the ruling circle at any cost. The spectre of civil disorder thus fused with the idea of military assistance to a decaying regime to make Lansana's martial law declaration very logical. Lansana declared martial law on the grounds that party conflict would cause disorder.[7] It was at best a tenuous argument and Lansana was quick to reassure the population of his good intentions.

> I want to make it clear that the Army – and I say this after consultation with my senior officers – does not, I repeat, does not, intend to impose a Military Government on the people of Sierra Leone. This country has a record of Constitutional Government.[8]

Lansana's rule was longer than that of Stevens's initial tenure but not by much. Within three days Lansana was removed by his fellow officers. Five hours after the arrest of Brigadier David Lansana and Albert Margai, Major Charles Augustine Blake delivered a statement to the nation announcing the overthrow of the army commander and the formation of a military government. Blake explained that the senior officers 'had since noticed that the attitude of the brigadier was not to bring about the creation of a national government but to impose Sir Albert Margai as the prime minister of this country'. Confronted with Lansana's obstinacy, they were left with no choice but to dissociate themselves from Lansana and 'to divest the Brigadier of control of this country'. Furthermore, Blake in his 23 March radio broadcast announced the formation of a National Reformation Council: strictly as 'an interim measure'. Speaking for all the members of the NRC, Blake stressed most emphatically that 'we are soldiers, and want to remain soldiers, and politics is not our mission'. The new regime, Blake continued, would 'do all in its power to bring about a civilian government in the shortest possible time', but added one stipulation – such a transition would have to wait 'until the situation is favourable'.[9] Thus, the National Reformation Council, Sierra Leone's first experiment with military government, formally came into being on 25 March 1967. Brought back from London to lead the military was Lt Col. Andrew Juxon-Smith, apparently chosen because he was the highest-ranking officer not to have any ties with the controversial election events.

The NRC was forced to confront a great deal of opposition to its continuation in office. The banning of organized politics by the NRC prevented any formal parties from acting but there remained among the population an almost universal resentment of Sierra Leone soldiers acting as government administrators. If these various components of opposition, ranging from university professors to army privates, had a common objective, it was to do away with military rule and to re-establish some form of civilian government. The absence of all formal manifestations of political power meant, however, that pressure groups or individuals sympathetic to the APC but not explicitly political had to take up the party's cause. The growth of opposition among civilian elements in society was made particularly difficult by the NRC's over-sensitive reaction to any statement of criticism or public demonstration which might be interpreted as insolence or insubordination.

Despite these difficulties, opposition to the NRC appeared almost immediately and soon was exasperated by the limitless power which Juxon-Smith and the NRC captains seemed to enthusiastically wield. By treating most civilians with whom they came in direct contact as inferiors the NRC compensated for the civilian's negative image of soldiers during both the colonial administration and under the two Margai governments. Some of the young captains who served in the Department of the Interior were especially prone to behave with arrogance if not only because of their low rank in the officer corps, their upcountry origins, their inferior educational qualifications, and their lack of prominent connections with SLPP 'big men'. Furthermore, there was the continuing problem of building consensus within the officer corps itself that only became aggravated once these officers found themselves in charge of an entire state apparatus and not simply a 1500-man battalion. As in the past, the military suffered from the divisions endemic of a small, poorly trained, ethnically heterogeneous, and factionalized officer corp such as existed in Sierra Leone.[10]

Part of the problem was that, with Juxon-Smith at the helm, the regime no longer felt committed to maintaining a dialogue with any group of politicians, including those of the SLPP variety who toiled for the Advisory Council. Disagreements between the NRC and its civilian advisors occurred continuously.[11] In discussions held with the Civilian Rule Committee, Juxon-Smith emphasized that once Sierra Leone had returned to civilian rule, the country should immediately adopt a republican constitution with an executive president. The council, however, recommended the eventual adoption of a republican constitution with a ceremonial president and by so doing incurred Juxon-Smith's displeasure. Furthermore, by declaring the APC a clearcut victor in the general elections, the Dove–Edwin Commission automatically repudiated most of the NRC's arguments for seizing power. The junta was now placed clearly on the defensive. Particularly since the NRC chairman was reported to have declared 'that he will be Sierra Leone's first president'.[12] Unlike most of the other members of the NRC who, with few illusions of budding political careers, had initially forsaken the comforts of barracks life to protect civilian friends from displacement by the APC,

Juxon-Smith viewed himself as the future ruler of Sierra Leone, with or without the NRC.

By the end of 1967, Siaka Stevens, angered by the British government's refusal to aid his party, left London in mid-December, re-established contacts with President Toure of Guinea, and went into exile there. Word of his voluntary exile in the Guinean capital soon spread to Freetown and served as a rallying point for those in the APC who sought the immediate ousting of the NRC. Stevens then met with APC leaders and other interested parties who slipped back and forth across the border. Not long after Stevens' arrival in Guinea, Colonel Bangura, leader of the February coup plot against Albert Margai, departed from his post at the Sierra Leone embassy in Washington to join the APC leader.

The preparations of the APC to return to power culminated with a rebellion of the rank and file. Throughout the late evening hours of 17 April 1968 and on into the early morning, teams of warrant officers, NCOs, and privates searched houses and bars in Freetown for commissioned army officers and their counterparts in the gazetted ranks of the 2400-man police force. Juxon-Smith was the first to be arrested at his Hill Station lodge because he held the keys to the armoury. Once having acquired substantial numbers of weapons, the mutineers surrounded the officers' mess and began a systematic search for any officers thought to be hiding in Freetown. Some 76 army and 48 police officers were arrested and imprisoned during the course of the mutiny.[13]

The privates' mutiny of April 17 and 18 brought an end to months of discontent within the lower echelons of the army, most induced by the NCR's neglect of the rank and file. After the military takeover the previous March, enlisted men and noncommissioned and commissioned officers gained the impression that the army as a whole would benefit immediately as a result of pay raises, new uniforms, reconditioned barracks, the acquisition of new automobiles, and the like. Juxon-Smith's public statements to the effect that soldiers 'were the most important element in the country' certainly contributed to these hopes.[14] Some individuals, of course, did stand to gain from army rule. Most of the members of the NRC promoted themselves and thus drew higher salaries. They participated in numerous extended junkets abroad. They apparently spent most of their waking hours in Freetown nightclubs. Furthermore, the brigadier, in complete violation of his call for fiscal austerity, established the use of cars for all officers down to the rank of first lieutenant. This meant that a number of officers who previously had ridden public transport or army landrovers suddenly appeared in brand-new Mercedes. For many of the rank and file it appeared that the senior officers were more interested in feathering their own nests than restoring civilian government.

All facets of the operation were successfully concluded on the morning of 18 April. Warrant Officer Patrick Conteh then announced the formation of an Anti-Corruption Revolutionary Movement (ACRM) as the successor to the NRC. The ACRM consisted of Conteh as chairman together with ten other warrant officers and two sub-inspectors from the police. In his address to the nation, Conteh noted that when the NRC assumed power 'little did we realize that the people we had chosen to direct our Nation's affairs were more corrupt and selfish than the ousted Civilian Regime'. In conclusion, he stated that 'soldiers and police have no business in running this country. Our immediate aim is to return to civilian rule'.[15] Accordingly, civilian rule was to be re-established by a military coup designed to end a previous armed intervention. On the afternoon of 26 April, 1968, seven years after Sierra Leone's entry into a world of independent states and a little over thirteen months following a military coup d'état, that country regained civilian rule. In a brief ceremony at State House, Siaka Stevens was again sworn in as prime minister, this time with the full backing of the Sierra Leone military.

The NRC was little more than a coalition of one-and two-man army cliques that had stumbled into the act of intervention without much commitment to any specific political programme. The regime was especially incapable of building bridges to a popularly based civilian sector, epitomized by the APC and Siaka Stevens. Subsequently, the NRC's unwillingness to espouse the basic right of the country to be inspired by civilian political values had undermined whatever support it had among the general population and the army.

SIAKA STEVENS' RULE

Siaka Stevens strove to avoid the excesses of the NRC and eliminate opposition by more subtle methods. Following a call for national unity, opposition leaders were persuaded to join Stevens's government and were offered cabinet posts. To accomplish this the number of ministries had to be increased; new ones were created and old ones divided up. Eventually, the cabinet would expand into a hall of residence accommodating a larger contingent of senior and junior ministers (from 1968–78) than in most Third World countries. Stevens's policy of 'absorption' also applied to the senior civil service, which expanded from just under 600 to just under 900 during this period. This expansion was especially noticeable in the foreign service, where the number of high commissioners and other foreign accreditations doubled.[16]

Stevens was particularly aware of the importance of first neutralizing and then gaining the support of the military. The army was given a joyful farewell to arms and marched off into the hills, where newly built barracks, better pay and conditions, and extra rice and alcohol rations kept their minds wonderfully concentrated on the pursuit of pleasure rather than of politics. Whereas the 1968 estimates provided for defence expenditures of Le2,091,824, in fiscal 1969–70 the figures for this same category had increased to Le2,353,309. For 1970–71, the estimates called for military expenditures of Le2,725,740, a 45 per cent increase over an actual outlay of Le1,500,000 in 1966–7, the last year of Sir Albert's administration. In a debate over the proposed military budget for 1969–70 one SLPP member offered his assessment of the APC's approach to civil–military relations:

> The fact is that this Government is playing with Army rule under the cloak of civilian rule. Their strength lies in the Army and they will stay by force and rule by force. This is why they are spending so much money for the Army and carrying the Army like a baby.[17]

Despite these protests expenditure on the military grew from Le2,091,824 to Le11,323,328, trebling in real terms, between 1968 and 1978.[18]

Yet, to balance these rewards Stevens took precautions against the military. He was in office less than two months before he purged the army of several officers and warrant officers alleged to have participated with some SLPP politicians in attempts to cause unrest. Among those dismissed and later arrested were the self-promoted Captain Patrick Conteh and warrant officers John Kengenyeh and Emadu Rogers. All three belonged to the Mende tribe and had joined with army privates to from the Anti-Corruption Revolutionary Movement. The detention of these men was followed by the forced retirement of Lieutenant-Colonel Ambrose Genda, a Mende, who together with Colonel John Bangura had constituted the entire officer corps of the Sierra Leone army since the privates' mutiny of April 18. In August 1968, Soloman Pratt, the minister of development under the national government, was quoted as saying that 'Sierra Leone wants to be the first country in Africa to let the military know it is treasonable to take over power because you have a gun'.[19]

Stevens had altered Albert Margai's policy of benign neglect of the army as an organization but he did continue the SLPP system of civilian control over an officer sympathetic to the regime in power and prepared to defend that regime against internal threats. Accordingly, to eliminate links with past political–military alliances Lansana, Blake, and their fellow conspirators were removed from the army list. This destroyed the old SLPP civilian–military coalition. Since the APC received the bulk of its support from northerners of various tribes and from Freetown Creoles, it was clear that these groups would have to predominate in the army's senior ranks. Throughout 1968 and 1969, the APC eliminated as many Mendes as possible from the officer corps. Taking the officer corps as a whole, the Mende proportion became 32 per cent and the Temne proportion, 35 per cent, which meant that an earlier imbalance in favour of the Mendes had been wiped out completely. Furthermore, minority northern tribes constituted 29 per cent of the total.[20] These were principally the Korankos and the Yalunkas which together represented only 4.4 per cent of the Sierra Leone population. Colonel John Bangura (promoted to brigadier on 1 May, 1969), a Loko, was acceptable for the position of force commander. The commander of the first battalion, Lieutenant-Colonel Joseph Saidu Momoh, belonged to the prime minister's minority Limba tribe and, being untainted by prior involvement with military or civilian–military cliques, was brought into the ruling elite.

In 1969 a group of university graduates returned from abroad to form the Sierra Leone Provincial Organization (SLPO), an ostensibly nonpolitical group. However, despite its rhetoric, it became clear that the SLPO was primarily the mouthpiece of Temne northerners who believed that Stevens had allowed the Creoles to perpetuate, if not to strengthen their monopoly on senior positions in the civil service and elsewhere. On 10 May 1970 the SLPO was superseded by the National Democratic Party (NDP) which, although it held no seats in the House of Representatives, became Sierra Leone's third registered political party.

The NDP was headed by Hamid Taqi whose older brother Ibrahim had served previously as the APC Minister of Information. The NDP charged that Stevens was planning to transform Sierra Leone into a republic, followed by the creation of an autocratic executive presidency. Stevens's reaction to this threat came quickly. On 12 September the government formally suspended the holding of public meetings. Dr Karefa-Smart formed the United Democratic Party (UDP) on 20 September and immediately incorporated Hamid Taqi's NDP. Stevens soon counterattacked, however, and on 8 October banned the new political party and detained thirty of its members under the emergency regulations. Thus, on the night of 8 October and throughout the following week, the army was used to carry out the arrests of the UDP leadership including Dr Karefa-Smart.[21]

The use of the army in arresting opposition politicians and some of the UDP's major supporters angered Brigadier Bangura who was known to be sympathetic to the UDP. Rumour held that Bangura had been contacted by Karefa-Smart and other UDP members on several occasions. On 13 October, five days after the banning of the UDP, Bangura's standing was further eroded. On that day, two senior officers, Majors Benedict Kargbo and Yankay Sesay, who were both Temne and known to be among Bangur's most trusted confidants, were suddenly pensioned off on suspicion of working for the CIA. Immediately following the dismissal of Kargbo and Sesay, Stevens ordered the arrest of twelve army warrant officers and NCOs, most of them

Temne, and charged them with an attempted mutiny on the night of 13 October.[22]

The situation continued to deteriorate and on the 23 March 1971, Brigadier Bangura appeared on Sierra Leone radio to announce that 'owing to the current state of affairs, the army had been compelled to take control of the situation until further notice'. He added further that his statements had the 'full backing and support of all members of the armed forces' and warned that 'any undue outside interference will be viewed with disfavour'.[23] During the day there had been two attempts to assassinate Stevens by pro-Bangura troops. Both had failed and Stevens took to hiking but his absence allowed Bangura to proclaim what appeared to be a successful military coup. Unfortunately for Bangura his support among the military was not sufficient for him to maintain control and within a few hours he found himself arrested by a pro-Stevens army clique led by Lieutenant-Colonel Sam King.

King announced that 'a large percentage of Sierra Leone's armed forces' wished to dissociate themselves from Brigadier Bangura's coup. Furthermore, he and his fellow officers regarded the Stevens's government as the only legally constituted authority in the country.[24] Following the lieutenant-colonel's radio broadcast, Bangura was placed under arrest and a search conducted for other pro-Bangura army officers believed to have gone into hiding. On 26 March loyalist troops arrested six other officers alleged to have participated in the Bangura coup attempt. In the next several days an additional five officers were apprehended and detained.

To strengthen his position Stevens decided to reintroduce the Guinean factor into Sierra Leone's civil–military relations. Sekou Toure was more than ready to oblige and on 28 March the two leaders announced the formal signing of a mutual defence pact. That same day, Guinean paratroopers were dropped into Freetown to take up positions at the prime minister's residence and other key points in the capital. By 31 March there were some two hundred Guinean soldiers in Freetown with promises from Conakry to send the entire Guinean army if it were needed. The newly promoted Colonel Joseph Saidu Momoh succeeded Brigadier Bangura as force commander of the Sierra Leone army. For his part, Dr Karefa-Smart feared being associated with the coup attempt, and on 24 March the leader of the banned UDP boarded a plane for Geneva. Of the nine officers eventually brought to trial on charges of mutiny and incitement to mutiny by violence, there were five Mendes, a Kono, a Koranko, and two Temnes. Death sentences were passed on four officers linked to the assassination attempts of 23 March. These included Brigadier Bangura, Major S. E. Momoh, Major F. Jawara, and Lieutenant J. B. Kolugbonda, all executed by firing squad on the morning of 29 June 1971.[25]

Stevens planned to preserve civilian control of the military by nurturing pro-government cliques of officers and by surrounding himself with troops from the Guinean unit of the Sierra Leone army. The success of his strategy was verified in April 1971 when he made Sierra Leone a republic and became its first president. In March 1971 *The New York Times* noted that 'for Siaka Stevens ... the problem has been to work out a stable relationship with his country's 1500-man Army'.[26] Subsequently, while the Guinean troops were being phased out, the last contingent leaving in mid–1973, Stevens requested and received Cuban assistance to train an APC militia as a counterpoise to the regular army. This militia was later dubbed the Internal Security Unit (ISU).

Beginning 2 August 1974, the Sierra Leone government authorized the detention of eighty-three civilians and army NCOs. Included in the list were Ibrahim Taqui and Mohammad Forna who had been among the founding members of the United Democratic Party and who had been detained in October 1970, only to be released in July 1973. Also included were the former chairman of the National Reformation Council, Andrew T. Juxon-Smith, and the former brigadier and army commander, David Lansana. Fifteen of those detained, including Forna, Taqi, and Lansana, eventually were brought to trial and charged with attempting to overthrow the government by violence. On 16 November all of the accused were found guilty of treason and sentenced to death by firing squad. On 19 July 1975 Forna, Taqi and Lansana were hanged along with Lansana Kamara, another civilian, a paramount chief, Bai Makri N'Silk, an NCO and a warrant officer.[27]

A major threat to the APC government came in 1977 starting with student demonstrations against Stevens during a congregation ceremony at Fourah Bay College in January. The harsh reaction of the government contributed to a spread of violent protests in many parts of the country.[28] Stevens quickly called up general elections for May of that year. While the APC won most seats unopposed, the SLPP returned to Parliament with 15 seats. In 1978 Sierra Leone's multiparty system was abandoned with the approval of a new constitution providing for APC one-party rule. The use of subtle bureaucratic obstructions and bribery against his political opponents were so successful that Siaka seldom had to use his private army against his political rivals. Accordingly, the Internal Security Unit was incorporated into the police force in December 1979; it was renamed the Special Security Division. Stevens argued in 1980 that the move to a one-party state had been necessary because 'We don't understand the concept of a loyal opposition'.[29]

During the first half of the 1980s Stevens maintained his control over both the military and civilian government. This was particularly impressive considering the country's economic decline, corruption, and authoritarian policies which plagued the government. Furthermore, Stevens survived the opposition caused by the $200 million cost of the Organization of African Unity summit meeting in 1980; which he hosted.[30] There was some apprehension in late 1981 when a military coup in Ghana caused alarm in Sierra Leone. *The New York Times* commented that Stevens's 'authoritarian rule under the All People's Congress has lately been reported to have become more repressive, with scores of journalists and political dissenters being jailed. The threat to Mr. Stevens may come from the 3,000-man military'.[31] Yet, his use of tribal loyalties and client–patron relationships enabled Stevens to avoid a Ghana-style coup. The Sierra Leone military, led by Stevens's ally Brigadier-General Momoh, continued to protect its special privileges by remaining loyal to the APC. By incorporating those tribes who opposed the SLPP, and their Mende supporters, into the army ranks Stevens ensured his survival.

MOMOH AND THE SINGLE PARTY CIVILIAN–MILITARY REPUBLIC

At the end of 1985, after a period of relative calm, Stevens announced his retirement. Stevens's hand-picked successor, Major-General Joseph Momoh was then selected by the APC as his successor. Wishing to retire in order to enjoy the rewards of 17 unbroken years as leader of Sierra Leone, and what was left of his health, Stevens was determined that the next administration would leave him in peace. With the steady decline of the country's economy, continued reports of government corruption, and the stigma of his personalistic rule, it was not unreasonable to suspect that succeeding political leaders might punish him as a means of misdirecting public criticism. Momoh represented the best alternative. He shared Stevens's multitribal background, his father was a Limba, his mother a Temne, and he was educated as a Creole. Furthermore, as commander of the army Momoh could maintain discipline over the politicians as well as the public. Subsequently, with the APC sufficiently cowed by Stevens, Momoh ran as the only candidate for president in the election of 1985 and won a reported 99 per cent of the vote.

Before he was in office Momoh had made it clear that he intended to bring the army more directly into government affairs, 'over and above normal duties like security'. It was his belief that many Sierra Leoneans were 'wanting in patriotism ... [and] have decided to put themselves before the country'.[32] Therefore, the discipline and loyalty of military life would be transferred to the civilian population to eliminate smuggling, corruption, and to enforce price controls. Apparently, Momoh enjoyed the full support of Stevens who argued that, 'If a civilian is good to be president, then the army man [is not] too bad'.[33]

Despite the optimism which accompanied Momoh's ascension to the presidency conditions in Sierra Leone did not improve and in fact worsened. By the end of 1986 Momoh was appealing for time to overcome 'this very difficult economic period'. Typically, he offered a military philosophy to the public declaring,

> People must be prepared to work hard and be productive. We shall separate the weak from the strong ... the average Sierra Leonean must appreciate that money is not all that matters; this is where patriotism comes in.[34]

This type of rhetoric was associated with what was being called the 'New Order' which emphasized discipline and loyalty to solve the country's problems. To ensure his position Momoh incorporated into the army large numbers of those tribes – in particular, his own, the Limba – who could be counted on through tribal loyalty and mutual interests to support his rule. Accordingly, the Sierra Leone government was transformed into a civilian–military run state under the guise of a civilian republic. Subsequently, while specific answers to problems remained absent, Momoh depended on the army to enforce economic regulations and generally alienated political advisors who criticized his methods.

By the end of 1989 Momoh's control of the military had enabled him to successfully crush one attempted civilian coup in 1987.[35] Meanwhile, the population continued to endure mounting hardships with the almost total collapse of the economy. The Leone had been devalued numerous times and by 1989 black market rates were Le100 to the dollar; the official rate was 45–1. Reports of government corruption and free spending continued to proliferate with accounts of officials buying luxury automobiles, at a cost estimated to be Le3 million, as well as a political convention in Makeni rumoured to cost Le10 million.[36] This was particular galling to the average citizen since a bag of rice, 1 month's supply, can cost over Le1000 while an average teacher's monthly salary is seldom more than Le750. Yet, significantly, the military has apparently been unaffected by these economic woes. Among many people it is believed that the soldiers obtained rice, the staple diet, at extremely low prices, possibly Le80 for a bag normally costing Le1000.[37] Officers and political officials are able to buy rice at extremely low prices or obtain it free. Thus, the population suffers from economic decline while being exhorted by the president to 'fight with all the might and determination we can muster.[38]

How long can this situation continue? The answer may be indefinitely. While there remains a political–military relationship that supports one party and one man then there can be little chance of a successful civilian revolution without a complete social upheaval. In Sierra Leone this kind of solution would be extremely difficult to accomplish. The fragmented nature of its tribal society and the client–patron network that exist perpetuate disunity. Those who have reached a level of relevant affluency have done so by working within and protecting the status quo. Few in that kind of situation wish to experience the hardships endured by the general population. Subsequently, Momoh and the APC have filled the ranks of the military with those tribes and supporters who will continue their support as long as the special privileges they enjoy continue. Thus, those in power cannot afford to change the system without risking a coup from either the army officers or the rank and file.

NOTES

1. I would like to thank Clarke Speed and Lisa Jondro for their advice and assistance.
2. *Shekpendeh*, 28 March 1961.
3. Biographical information primarily from: Mark R. Lipschutz and R. Kent Rasmussen, *Dictionary of African Biography*, (Berkeley: University of California Press, 1989).
4. Christopher Clapham, *Liberia and Sierra Leone*, (Cambridge, Mass., Cambridge University Press, 1976), p. 14.
5. Thomas Cox, *Civil–Military Relations in Sierra Leone: A Case Study of African Soldiers in Politics*, (Boston: Harvard University Press, 1976), p. 95.
6. John R. Cartwright, *Politics in Sierra Leone 1947–67*, (Toronto: University of Toronto Press, 1970), p. 252.
7. Ibid., p. 253.
8. Cox, p. 128.
9. Ibid., p. 133.
10. Eric A. Nordlinger, *Soldiers in Politics: Military Coups and Governments*, (Englewood Cliffs, NJ: Prentice-Hall Inc., 1977), p. 61.
11. Cartwright, p. 254.
12. *Times*, 29 March 1967.
13. *Times*, 29 March 1968.
14. *Daily Mail*, 29 July 1967.
15. *Africa Research Bulletin 5*, 1985, Col. 1035A.
16. Frank Ly, 'Sierra Leone: The Paradox of Economic Decline and Political Stability', *Monthly Review*, (June 1980), p. 20.
17. Cox, p. 208.
18. Ly, p. 20.
19. Cox, pp. 206–9.
20. Ibid.
21. *West Africa*, 17 October 1970.
22. Ibid.
23. *West Africa*, 2 April 1971.
24. Ibid.
25. *West Africa*, 9 July 1971.
26. *The New York Times*, 28 March 1971.
27. *West Africa*, 28 July 1975.

28. C. Maghaily Fyle, *The History of Sierra Leone*, (London: Evans Brothers Limited, 1981), p. 143.
29. *Time Magazine*, 28 July 1980.
30. Ibid.
31. *The New York Times*, 4 January 1982.
32. *West Africa*, 9 September 1985.
33. Ibid.
34. *West Africa*, 1 December 1986, p. 1986.
35. *The New York Times*, 11 October 1987.
36. *West Africa*, 27 March – 2 April 1989.
37. Amounts were obtained through personal experiences in Sierra Leone from 1988 to 1989.
38. *West Africa*, 27 March – 2 April.

12 Military intervention and withdrawal in Africa: problems and perspectives

Karl P. Magyar

Most nations of Africa have attained their independence starting in the 1950s. In their brief but tumultuous histories, many of these emerging nations witnessed considerable military intervention in political affairs – and an occasional military withdrawal after such intervention. These relatively infrequent cases of withdrawal, and the rarer cases of unbroken civilian government, are certainly exceptions to the general rule of active military interference in the affairs of state throughout Africa.

A substantial body of literature has been produced on the topic of Africa's coups d'état, with the most frequent question addressing the causes for military take-overs. This particular issue has produced wide disagreement among analysts searching for explanations among a wide array of plausible answers which at best remain conjecture. Attempts to explain military disengagement or withdrawal are even more tentative, if for no reason other than the infrequency or the temporary nature of such withdrawals.

With over fifty African countries, it is tempting to engage in quantified comparative studies of military regimes taking over from civilian governments and to arrive at some respectable empirically based conclusions. Comparative studies of African military governments, however, are impeded by complications which defy generalizations. For example, most coups are perpetrated against military governments which had themselves come to power by prior coups against original civilian governments. Hence, a distinction must be made between coups against civilian or against military regimes. In other cases, some governments since independence have been comprised of fused party–military structures, such as those in Angola or Mozambique. These differ fundamentally from the greater incidence of countries which attained independence under multi-party structures, but soon developed into single-party civilian states against which coups were then executed. It may indeed be easier to study the rare cases of coups or military governments in the socially homogeneous and economically more developed states such as those in Portugal or Greece, than in Africa, where coups are much more frequent – but meaningful generalizations much more elusive.

Finally, by way of introduction, the purpose for such studies must be elucidated. A study of coups tends towards the divination of the motives for such actions, with the presumed intent of ultimately contributing to the development of stable civil–military relations. And studies of the 'back to the barracks' movement focus on which conditions generate such movements, and what it takes to keep the 'men on horseback' at the stables.

These analyses of military withdrawal may overlook a deeper dimension of the problem. Simple success in preventing coups and keeping the military in the barracks does not address the underlying causes and conditions which gave rise to pervasive military interventions. By way of obvious example, if it could be proved that the motive for a projected coup concerned the need to remove an undisputably corrupt regime, dissuading the plotters from carrying out their actions does not address the issue of corruption. Consequently, keeping the soldiers in the barracks could lead to even increased corruption by a more secure civilian administration.

Studies of coups are almost always biased against such interventions, and they are not sympathetic to any potentially positive dimensions. The original military junta which ousted Emperor Haile Selassie in Ethiopia in a revolutionary coup in 1975 argued (rather persuasively) that the Emperor was totally inept because he could not satisfy the needs of the hundreds of thousands of starving Ethiopians. Could a military government do worse? And the succession of corrupt or inept civilian governments in Ghana and Nigeria support the conclusion that keeping the soldiers in the barracks does not solve the fundamental problems of those countries, where the soldiers have repeatedly re-emerged to right the wrongs – thereby becoming part of the problem. This should not be construed to be a veiled preference on the part of the author for non-democratic military governments, but it is a call for new directions in research. If the goals to be pursued in Africa include prosperity, stability, human rights, and eventually, Western-type democratic institutions, and if we agree that the civilian regimes as constituted at independence have failed to progress towards these goals, then perhaps academic analysts have been asking the wrong questions.

A major analytic problem regarding Africa's proclivities towards intervention stems from the tendency to make global comparisons. Those of us in the economically developed and functioning multiparty states are repelled at the very thought of praetorian governmental controls over the state. Our militaries know this, and respond accordingly. But this Western paradigm of civilian rule does not necessarily connote the same liberal and progressive attitudes in all parts of the Third World. Our bias may be inappropriately universalistic, in that we do not account for the objective, historical, cultural, and specific conditions which prevail in the Third World, which at this point may require divergent social structures from those we prefer.

Where we in the First World enjoy prosperity and (mostly) competently-managed administrations, the Third World suffers from poverty, the absence of developed political institutions, a lack of wide legitimacy in all corners of the land, an absence of competitive abilities at the international level, excessive historically-derived ethnic-based pluralistic tendencies, insufficient quantities of capable administrators, and in many cases, a lack of the basic conditions required to attain sovereignty and basic 'viability'. In the case of Sub-Saharan Africa, most countries are in the early stages of their consolidative period which is characterized by a plethora of constraining conditions. For most – if not all – countries throughout history, these were always very volatile periods. Africa differs only in that these constraining factors have been greatly concentrated into a few intense decades.

The American civil war, we should not forget, occurred almost a century after independence – and under comparatively favourable economic conditions. At issue in the American civil war was the acceptance of governmental legitimacy nation-wide, which implies that internal conflicts are to be peacefully settled. And if we go by the standards of Latin America's progress towards liberal-based legitimacy, we can expect that these volatile conditions in Africa will remain, in the words of Claude E. Welch, Jr, 'for several decades to come'.[1]

Adda Bozeman raises yet another dimension of our analytic problems. We tend to classify conflicts into neat typologies and to search for statistically-significant patterns which may yield unambiguous clues as to the origins of coups. Surely they must have rationally-based motives, and hence prescriptions for their elimination may be offered. But Professor Bozeman states: 'it is difficult today to isolate a military coup from the mutiny, rebellion, movement of secession or liberation, civil wars, interracial massacre, or other flight into violence with which it was entangled'.[2] This describes better the succession of coups, a problem which goes beyond merely explaining the initial military interference in the original civilian regime. Coups are merely the most frequent expression of the utter frustrations encountered in nation-building in Africa, attempted under the most severe socio-historical conditions. As such, analytic comparisons and value judgements based on the prevailing First World paradigm will hardly inform those who more modestly seek to lessen the negative impact of coups and to hasten the legitimating process of Africa's fragile countries.

AFRICAN COUPS: ANALYTIC PERSPECTIVES

It may be hypothesized that to best explain why soldiers remain or return to the barracks, we need to examine the evident motives which led them to the accession to power. While the best overarching explanation lies in the very nature of fragile states in their consolidative stage, specific reasons were offered by numerous analysts writing in the mid-1960s – by which time this phenomenon had been well established. Two notable features characterize these explanations. The first is that military intervention had not been widely anticipated when these colonies were considered for independence. Indeed, Tanganyika at independence seriously contemplated becoming a state without a military at all. The second feature of such explanations of coups concerned the multifarious reasons offered – which in itself may express the likelihood that we have not really understood the coup phenomenon, and also, that the many specific reasons may perhaps be better treated collectively. (This I attempt to do by reference to the travails of states in their early consolidative stages.)

The first Sub-Saharan coup took place in Sudan in 1958. Congo was next in 1960, and Togo, Congo–Brazzaville, and Dahomey followed in rapid succession with coups in 1963. In 1965 there were 4, and 1966 saw 7 more successful coups d'état. Pretoria's Africa Institute counted 68 African coups from 1963 to 1987. Thirteen countries had 1 violent change; 18 had more than 1. Seventy-two leaders were ousted from office by any one of several violent methods; 21 were assassinated.[3] Another study calculated that 230 military interventions occurred in Africa between 1956 and 1984. This included coups, attempted coups, and reported plots.[4] Some of the data excludes the activities in the radical-tending states which fuse the party and military functions, making it difficult to distinguish between military and civilian governments. Other states in which the military have extraordinary influence on policy, but power remains technically in civilian hands, also comprise part of this militarist history.

Early scholarship regarding military intervention in public affairs examined Europe, and in the Third World, Latin America. S. E. Finer's *The Man on Horseback* was perhaps the most influential such effort in the early 1960s.[5] Finer lists as motives for military intervention the 'manifest destiny' of soldiers; the motive of the 'national interest'; sectional interests such as class, regional, and corporate self-interest of the armed forces and individual self-interest; and the 'mixed' motives of the military. Claude E. Welch, Jr, offered another list in 1967: the declining prestige of the political party, political schisms, lessened likelihood of external intervention, contagion, domestic social antagonisms, economic malaise, government corruption and inefficiency, and a heightened awareness by the army of its own power.[6] Ruth

First accords a prominent position to the issue of pay in many early mutinies and coups.[7]

These early analyses are illustrative of the generally frustrating attempts to isolate causes – along with the usual well-intended attempt to project the consequences of the continuation of such tendencies, and to address the conditions required to bring military interventionism to an end.

The explanations of 'contagion' and 'ease' were the most pervasive themes offered by these early analysts.[8] The first referred to the contagious process of influence by one country's military take-over on another. Such processes ironically unified Africa in a pattern of common behaviour which subsequently influenced relations also in the political and economic realism. The explanation concerning 'ease' remains attractive, but also one that harbours the need for more revealing analyses. Just which conditions make it 'easy' for military intervention? Coups are like vultures who pick on dead prey, but we need to know what killed the prey in the first place.

Another characteristic of early analyses of Africa's military intervention concerned the varieties of such interventions. The Congo in 1960 experienced revolts and rebellions, [9] while in East Africa, the major problem was mutinies.[10] Welch notes that although the mutinies were not political in objective, they did have political consequences: they represented insubordination to officers and not to elected officials. We may speculate today that such mutinies may have laid the groundwork for subsequent tendencies of younger military men to disregard the legitimacy of their own military power hierarchies much as entire armies would soon disregard the fragile civilian power structures. Pretexts offered for such mutinies concerned the resentment towards the retention of expatriate military officers, the fear of not reaping the rewards of independence, and of course, the demand for more pay. In any event, the 'ease' with which coups were waged was preceded by the ease with which mutinies had been conducted.

Analysts also focused on the nature of the emerging political institutions whose fragility had not been sufficiently anticipated. 'Political development' became a topic which in the African context centred on 'modernization'. As original constitutions would soon be modified, pluralistic competition emerged from various regions within the land. Political institutions would weaken due to rapid personnel changes – exacerbated by a lack of administrative funds. Hence the military was often seen as the most logical social institution which could promote national integration and generate stability. If the state would require a period of depoliticization in order to advance development, the military was seen as the most appropriate depoliticized agency, one not subject to particularistic and competing pressures. Richard Hodder-Williams expresses it: 'For some people, the army in Africa was assumed to be cohesive, non-tribal, and the modernizing agency *par excellence*.[11] But he notes that this was not the case.

Welch cites several analysts who note that indeed, in (other) Third World states, the military may well oppose modernization.[12] Even where the military may genuinely set out to rule a country more competently than did the ousted civilian regime, the results are hardly more encouraging, nor are policy alterations always significant.[13] F. W. Gutteridge offers his conclusion on this topic: 'No overall generalization about the army as a national melting pot and symbol of unity can survive the litmus tests of behaviour of the Nigerian Army in 1966 and of the exploitation of the tribal divisions in the Ugandan force by Obote and Amin'.[14] He also notes the general characteristic of the military often lacking 'any clear-cut objectives'. And Ruth First produced the most often quoted observation when she referred to a coup as 'a method of change that changes little'.[15]

In summary, a review of the early analytic literature regarding military intervention in African politics reveals that coups were preceded by a variety of other interventionist methods; that a few specific motives could not explain the full spate of such phenomena; and that there is no generally accepted conclusion that military rule is decisively more efficient or desirable than civilian rule.

Subsequent scholarship included quantified analyses aimed at understanding the structural environment, which, presumably, would yield information of a predictive nature.[16] One such study, based on a series by several analysts, devised a table of high, moderate and low probability rankings of 'serious military intervention' for 1985.[17] Considering that there had been an average of three successful coups per year in Africa, and that in recent years the annual average was two, such predictions can be made safely without identifying the specific victims. But even at that, it was disconcerting to read the analysis in question which had rated Lesotho as a 'low probability state' – a week after a coup had been successfully conducted there. In this regard, quantified studies have likewise failed to contribute a decisive explanation for military interventionism – which implies that our analytic energies may be perhaps more appropriately channelled towards the consequences of such interventions.

MILITARY INTERVENTION: A CONTEMPORARY PROFILE

A broad review of military intervention in the politics of African states during the last three decades yields few definitive insights of a causal, regional, ideological or socio-environmental nature.

Several coups occurred in Burundi, but only one in Rwanda – where similar economic, ethnic and conflictual conditions prevail. Uganda, Chad,

Sudan, and Ethiopia have each had more than one coup and all have fought protracted conflicts. Angola and Mozambique, however, have also experienced long wars but to date have avoided successful coups. And Ghana, Nigeria, Burkina Faso and Benin have each had multiple coups – and have experienced no major wars except for Nigeria's internal civil war in the 1960s. Nor can regionally-based conclusions be drawn, for both East and West Africa contain some of the most stable – as well as some of the most volatile – countries.

A parallel may be drawn between the attempt to explain coups and the difficulties encountered in making decisive judgements regarding Africa's wars. On a purely statistical basis, there are evident similarities among the countries which have fought the most protracted conflicts, be they liberation wars, civil wars, or truly transnational wars, or a combination of such types of conflicts. In broad terms, to list Africa's countries involved in wars is to list Africa's poorest countries. But there are exceptions such as Nigeria, which is not usually ranked among the poorest, and Angola, which has more than sufficient resources to develop into a prosperous state. We are, however, at a loss to explain the coincidence between violent conflicts and the state of the economy, even if the general observation is valid, that the more prosperous states are internally more stable and are likely to be dominated by civilian governments. (Examples include Ivory Coast, Senegal, Gabon, Kenya, Zimbabwe, Mauritius, and Botswana.) It must be stressed that even some of these have experienced attempted coups, but the attempts were not successful – which could be interesting in itself.

Perhaps the key to understanding Africa's militarist tendencies lies in the domain of economic development, but that explanation has yet to be convincingly articulated. Sheer poverty alone is hardly the prime motive for violent conflict or the justification for the installation of praetorian governments. The military has no innate claim to developmental talents – at least within a peaceful democratic context, unless we are willing to entertain its capacity for forced labour and austerity. We are also soberly reminded that the greatest wars in our century have been fought by the richest nations. At best, then, we can hypothesize that those nations not progressing economically under civilian rule leave themselves open to military intervention, which, while it constitutes no automatic panacea, offers at least the hope that a different set of decision-makers may produce different policies. As for the military's acceptance of such challenges, the immorality of economic and political stagnation sanctions the morality of intervention.

Whatever the cause, coups continue to occur in Africa. Three decades since the Congo mutiny have not produced acceptable explanations for coups, but they have become an established institution. Particularly disturbing to Western analysts was the attempted coup in Kenya in 1982 which resulted in 250 deaths, 1500 persons detained, and the disbanding of the Kenyan air force due to its role in the attempt. In 1987, Africans throughout the continent expressed shock at the seemingly senseless coup in Burkina Faso and the brutal assassination of Capt. Thomas Sankara – who himself had taken over in a previous coup.[18] True to Ruth First's pronouncement, nothing had changed. In 1989 the military took over again in Sudan, after giving substantial notice to the civilian government of Sadiq el-Mahdi, who could not resolve the civil conflict. That same year, coup plots were uncovered or coups were prevented in Gabon, Burkina Faso, and in Liberia, while in Comoros, the president was assassinated under what may generously be called bizarre circumstances. Talk of yet another coup was ripe in Benin; and Ethiopia offered that year's bloodiest but successful defence against a coup attempt.

These numerous recent coups or attempted coups produced no significant changes, except perhaps that more successful defences have been demonstrated by governments in power. Most of the coup attempts are at this point aimed at military governments. Nor do the profiles of the countries in which these recent coups are attempted differ from those in the first decade of independence. This is emphasized as we are still confronted with the same diversity of countries which indicates that none are immune to military intervention. The soldiers are certainly neither staying in, nor returning to the barracks.

SOLDIERS AND BARRACKS IN AFRICA

The preceding has argued that the general assumptions about military intervention in politics in Africa need to be re-examined in light of that continent's unique historical circumstances and especially the problems associated with the drive for national consolidation under very austere socio-political conditions. Active military intervention and coups d' etat are in fact the norm for most of Africa's independent countries. Nevertheless, there are soldiers in some African countries who have never intervened, while in others, the military has withdrawn for a 'significant' period of time after having toppled civilian regimes. A third category consists of those states in which coups were hatched and attempted, but failed.

The 'barracks-loving' soldiers, those who never attempted a coup, are in a small minority, and there is no question that this phenomenon should be closely examined in a more comprehensive study than can be provided presently. However, just as we acknowledge that the precise identification of motives which inspire coups is elusive, we should also not expect to arrive soon at more definitive judgements regarding the decisions to stay in, or to return to the barracks.

The literature concerning successful coups is relatively extensive in comparison to the analyses concerned with the 'back to the barracks' phenomenon. In part, this may logically stem from the greater infrequency of such withdrawals, but also because such analyses may have to be more speculative. Ruth First offered only limited comments on the back to the barracks phenomenon, and she observed: 'it is easier to step into than out of power'.[19] She raised another interesting point with her observation that most coup leaders quickly disavow long-term political ambition – but then succumb to it. We may deduce from this almost standard pattern that the military acknowledges by these initial promises that they ought not to be in power. This may be an important point in that African military governments may concede that legitimacy will not accrue to any but civilian governments.

The early literature on military abstention or withdrawal demonstrates yet again the reliance – however inappropriate – on non-African patterns. S. E. Finer referred to S. P. Huntington's notion of military 'professionalism', which keeps soldiers out of politics.[20] However, within the context of Africa, we will soon realize the inadequacy of such conceptions as we have little reason to expect the military to be any more – or less – professional than civilian governments. Should the military attain and respect such professionalism and abstain from intervention, it would still exist within the context of a non-professionally administered state. In short, Africa, in its consolidative period characterized by laborious institutional development, will experience structural inadequacies in all social organizations – hence the military cannot be examined as a separate institution in society. In fact, the military's lack of professionalism reflects the inadequacies of the entire social fabric in Africa's transitional period.

Some fifteen Sub-Saharan African mainland countries have to date not experienced successful coups. However, no major discernible pattern emerges from this group which could enlighten us. These stable countries range from Gambia and Senegal to Djibouti, and south to Botswana and Swaziland. Seven of these countries are concentrated in Southern Africa, a region characterized by histories of substantial anti-colonial or anti-white struggles; by the radiating economic influence and interventionist tendencies of South Africa; and by the socialist orientation of several regimes. If Kenya is included, an argument may be made that most of Southern Africa's countries were settled by substantial numbers of Europeans during the colonial days, and in several, many whites remained after independence. But exceptions include 'coupless' Malawi, Botswana, and Swaziland – which had no great concentrations of European settlers, nor are they today inclined towards socialism.[21]

A thorough analysis should investigate the economic dimension, for several of these stable countries also exhibit respectable economic progress, but as previously noted there are exceptions. And it must be recalled that several countries on this short list have experienced coup attempts – they merely failed!

Except for the countries which experienced no coups, the next category of interest concerns those countries which experienced one coup and then either a military government was installed and remained in power, or a civilian government took over again after the soldiers actually returned to the barracks. A new analytic problem is raised in the case of single-coup countries with military regimes which remain in power. The military component of such regimes may become diluted, giving the outward appearance of virtual civilian rule as the military man at the top finds it advantageous to blur the distinctions between the two sectors.[22] This characteristic may describe Somalia, Madagascar, Rwanda, Mali, Togo, Equatorial Guinea and Niger. Technically, the military still rules, but after being in power so long, the leader's tendency to exchange military uniforms for civilian garb symbolizes the act of wilfully demoting the militarist image. Zaire's Mobutu represents perhaps the best example of this. In the words of Ali A. Mazrui and Michael Tidy: 'Zaire's government is more civilian than military'[23]

The phenomenon of successful long-term military rule which manages to avoid internal coups may also be a topic that deserves more attention – if peace and stability are the desired end-product. At the outset of military rule, most positions of authority may be in the hands of military men but 'civilianization' could progressively introduce greater non-military components. This long interlude would enable both the military and civilian administrators to 'professionalize' and to progress towards the attainment of well-grounded legitimacy.

Claude E. Welch, Jr, presents an interesting analytic framework in his investigation of Ghana and Nigeria.[24] Although these two countries are controlled most of the time by military regimes, they do offer occasional opportunities to study the return of soldiers to barracks, even if they don't stay there. He observes that disengagement of the armed forces from politics will be temporary if not accompanied by effective institution building. Such repeated coups within a specific country offer another version of the 'contagion' effect, in that the initial coup may inspire subsequent coups, but all within the same country.

Theories have been offered to portray the conditions surrounding the return to the barracks. Mazrui and Tidy postulate that such returns occur when military rulers 'tire of trying to deal with intractable problems, mainly in economic management'.[25] By itself, this is an inadequate explanation, for we have noted that most coups in Africa are in fact against ruling military regimes, hence the next set simply inherits the same economic problems, although it could be plausibly argued that the new coup aspirants have not learned anything by observation of their military colleagues in power. Mazrui and Tidy cite the cases of Sudan in 1964, Sierra Leone in 1968, and Ghana in 1969 and 1979 as examples of military regimes withdrawing 'after discovering that they were no better equipped for coping with severe economic and social problems'.[26] Mazrui and Tidy observe that in Sudan, the military yielded to civilian rule due to its failure to solve the southern question. Yet this is precisely the same reason for staging the coup of 1989. In the case of Sierra Leone, they note that the army itself began to weaken and to divide after its initial coup, with substantial numbers opposing continued military rule. Ethnic factors also played a complex role. In the case of Ghana, Mazrui and Tidy explain the return to the barracks as being the consequence of pressures exerted by the educated elite; the military feared a counter-coup; the first ruling military general soon became corrupt; and in Kofi Busia, the military thought they found a civilian of sufficient stature to be able to rule the country again.

One of the earlier comprehensive studies of demilitarization is that by Thomas S. Cox, who examined Sierra Leone's return to civilian rule. He offers a valuable detailed study of that case history, but while it analyses that single incidence of military rule and withdrawal, we would do well to learn more about the other dimension of the event: why the soldiers stayed in the barracks.[27] Cox portrays a military government under Brigadier Juxon-Smith, whose aspirations included ruling Sierra Leone beyond the originally estimated 15 months of intended military rule, following the coup of 1967. However, in April 1968, a small group of junior officers overthrew Juxon-Smith and soon restored civilian government. Cox quotes one of these original coup leaders, Major Blake, as having stressed that '"they were soldiers"' and '"politics is not our mission"'.[28]

Cox also refers to the influence of Sierra Leone's public which saw the military as obstructionists, and also the perception that the economy would not be developed under military rule. Another factor concerned the vast financial abuses of the many officers of the National Reformation Council, whose advantages stood in sharp contrast to the soldiers of lower rank. All these ostensible explanations for the move back to the barracks may be summed up: the civilian population was in a position to exert its sentiments, the military showed divisiveness in its own ranks, and there appeared an almost naive puritanical streak among junior members of the military. But again, there was no universal lesson to be learned of relevance for other African states. Once civilian power was in the hands of Siaka Stevens (who then governed until 1985,) he soon set about to purge the remaining military; adjustments were made among certain military leaders but in consideration of their tribal origins; and it was not long before generous financial benefits were extended to the armed forces.[29] Interestingly, although the public's anti-military attitudes remained consistent, little sentiment supported democracy as the country reverted to one-party rule. Cox also notes that in 1974, another coup had been started, but was successfully suppressed.

Claude E. Welch, Jr. also investigates military disengagement in a comparative study that examines Latin America and Africa. His analytic framework includes the following considerations which favour disengagement: economic decline, professionalism of the military, budgetary enhancement of the military, constitutional means for change, availability of civilian successors, and economic growth.[30] Welch draws several significant conclusions regarding reasons for disengagement. Two themes predominate: the major influence of emerging divisions within the military ruling ranks, and the failure to stimulate significant economic progress. 'Returns to the barracks, in other words, could well result from seeming failure'.[31] Two types of military regimes are postulated: the 'ruler' and the 'arbiter' types. The former is frustrated by the difficulties of realizing structural transformation and socio-economic success. This serves as an incentive to return to the barracks. The arbiter types, however, have more limited agendas and realize their innate limitations – hence they intend to return to the barracks as soon as possible. Welch's analysis provides a sophisticated review, but his conclusions only add support to the broader explanations which focus on states in their consolidative stages, embarked on the frustrating attempt to pursue legitimacy. Divisions in the ruling military ranks can actually contribute to their march back to the barracks, but these divisions reflect the entire society, which hardly unites despite the newly-exposed fragility which the military's interference in the governing process demonstrated. Little changes as a consequence.

Although S. E. Finer's influential *The Man on Horseback* was originally published in 1962, a second edition in 1988 included a brief section on the retreat to the barracks. His earlier comments listed four conditions for disengagement: the leader must positively want his troops to quit politics; a regime must be established which can function without military support; the new regime must be favourable to the armed forces; and the armed forces must have confidence in their leader.[32] But Finer notes that these conditions do not prevail in Africa. The new appendix lists as motives for abdication: the armed forces may subscribe to the doctrine of civil supremacy; they may perceive threats to their own cohesiveness and capability; they may lose their self-confidence due to the problems associated with governing; internal opposition forces may challenge the military (he cites the case of the professional ranks which organized in Ghana); and external intervention can (though rarely does) defeat a regime as it did in the case of Tanzania's ousting of Idi Amin.[33]

Arguing against a popular theme, Samuel Decalo debunked the myth of African armies as representing 'cohesive, nontribal, disciplined, and national units', and that they are 'modern, Westernized, and efficient organizations'.[34] They are rarely so, he notes. The consequences are obvious: the military 'is frequently not able to provide an efficient, nationally oriented, and stable administration'. For us, this implies that the public's expectations are not satisfied, and that the ensuing disillusionment facilitates the emergence of fissures in the military ranks, as the older generation of top officers may aspire to replace the civilian rulers they ousted on a more permanent basis, while the younger military contingents may acknowledge the innate limitations in the military's preparedness to rule. William Gutteridge presents another version of this interpretation when he lists reasons for military rulers leaving power which include being 'tired of power' and 'they think it wrong to examine it other than temporarily' or because 'they realize they have lost control and cannot command popular consensus'.[35] He also observes that demilitarization can be even more complex than decolonization. Another scholar, Roger Hamburg, sets the tone for a volume devoted to the topic of military disengagement from politics. He lists as reasons: public pressures, having been discredited in a foreign war, failure in the domestic policy arena, fissures in the ranks, desire for the return to professionalism, external pressures, and the realization of their inability to deal effectively with inherited political problems.[36] Not all reasons are evident in Africa.

This review of some of the prominent literature on the subject of the back to barracks movement is characterized by several features. The earlier studies of such tendencies in Africa focused heavily on Nigeria, Ghana, and Sierra Leone, all three of which yielded interesting, but mostly, situational information. Nigeria and Ghana remain under virtually perpetual military control, and Sierra Leone saw several unsuccessful coup attempts during its comparatively long period of civilian rule. Hence the availability of analyses of those instances remains of interest to the historian, but they did not yield definitive Africa-wide insight. The literature on the 'barracks' remains highly theoretical, but again, a wide array of hypotheses are postulated.

So varied are the explanations regarding coup or back to the barracks motives in Africa that we may safely assert that these affairs await more persuasive elucidations. The comparative dimension with respect to Latin America – though interesting – may be questioned. If we agree that we cannot convincingly deduce conclusive lessons from a comparative perspective of states within only Africa (as is my contention), then the reference to Latin America remains more tenuous. And finally, few speculate on the ramifications of the small African states which may never develop a sufficient level of 'viability'. Most analyses are indeed optimistic that as long as the soldiers stay in barracks, the civilian regime will be able to develop and modernize the state. Yet even this remains an assumption which, for many African countries, may be unwarranted. In this respect, I question if soldiers staying in barracks addresses the greater issue of the lack of effective legitimacy, development, and viability.

CONCLUSION

Going back to the barracks in Africa is analogous to a man who stops smoking. He stops at the end of every cigarette – before he lights up a new one. The recurrence of coups is perhaps the most striking characteristic of Africa's military interventionism. While we may judge as successful a specific instance of soldiers returning to the barracks, keeping them there is the next challenge, especially in view of new personnel continuously entering the military ranks.

The general thesis has been that to best understand the soldiers' enthusiasm for governing, we need to examine the conditions that encourage coups. Presumably, if such conditions are rectified, the causes for intervention will be eliminated. But we examined analyses which remind us that uncovering hard, structural, and readily observable conditions is difficult. And the patterns we uncover may not be applicable throughout all of Africa. Personal ambition may transcend standard institutional explanations, and hence the 'ease factor', which facilitates or encourages coups, cannot be dismissed too lightly.

The economic arena offers the greatest opportunities to investigate coup motives in depth. Africa's states in their early consolidative stages are characterized by economic fragility, which hardly supports national social integration. Where the economy offers competitive prospects to only a few, and the civilian administration is glutted with the educated and ambitious, the military will be the only other major institution which can offer the ambitious another competitive arena. Hence we could reason that more outlets will have to be established in the economic and political realms to absorb the ambitious military men.

The wealthy OECD states of the First World demonstrate a universal disdain for praetorian politics. This remains a proper distant model, but one not likely to be realized in the near future in Africa. In the meantime, the substantial influence of foreign capital and its natural attraction to socially stable states (barring those like Nigeria, which have oil) should soon exert a moderating influence on the domestic situation if these states are characterized by non-socialist orientations. Zimbabwe has to date avoided military interventionism, but the socialist tinge of the regime alone has kept foreign capital away. Market size is another major consideration in the attraction of foreign capital, and this could be abetted in Africa by regional economic integration. Hence intensified economic relations could, as a by-product of development, encourage political stability as well. Soldiers may be pressured to stay in the barracks if their emergence would be resisted by fellow members of an economic community in a position to impose economic sanctions on a member's military regime.

Another problem of keeping the soldiers in the barracks is raised by Richard Hodder-Williams. He refers to Milton Obote, who called out the Ugandan army to control the Buganda people in his country. Once this was accomplished, Obote came to rely increasingly on the army.[37] This was understood by Joseph Schumpeter, who postulated that once a state does utilize its military for its intended purposes, the militarist tendency remains thereafter. This militarist tendency bodes ill for the numerous countries in Africa which have fought transnational, civil, or secessionist wars, and it is already evident in Angola and Mozambique where conflicts persist long after the anti-colonial struggle ended. Similarly, one coup inspires subsequent coups, which then institutionalize the interventionist proclivity. The only way to defang the monster may be to continuously co-opt the leadership ranks into the civilian regime while presiding over the demise of the military rank and file, or to await the distant day when consolidation has been accomplished, and the new recruits and officer corps respect the unquestioned legitimacy of the civilian administration. However, since Africa is not progressing economically, nor is the conflict environment abating, a more plausible solution may have to be found.

Our analytic paradigm regarding soldiers in barracks will be misleading if we do not account for the greater historical context of the evolution of the African state. S. E. Finer referred to countries of 'low' or 'minimal' political culture, implying an evolutionary scale.[38] W. F. Gutteridge refers to countries with immature political systems.[39] And Gutteridge also writes of Africa's states which have yet to be firmly 'consolidated'.[40] These are perhaps unrefined analytic assertions but potentially very enlightening to those who do not realize that most presently-constituted African countries are synonymous with neither 'nations' nor 'states'.

While the methods of keeping soldiers in the barracks should be monitored, two groups of countries also deserve analytic scrutiny in Africa. As noted, there are some African countries where coups have never been attempted, or if attempted, have not succeeded. The second group included those countries in which a coup installed a military government which remained firmly in power, but gradually civilianized the regime. Both of these types could offer some advantageous insights if the ultimate goal is not the usual demand to introduce viable multi-party systems but instead, to encourage domestic stability, economic expansion, and civilian control, so no new upstarts embark upon yet another campaign of national salvation.

The international community may be in a position to influence events in this regard.

Southern Africa is an area largely neglected in the literature regarding coups and barracks. As noted, there is a relative paucity of coups in the region – although as the most recent area to attain independence, it may yet undergo its own coup experiences. But a new development should be of interest to military analysts and to South Africa specialists, that of the militarist histories of South Africa's homelands. Ostensibly, four homelands have attained 'independence' (which is not recognized by any government save South Africa). In the mid–1980s, five instances of extraconstitutional exercises of military power were exhibited by the fledgling armies of three of these homelands. In Transkei, an actual coup ousted Prime Minister Sigcau, and introduced B. Holomisa, who subsequently became major general, as the military ruler.

The interesting feature of these homeland military interventions is how closely they resemble the more prevalent African mould. In Transkei the army which ousted the civilian South African-backed administration rebelled against evident corruption, but other standard African characteristics were evident.[41] These included abject poverty, an entrenched political family oligarchy, and the resentment towards the usual expatriate white officers who remained after 'independence', as well as a younger disenchanted generation, epitomized by Holomisa (who was 32 at the time of his coup). Before ousting Sigcau, the reformist army also ousted the previous government of the despotic George Matanzima; followed by the Rawlings-like emergence of Holomisa, intent on clean government.[42]

South Africa exhibited its own internal 'mini-zone of contagion'. Perhaps impressed by Transkei's military takeover, junior officers of another homeland, Bophuthatswana, attempted their own coup a few months later. Again, the issue of government misuse of funds was offered as a motive, but also included were resentment towards expatriate commanders, especially Brigadier Rieckert of the South African Defence Force, who had been a member of South Africa's right-wing Broederbond. Other plotters referred to pay, lack of promotion, and service unwittingly in an active capacity in Angola – which, they claimed, had nothing to do with the interests of Bophuthatswana. This time South Africa played the role of France or Great Britain of another day, repulsing the coup and restoring Bophuthatswana's administration.[43] Keeping the soldiers in the barracks was a concern soon expressed in Ciskei, another 'independent homeland'. One week after Bophuthatswana's coup attempt, Ciskei's President Sebe suddenly praised his loyal troops and their commanders and promoted 25 officers, some up to the rank of general. Coincidentally, he had also survived an attempted coup shortly before! [44] In South Africa's homelands, of course, keeping the soldiers in the barracks can be done efficiently if needed. South Africa can intervene on short notice, as it did in Bophuthatswana.

Finally, if Africa will not soon conform to the prevailing worldwide tide of demilitarization, the challenge then may be, not to force conformity, but to deal with the consequences of military involvement. Whether regimes are civilian or military dominated, they may both encounter frustrations and ineptitude. But there is one difference. If a civilian regime falters, or if it gains only modest success, the military, which has been constantly peering over its shoulders, may step in. But if a military regime is in power, at least it faces prospects of disruption only from among its own colleagues – if at all. In itself this may, at least in theory, favour the military in the context of who will more likely provide greater stability. Unfortunately, this logical deduction is offset by the paradox that the military may not be as successful at developing the state and hence may inadvertently perpetuate an austere socio-economic environment. Nevertheless, if we do accept that some military or (more likely) quasi-military regimes will remain a prevalent feature in Africa's short-to medium-term future, then the goal of merely sending the soldiers back to the barracks does not really respond to the actual realities. The task, instead, may be to ensure that the military governors are rapidly trained and properly advised in matters of public administration, and to prepare them to respect competent civilian authorities if, and when, they do emerge, and to facilitate civilian ascendancy to positions of authority.

Under the present circumstances, the numerous contentious debates among academic analysts as to whether civilian or military men are better equipped to run the affairs of state, and whether soldiers should be in the statehouse or barracks, is tantamount to arguing about who should command the Titanic – which is already well out to sea.

NOTES

1. Claude E. Welch, Jr, *No Farewell to Arms?* (Boulder, Colorado: Westview Press, 1987), p. 204.
2. Adda Bozeman, *Conflict in Africa: Concepts and Realities*, (Princeton, New Jersey: Princeton University Press, 1970), pp. 27–8.
3. *Africa Insight*, 17: 4, 1987, section 3.
4. Pat McGowan and Thomas H. Johnson, 'African Military Coups d'Etat and Underdevelopment: A Quantitative Historical Analysis', *Journal of Modern African Studies*, 22: 4, 1984, p. 638.
5. S. E. Finer, *The Man on Horseback: The Role of the Military in Politics*, (Boulder, Colorado: Westview Press, 1988), 2nd edition, ch. 4.
6. Claude E. Welch, Jr, 'Soldier and State in Africa', in *Journal of Modern African Studies*, 5: 3, November 1967, pp. 305–22.
7. Ruth First, *Power in Africa*, (New York: Pantheon Books, 1970), pp. 205ff.

8. See Welch, 'Soldier and State in Africa'; First, *Power in Africa*; W. F. Gutteridge, *Military Regimes in Africa*, (London: Methuen, 1975), p. 16; and Richard Hodder-Williams, *An Introduction to the Politics of Tropical Africa*, (London: George Allen and Unwin, 1984), p. 131.

9. See Edward Feit, 'Military Coups and Political Development', *World Politics*, 20: 2, 1968, pp. 179–80.

10. Welch, 'Soldier and State in Africa'.

11. Williams, *An Introduction to the Politics of Tropical Africa*, p. 134.

12. Claude E. Welch, Jr, 'African Military and Political Development: Reflections on a Score of Years, and Several Score of Studies', *Issue*, 13, 1984, p. 43.

13. See Claude E. Welch, Jr, 'Emerging Patterns of Civil-Military Relations in Africa: Radical Coups d' Etat and Political Stability', in Bruce E. Arlinghaus, ed., *African Security Issues: Sovereignty, Stability, and Solidarity*, (Boulder, Colorado: Westview Press, 1984) p. 127.

14. Gutteridge, *Military Regimes in Africa*, pp. 185–6.

15. First, *Power in Africa*, p. 22.

16. See the critique of such approaches by David Goldsworthy, 'On the Structural Explanation of African Military Interventions', *Journal of Modern African Studies*, 24: 1, 1986.

17. Pat McGowan and Thomas H. Jackson, 'Forecasting African Coups d'Etat', *Politikon*, (South Africa), 12: 2, 1985, p. 18.

18. An analysis is offered by Claude E. Welch, Jr, 'Obstacles to Disengagement and Democratization: Military Regimes in Benin and Burkina Faso', in Constantine P. Danopoulos, ed., *The Decline of Military Regimes: The Civilian Influence*, (Boulder, Colorado: Westview Press, 1988), ch. 2.

19. First, *Power in Africa*, p. 439.

20. Finer, *The Man on Horseback*, p. 21.

21. I. L. Griffiths offers a somewhat cynical explanation for the relatively coup-less Southern Africa region: it may be 'related to later dates of independence implying that their turn is yet to come'. *An Atlas of African Affairs*, (London: Methuen, 1984) p. 68.

22. Ali A. Mazrui and Michael Tidy refer to this process as 'civilianization of military rule'. See their *Nationalism and New States in Africa*, (London: Heinemann, 1984), p. 274

23. Ibid., p. 275.

24. Welch, *No Farewell to Arms?*, p. 199.

25. Mazrui and Tidy, *Nationalism and New States in Africa*, p. 263.

26. Ibid., pp. 281–2.

27. Thomas S. Cox, *Civil–Military Relations in Sierra Leone*, (Cambridge, Massachusetts: Harvard University Press, 1976) see ch. 10.

28. Ibid., p. 177.

29. Ibid., pp. 205–7.

30. Welch, *No Farewell to Arms?*, p. 25.

31. Ibid., p. 196.

32. Finer, *The Man on Horseback*, 2nd edition, p. 286.

33. Ibid., pp. 301–2.

34. Samuel Decalo, *Coups and Army Rule in Africa: Studies in Military Style*, (New Haven: Yale University Press, 1976), p. 14.

35. William Gutteridge, 'Undoing Military Coups in Africa', *Third World Quarterly*, 7: 1, 1985, p. 87.

36. Roger Hamburg, 'Military Withdrawal from Politics', in Constantine P. Dano-poulos, ed., *Military Disengagement from Politics*, (London: Routledge, 1988), p. 1.
37. Williams, *An Introduction to the Politics of Tropical Africa*, p. 129.
38. Finer, *The Man on Horseback*, pp. 78ff; 117ff.
39. Gutteridge, *Military Regimes in Africa*, p. 181.
40. Gutteridge, 'Undoing Military Coups in Africa', p. 80.
41. Reported in *The Star*, (Johannesburg) 18 February 1988.
42. *Financial Mail*, (Johannesburg) 8 January 1988.
43. Karl P. Magyar, 'Failed Coup Highlights SA's "Generation Gap"', *Sunday Times*, (Johannesburg) 15 February 1988.
44. *Weekly Mail* (Johannesburg) 19 February 1988.

Index

For Product Safety Concerns and Information please contact our EU
representative GPSR@taylorandfrancis.com
Taylor & Francis Verlag GmbH, Kaufingerstraße 24, 80331 München, Germany

www.ingramcontent.com/pod-product-compliance
Lightning Source LLC
Chambersburg PA
CBHW071848270326
41929CB00013B/2143